BUS

You Can Do It!

The BOOMER'S GUIDE to a GREAT RETIREMENT

Jonathan D. Pond

Collins

An Imprint of HarperCollinsPublishers

HarperCollins books may be purchased for educational, business, or sales promotional use. For information, please write to: Special Markets Department, HarperCollins Publishers, 10 East 53rd Street, New York, NY 10022.

Designed by Jaime Putorti

Library of Congress Cataloging-in-Publication has been applied for.

ISBN-10: 0-06-112138-X
ISBN-13: 978-0-06112138-8

07   08   09   10   11   WBC/RRD   10   9   8   7   6   5   4   3   2   1

Disclaimer

This book is meant to provide general investment and financial advice. It is not designed to be a definitive investment guide or to take the place of advice from a qualified financial planner or other professional. Given the risk involved in investing of almost any kind, there is no guarantee that the investment methods suggested in this book will be profitable. Thus, neither the publisher nor the author assume liability of any kind for any losses that may be sustained as a result of applying the methods suggested in this book, and any such liability is hereby expressly disclaimed.

The names of certain individuals throughout have been changed to protect their privacy.

Acknowledgments

While the author garners most of the glory (or the brickbats), producing a book requires the efforts of numerous people. I am indeed fortunate to have a very talented group of professionals supporting me every step of the way.

Joe Tessitore, group president at Collins, has been my friend for more years than we care to admit. He's now a "mature" boomer who has already downsized his home. Good for you, Joe. I wish my agent, Peter Ginsberg, would also heed my advice. His wise counsel is always appreciated, but he persists on leasing cars, although at least he now feels guilty about doing so. Marion Maneker, vice president and publisher at Collins, is one of the most perceptive people I have ever met. Marion's suggestions and wit are much appreciated, as are the contributions of Alex Scordelis, editorial assistant.

As you will soon observe, this book was a nightmare to copyedit, proofread, design, and typeset, but all of the wonderfully skilled people involved in the process pulled it off with aplomb. Special thanks for the titanic efforts of the copyediting team, including Donna Ruvituso, executive managing editor, Diane Aronson, copy chief, Matthew Inman, assistant managing editor, Steven Boldt, copyeditor, and Christine Michaud, indexer.

I am particularly appreciative of the poor souls who were charged with the complex typesetting required of *You Can Do It!* Thanks to the great people at Westchester Book Group as well as Nyamekye Waliyaya, production manager, and Shana Jones, proofreader.

Grateful acknowledgment is also accorded those involved in design, including art director Georgia Morrissey, senior designer William Ruoto, designer Jaime Putorti, and cover designer Erica Heitman-Ford at Mucca Design.

Those involved in the promotion of *You Can Do It!* are both very talented and enthusiastic. Special thanks to Angie Lee, marketing director, for her great suggestions and for coordinating the extensive promotional program. Thanks as well to Beth Mellow, publicity manager, Larry Hughes, publicity director, George Bick, senior vice president of sales, Janina Wong, marketing coordinator, as well as Felicia Sullivan, online marketing manager.

I would like to single out two special people at HarperCollins who contributed immensely throughout the production of this book. Helen Song, senior production editor, oversaw the process with considerable skill, and her efforts are very much appreciated.

My editor, pre-boomer Ethan Friedman, is a rising star in the publishing business. His suggestions and encouragement have resulted in a much better book. Ethan is a very able guy. Ever tactful, he gently encouraged me to write in everyday English and minimize the use of Latin. I think he would prefer that I get rid of my beloved OED, to which I respond: flumadiddle.

Betsy Peterson was very helpful in editing the early versions of the manuscript. Thanks as well to John Annino and Richard Merrill in my office who helped both with the book development and the reader Web site. Thanks also to Adreck McDonald for his help in designing the reader Web site.

Finally, and most importantly, I thank my family: my wife Lois and our three Puddles, Elizabeth, Laura, and Emily, for their forbearance during my long absences. Book writing is never easy on a family. I have frequently told them that the best jobs in the world are those that make a positive difference in people's lives. I sincerely hope that *You Can Do It!* makes a positive difference in yours. If so, all of our efforts and sacrifices will be amply rewarded.

Contents

Introduction

Statistics Are Curious Things

Good news: Baby boomers are in a lot better financial shape than the media portrays, and *You Can Do It!* will help you achieve not just a good retirement, but a great retirement.

A few years ago, I was asked by a giant financial company to do some work on their "groundbreaking" research into baby boomer retirement preparedness. This was a time when all of the big investment and insurance companies were coming out with their own studies, all coming to the same conclusion: if baby boomers don't straighten out their acts, they're headed for retirement perdition.

Before my final interview, I did some of my own research, comparing their raw data with government statistics on the financial status of current retirees. I concluded that the baby boom generation was certainly no worse off than current retirees, who have the lowest poverty rate of any age group, and in all probability boomers were going to be better off than the current batch of retirees! So I went to the meeting with a bold suggestion: "Since all of your competitors are coming up with such dreadful prognostications, why don't you take a more positive approach by stating the facts: a healthy majority of baby boomers are in pretty good financial shape, but there's still some work to do to achieve a really good retirement."

The immediate and unanimous response from the firm's PR people was "Why would we want to do that?" I said, "Because that's what your raw data show before you cherry-picked the worst statistics." Well, I was shown the door. Since then, I have heard that some financial company employees have admitted that they would lose their jobs if their firms' research data were not massaged to portray a bleak situation.

It's not easy being a baby boomer these days. Sure, most of us are enjoying a pretty good life, but retirement looms. For the more "mature" boomers, retirement is just a few years off. Judging from the news headlines, most of us are headed for the poorhouse. We could become discouraged by all of the studies and reports that seem to draw the same conclusion: baby boomers are going to pay a heavy price for their profligacy.

But the reality is quite the contrary. Across almost all income levels, baby boomers are better prepared for retirement than any previous generation. In fact, boomers are far better prepared than their parents were at the same age.

Advice for Financial Malingerers

I, for one, long ago tired of the overabundance of financial guidance based upon the premise that baby boomers are a bunch of ignorant slackers who need to be told and retold the same old condescending tripe. Here are some of my favorite advisories (how many times have your read these?):

✦ "You're not saving enough." (Fortunately, here the "experts" give us a solution to the problem: save more.)

✦ "You need to prepare a budget to rein in your spending." (Who has time to budget, anyway?) The only fill-in-the-blanks budget you'll find here is in an appendix.

✦ "You need a big mortgage to take advantage of the tax deduction." (Big deal: for every $10,000 paid in mortgage interest, the average home owner saves a mere $2,500 in federal income taxes.)

✦ "You'll end up in poverty if you don't take out a long-term-care insurance policy." (Many people either can't afford the coverage or can afford to self-insure.)

✦ "When you get ready to retire, you need to move most of your money into safe interest-earning securities rather than stocks." (Do that and you'll probably run out of money before you die.)

If you're sick of being told and retold what you already know, this guide is for you.

Why *You Can Do It!* Is Not "Just Another Retirement Book"

Several retirement books are on the bookshelves, but none is like *You Can Do It!* First, this guide doesn't rely on the timeworn tactics of the financial-planning-book genre, to wit:

No bizarre strategies here. A recent financial author suggested that people preparing for retirement should buy two additional houses, because real estate was a sure winner. Unfortunately for those readers who heeded his advice, that recommendation came in late 2005, a couple of months before the U.S. housing market began to slump. Also, forgoing a designer cup of coffee a day, while a good thing to do financially, and it's something I recommend, isn't going to insure your wealth unless you do it for several decades and manage to earn about twice as much money on your forgone-coffee savings as the average investor. Conversely, many of the strategies in *You Can Do It!* are either not known or not well understood by most people. But they make sense and don't require you to do bizarre things with your money.

No get-rich-quick schemes here. Whether it's a "can't miss" business idea or a way to make a quick killing in the stock market or in real estate, you won't find such schemes in here; rather, my objective is to allow you to retire confident in the knowledge that you'll be financially secure for the rest of your life.

No tales of the rich here. Some authors think there's nothing more inspiring to readers than describing the retirement plans of someone who has $10 million. You wonder if they realize that many people may never have $10 million, and describing the lifestyles and plans of multimillionaires is hardly encouraging. *You Can Do It!* assumes that you have what you have, and my goal is to help you make the most of that and to encourage you to make the right decisions between now and the time you retire to brighten your retirement prospects.

No long and boring passages detailing arcane rules and complex investments. The standard fare in financial books is agonizing details on tax rules, estate planning regulations, and retirement plan alternatives, some of which are outdated by the time the book is published. Readers are left perplexed by the long delineation of alternatives with little or no guidance on what to do. *You Can Do It!* cuts to the chase to help you make the right choices without delving into mind-numbing details. If you need more guidance, you'll find up-to-date information on the special reader Web site described on page xix.

No tales of woe here. A recent cover of a national financial magazine featured a supposed millionaire retiree eating dog food. The implication of this cover is that if you have only a million dollars, you're headed for an impoverished retirement. You won't need to worry about such stories here, although you will see many "Success Stories," including some that show how people who had been in varying degrees of financial difficulty managed to overcome their travails.

No sermonizing here. Some people want to be told in no uncertain terms what they should be doing with their financial lives, and some authors are good at telling you what you should do. But life isn't that simple, unless you're starting from scratch with your finances. Most baby boomers aren't starting out, so the overriding assumption in this guide is that you currently have some finances to plan and you'd prefer to have me help you make wise decisions rather than have me tell you, as some would have it, "It's my way or the highway (to financial ruin)."

Enough of what *You Can Do It!* isn't. Here's why it will be your single indispensable source of money guidance, now and for years to come.

Based on the reality of the financial condition of baby boomers. This book is based on the reality of the financial condition of the baby boom generation. Serious research (as opposed to a lot of cursory research that comes up with spurious conclusions) indicates that a sizable majority of baby boomers, approaching 80 percent, are in pretty good shape to retire comfortably. There's no need for scary statistics that we hear or read about almost every day, because they simply don't reflect reality. These encouraging statistics don't mean, however, that I'm not going to goad you into doing even better with your money.

Highlights real people. There's nothing like the stories of real people talking about how they have succeeded in their financial lives, often after misfortune. Chapter 2 is devoted to the "success secrets" of numerous retirees, highlighting the most important financial decisions they made during their working years. Thereafter, Success Stories are sprinkled throughout this guide, again highlighting real stories of real people (as opposed to centimillionaires). In my years of work on television and in speaking venues, I have always found that the stories of real people are the most compelling way to learn about wise personal financial management. I hope that you agree.

Exclusively for baby boomers. *You Can Do It!* is strictly for baby boomers, so it doesn't waste your time with matters pertaining to the Generation X and Generation Y youngsters or those youngsters-at-heart who are retired. Baby boomers are a harried lot who are constantly trying to make their overprogrammed lives more efficient and effective. You've come to the right place!

Lots of Decision Makers and Checklists. The chapters that follow are filled with Decision Makers and Checklists that will help you easily evaluate your situation and make important decisions about your current finances and eventual retirement. Gone are the days when you had to read extensively about a particular matter only to be left in a quandary as to what to do. You'll be able to complete a Checklist or answer a brief Decision Maker questionnaire and at last be able to confidently make a smart financial decision, free of bias and confusion.

Guidance for now and the future. You'll find advice in these pages to help you every year between now and the time you retire, including what changes you should make in your investments and financial planning *after* you retire. Planning for an exciting and fulfilling retirement is not just about money, either. And while money is my shtick, I'll also remind you about two other important ingredients of a successful retirement: lifestyle and health. You shouldn't wait until you retire to make important lifestyle decisions, not the least of which is: what are you going to do to occupy yourself while you're retired? And you don't want to spend a good chunk of your retirement years in lousy health. So I'll impart some words on important health matters to attend to now so that the decades you spend enjoying retirement are both wealthy and healthy.

Helpful and hopeful. Imagine a book for you much-maligned baby boomers that's both helpful and hopeful. Whatever your financial situation is, *You Can Do It!* will not shame you by denigrating your past financial foibles nor depress you by suggesting your financial future is hopeless. It will show you how to overcome the past and improve your future. You're probably like most baby boomers who are enervated by all the negative stories. But as most in-depth research into your collective condition has shown, the vast majority of boomers are on the road to a good retirement. Let the chapters that follow take you from a good retirement to a great retirement.

In short, this is a guide, not a book—a guide that will help you achieve your retirement dreams.

A Guide for All Boomers

As noted above, *You Can Do It!* contains many checklists and fill-in-the-blanks sections to help you plan a great retirement, no matter how far or near retirement you may be. I encourage you to complete those checklists and fill-in-the-blanks sections that are relevant to your situation, which will not only help you better identify important matters to attend to, but will also make the book harder to resell.

Depending on where you are on the baby boomer age spectrum, which ranges from those seasoned boomers born in 1946 all the way to fledgling boomers born in 1964, your retirement may be anywhere from a couple of years away to over twenty years hence. Those who are many years from retiring—a decade or more—may be most interested in the chapters on investing, choosing retirement plans, and avoiding expensive financial mistakes. On the other hand, those who are nearing retirement might focus on chapters that deal with key pre- and postretirement decisions. But don't pass over any of the chapters because you think they don't relate to your situation and needs, since each chapter contains important guidance for *all* members of, in the words of the demographers, the baby boom cohort.

Special note for younger boomers. The most common lament of retirees is that they didn't start planning soon enough. If you're a decade or two away from retirement, you need to start paying at least some attention to such matters as how much it's going to cost you to retire, how to improve your financial status before you retire, and even where you're going to retire and what you're going to do in retirement. This guide is designed to make sure you begin to pay attention to important retirement-planning topics even if you're as young as your early forties, which may seem antediluvian to a preschooler, but is a prime age to start seriously preparing for retirement.

Special note for veteran boomers. If retirement is looming like a Category 5 hurricane, you're going to make a lot of important, and in some instances irreversible, decisions over the next several years. This will naturally lead you to those sections of this guide that help you make decisions such as when to begin collecting Social Security. But please don't pass over matters that you may think are primarily the purview of more youthful boomers. Look at it this way: a lot of what goes on in successful financial planning involves what is euphemistically called the TR factor, which stands for "time remaining." You have decades of TR, during which you need to make sure that you pay as much attention as the younger members of the baby boom generation to such matters as diversifying your investments and preparing for the unexpected.

BREAKDOWN OF THE BABY BOOM GENERATION

DATES OF BIRTH	HEAD COUNT
1960–64	23 million
1955–59	22 million
1950–54	19 million
1946–49	13 million
Total	77 million

- Baby boomers comprise almost 27 percent of the U.S. population
- Over 32 million are over age fifty
- By the year 2030, when they are ages sixty-six to eighty-four, boomers will make up about 20 percent of the total population

Special Reader Web Site for Up-to-Date Financial and Investment Guidance . . .

Many areas of your financial life, from taxes to the investment markets, are moving targets. As you read the book you will frequently find the following notation:

www

This indicates that the accompanying text includes matters that may change or need further explanation. You can receive up-to-date information and guidance, *including my latest investment suggestions and all-star mutual fund recommendations,* and an up-to-date list of the best financial Web sites simply by visiting this special reader Web site:

www.jonathanpond.com

At the top of the Web page, click on the "You Can Do It! The Boomer's Guide to a Great Retirement" link.

For your convenience, here is a summary of areas that are kept up-to-date on the special reader Web site:

CHAPTER 1

Yes, You Can Achieve Your Retirement Dreams

"Are Americans Saving 'Optimally' for Retirement?" (*Journal of Political Economy*, August 2006) by Scholz, Seshadri, and Khitatrakun. The authors conducted a rigorous analysis of the financial status of working-age Americans and concluded that over 80 percent of the households surveyed met or exceeded their wealth targets, and most of those who were below missed by a relatively small amount. The data for these conclusions came from 1992 and 1993, before the big increases in the stock market later in the 1990s and the boom in real estate prices, so the financial outlook for boomers may be even better.

Woulda, coulda, shoulda. If only I had started earlier. How often have you lamented not having begun to save early enough or making such incredibly naive investment decisions? Is there *anyone*, at any age, who hasn't felt the same, other than the occasional socially marginal savings zealot who thrives on self-deprivation (and ends up on the cover of one of the consumer financial magazines to make you feel even worse)? You need to get over dwelling on your past financial omissions before you can rationally plan for the future. You've moved on from other past indiscretions. So why is it that we can't get over past pecuniary shortcomings? Because, while we can completely get over most of what we've regretted in the past, we have to live the rest of our lives thinking that we'd be in better shape if we had developed sounder financial habits earlier. Such misgivings are present whether you're forty-two, fifty-two, or sixty. Either you can be despondent or you can take at least some solace from the realization that most—virtually all—baby boomers have the same misgivings. Thanks to the yeoman's efforts of the media and financial services industry, you are reminded of your lamentable state daily. Learn to tune them out.

The retirement planning two-step. Presumably, you purchased or were given this guide to get some ideas about achieving a better retirement. If so, you can do yourself a lot of good by reading these pages with a positive attitude. If you're suffering from the "woulda, coulda, shoulda" syndrome, imagine that today you're are at a fork in the road. You can continue on the same route as you have in the past:

1. I regret my past financial dereliction, so

2. I'm afraid to face my financial future.

Or, you could view your future as an opportunity, rather than a problem:

1. There's nothing I can do about the past, but

2. I'm ready to improve my financial future.

If you'll promise to take the positive fork in the road, I'll make the following promises as you read these pages:

A. You won't be chided for your past financial mistakes, but you will be shown how to avoid making those same mistakes in the future.

B. I won't depress you with stories of people who got rich quick using cockamamy get-rich-quick schemes, like llama farming, but I will show you how to achieve a great retirement, even a rich retirement.

C. You won't find a Holy Grail leading to financial nirvana, but you will be given sensible guidance on all of the important financial decisions you need to make between now and the time you retire.

D. You won't be given a bunch of dubious "can't lose" investment ideas, but you will at last find out how to invest very successfully under all economic and market conditions.

Whether you are two years or twenty-two years from retirement, you'll find ways to retire on your own terms. As you read the pages that follow, my goal is to have you say, time and again, "I can do that," because you can.

Belaboring the Obvious: The Keys to Achieving a Great Retirement

Before launching into the nitty-gritty, a brief review of the keys to achieving a great retirement is in order. Here they are:

1. Living beneath your means.

2. Investing your savings wisely.

3. Eliminating debt.

4. Preventing financial disruptions.

5. Staying active and maintaining your health.

They're pretty obvious, aren't they? But they're still difficult to implement and maintain.

It's all or nothing. One major impediment is the national mentality, perfected by the baby boomer generation, toward "all or nothing," which even affects our financial planning. "I'm ten years from retirement, but have twenty-five years left on my mortgage. I could pay it off in ten years by adding an extra $600 to my mortgage payment." The result is predictable. The $600 extra payment proves impossible to maintain, so it's back to making the regular payments a couple of months later. By that time, the well-intended home owner feels even more disheartened about his financial future. More realistic: He would have a better chance of success by gradually working up to the high extra-payment level, even if it took a couple of years to get there.

That old devil human nature. Human nature also impedes making improvements in our financial lives. It's a lot easier to spend money, and to justify our expenditures as essential, than it is to forgo some spending to save for a retirement that seems a long way off—or may be too imminent, in which case, why bother? Human nature also causes us to avoid contemplating risks to our own and our family's financial futures—unpleasant events such as job loss, disability, and death.

Success tip. Resist the temptation to avoid confronting the future and, when changes need to be made, make them *gradually* rather than in one fell swoop.

This book is filled with guidance and checklists that will help you make some positive changes in your financial future as well as plan for a fulfilling retirement. But before delving in, here's an introduction to the problems—and opportunities—in grappling with the five aforementioned essential keys to achieving a great retirement.

1. Living Beneath Your Means

The problem. It's a lot easier to spend than to save. First, we have to spend a lot of our income on the basics, such as food and housing. After the basics, we have the Madison Avenue crowd bombarding us with ads that tell us how much better we would feel spending whatever's left over on all manner of fripperies. Spending money on self-indulgences feels good. It always has and always will.

The opportunity. Saving need not rob you of all of life's pleasures. Rather, spending less than you earn is really delayed gratification. The best way to reach an appropriate savings level, if you're not there yet, is to do so gradually and automatically. Build up to it and have the savings automatically transferred from your paycheck or bank account into a retirement or investment account. Even if you are an expert at spending your money, it's a lot tougher to spend money that you never receive. That's the beauty of an electronic funds transfer, the saver's best friend. That's pretty much the last saving exhortation you'll find in these pages. There are more important matters to attend to.

2. Investing Your Savings Wisely

The problem. On its face, investing seems difficult. Just look at the jargon: *equities, fixed-income securities, cash equivalents, diversification.* Sounds complicated, and many members of the investment fraternity are quite content to keep it that way. Too many boomers invest in extremes. Some are frightened of investment risk, which can result in anemic investment growth and potential income problems in retirement. Others take too much risk in the vain hope of hitting an investment home run. Hefty investment losses, the bane of many investors during the 2000 to 2002 bear market, can erode a retirement nest egg tout de suite. (A "bear" market is a declining overall stock market, while a "bull" market is a rising stock market.)

The opportunity. Investing successfully isn't that difficult, as you'll discover in chapters 3, 4, and 5. Whether you make your own investment decisions and/or use an investment adviser, it behooves you to understand the basics of investing, including diversification. Arming yourself with this knowledge and reviewing your investments periodically will help you and/or your adviser avoid problems and grow your money quite nicely over the years. If you're not knowledgeable about investing or could use a refresher course, please pay a visit to Appendix II.

3. Eliminating Debt

The problem. Debt is a convenient way to buy worthwhile and durable things—such as a house—sooner and pay for them later. But too many people have extended their borrowing to include "things" that are neither worthwhile nor durable. Reducing debt over time has proved challenging for many baby boomers.

The opportunity. Retiring free of debt or becoming debt-free early in your retirement has an astonishingly positive impact on your retirement prospects. I'm not going to waste time chiding you if you have credit-card debt. You know what you need to do. But I will help you devise a plan to pay off the home mortgage sooner rather than later. You'll be pleasantly surprised at how little extra it takes to greatly reduce the time it takes to pay off home equity loans and mortgages, particularly if you start with small additional payments and work up from there. See chapter 8.

4. Preventing Financial Disruptions

The problem. A single financial disruption can wipe out years, if not decades, of hard-earned savings. Many people haven't prepared for those unfortunate occurrences over which they can have at least some control, either because they fail to foresee these events or they find this area of financial planning to be irksome, if not depressing.

The opportunity. Most of the expensive unpleasantries that could befall you or a family member can be addressed with insurance, the one area in this list that does not lend itself to gradual implementation. Always have comprehensive insurance coverage. Other financial vexations can be prevented by, for example, investing in your relationships (I'm talking about preventing divorce, here), raising financially responsible children so you won't have to support them in perpetuity, and investing in your career to maximize your career earnings. While I don't intend to bore you with long passages on insurance, I'd be remiss in ignoring it and the risks to all that you've done over the decades to improve your financial outlook. "Preparing for the Unexpected" is the subject of chapter 10.

5. Staying Active and Maintaining Your Health

The problem. Baby boomers are so busy with their careers, families, and attending to the previous four financial items that they all too often fail to do the necessaries for enjoying a long, healthy, and active retirement. A poll of retirees indicated that only one in ten felt that he or she had devoted sufficient attention to planning for retirement during the working years, and a great majority of the other 90 percent greatly regretted not having done so.

The opportunity. Baby boomers are doing a lot better than their parents in exercising and paying attention to their health, but many of us still have room for improvement. A better diet and regular exercise have benefits that are as lasting as a prodigious retirement income. As someone once noted, "It's a lot better to be rich and healthy than poor and sick." As with matters financial, the problem many baby boomers have with diet and exercise is that they approach them with the same intensity as they do everything else, rather than gradually building up to the desired target. This often results in only temporary success. Because you can't reach some muscle-bound exercise guru's or emaciated nutritionist's opinion of what you should be doesn't mean you've failed. Just as with saving a bit more of your income, small improvements in diet and exercise are clearly beneficial. For example, I know I should cut out ice cream, but to me, life without ice cream is, well, death. But I have taken the advice of my beanpole youngest daughter and no longer eat ice cream directly out of the container. This has greatly reduced my consumption, but I still have something to live for.

Whatever your age or financial status, take small, incremental steps toward improving your retirement prospects.

RETIREMENT NIRVANA LONG SHOTS

Don't count on having some money fall from the sky to instantaneously eradicate a retirement-funding shortfall. Sadly, some people still harbor those desires:

Winning the lottery. If play you must, don't make lottery spending one of your bigger household expenses.

A child becoming enormously wealthy. This is a long shot for a couple of reasons. Do you actually think (be honest with yourself!) that your kids are going to amass a bundle of money? Even if they do strike it rich, will they really share that wealth with their doting and doddering parents? With one of our kids aspiring to be a teacher, the second majoring in Latin, and the youngest concentrating on video gaming, I'm not counting on the Pond "puddles" for future financial support.

Receiving an inheritance. Many baby boomers will in fact receive an inheritance, and an inheritance can provide a needed boost in a retirement nest egg, assuming that's where the money is put. But before using an expected inheritance as a foundation for your retirement planning, consider the following two questions. First, how much can you reasonably expect to receive? Most of us aren't blessed with parents who are simultaneously prosperous and parsimonious. Big expenses for health care and the like and long lives can substantially diminish, if not eliminate, an inheritance. Speaking of longevity, the second question is, when can you reasonably expect to receive said inheritance? Could it be that your inheritance won't arrive until you're already well into retirement, because not only are boomers living a long time, so are many of their parents. Don't overestimate the amount of the patrimony or underestimate the time until you receive it.

MYTH DEBUNKER: "BOOMERS ARE PALTRY SAVERS AND PRODIGIOUS BORROWERS"

One recent study (*Balance Sheets of Early Boomers: Are They Different from Pre-Boomers?* Finke, Huston, and Sharpe [2006]) compared baby boomer finances with the previous generation and found that boomers possess a significantly higher level of financial assets than their parents did at the same age. It concludes, "On average, boomers are taking seriously the responsibility to prepare for their financial future," rather than the common media portrayal of just the opposite.

The Great Retirement Pyramid: Achieving Your Retirement Dreams in Less Than an Hour a Month

Despite the dismal news stories, we now know that the baby boom generation is in far better financial shape than the previous generation, indeed all prior generations. But that doesn't mean your work is done. If you're on the road to financial security, but you're not yet there (like most of us), you need to avoid pitfalls that could impede your progress while doing what's necessary to close the gap between what you've got and what you'll need when you want to retire. If you're already in pretty good financial shape, you should protect what you have and continue to improve your situation to brighten your retirement prospects.

There's a lot to attend to as you approach retirement, and the closer you are to retirement age, the more you have to do. But that doesn't mean that planning your finances and monitoring your investments needs to be a full-time job. You've got more important things to do. I'll show you how to achieve a great retirement with only a few hours a year of effort. It's all contained in the Great Retirement Pyramid.

"Set It and Forget It" Financial Foundation

Like a pyramid, your finances need to rest on a strong foundation. That foundation includes protecting yourself from the unexpected by maintaining adequate insurance coverage, deciding about long-term-care insurance, and preparing essential estate-planning documents, for example. These are enumerated in chapter 10. If you haven't already, putting your savings on automatic is the easiest way to add to your retirement dough. The easy part about maintaining your financial foundation is that most of these matters need only be attended to once a year.

Putting Your Financial Life on Autopilot

Moving up the Great Retirement Pyramid, the middle section is, if you'll excuse the analogy, the "guts" of your financial future: retirement-plan participation, investing, and paying off the mortgage. These tasks need not be worrisome or time-consuming. I'll help you put your financial life on "autopilot" by showing you the

THE GREAT RETIREMENT PYRAMID

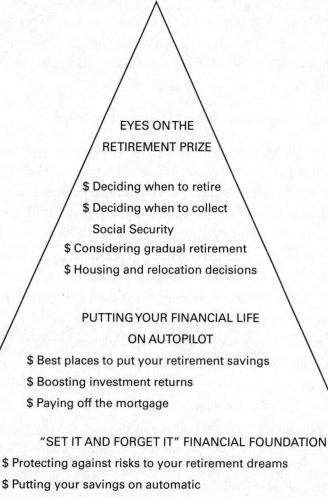

EYES ON THE
RETIREMENT PRIZE

$ Deciding when to retire
$ Deciding when to collect
Social Security
$ Considering gradual retirement
$ Housing and relocation decisions

PUTTING YOUR FINANCIAL LIFE
ON AUTOPILOT

$ Best places to put your retirement savings
$ Boosting investment returns
$ Paying off the mortgage

"SET IT AND FORGET IT" FINANCIAL FOUNDATION

$ Protecting against risks to your retirement dreams
$ Putting your savings on automatic
$ Protecting your loved ones through estate planning

best places to put your retirement savings in chapter 4. You'll also learn investment-diversification strategies in chapter 3 that are easy to set up and easy to maintain. One of the best things you can do to assure a great retirement is pay off your mortgage when or shortly after you retire. You'll be amazed at how painless paying off your mortgage early can be. I'll show you how in chapter 8.

Eyes on the Retirement Prize

The capstone of your retirement pyramid involves starting to make concrete plans about your retirement. If you're a "veteran" boomer, these matters should be prominent in your planning. If you're still a decade or two away from retirement, starting to think about how, when, and where you'll retire will be a big help in the way you plan your finances over the years. When you get down to the crux of planning your retirement, decisions aplenty will be front and center, including deciding when to retire, the subject of chapter 7. You'll also need to decide when to begin collecting Social Security, a complex and controversial decision that I'll lay out beginning on page 134. Increasingly, baby boomers are eschewing early retirement and are looking forward to working beyond age sixty-five. The financial advantages of gradual retirement are described on page 172. Chapter 8 will guide you through the perplexing and often terrifying process of deciding what to do with the family home, and chapter 9 will help you decide where to retire.

Three for the Money

The following chapters will offer many suggestions that will help you prepare for retirement. But whatever your age, pay particular attention to three key matters that can elevate you from a good retirement to a great retirement.

1. **Investment returns have a major bearing on your retirement income.** You can double the amount of income you withdraw from your retirement savings by paying attention to how your investments are diversified and selecting top-of-the-line investments. Chapters 3 and 5 will show you how.

2. **Paying off the mortgage could greatly reduce your retirement budget.** Planning now to pay off the mortgage when you retire or shortly thereafter can reduce your retirement living expenses by 20 percent or more. Mortgage-free retirees enjoy a much better lifestyle. A variety of ways to reach this goal are discussed in chapter 8.

3. **It may cost you a lot less to retire comfortably than you think.** Forget the often-quoted rules of thumb that suggest you'll need a retirement income that's close to (or some say in excess of) your preretirement income to live okay once you're retired. Everyone's situation is different, and many retirees have found that they can live quite well on 65 percent or less of their preretirement income (see page 126.) The following table will help you get a quick look at what your retirement expenses might be. More detailed budget work sheets and guidelines can be found in Appendix I.

QUICK RETIREMENT BUDGET WORK SHEET

You can retire on less than you think. Use the following work sheet to make a quick and dirty assessment of how much it's likely to cost you if you retired today, but without the expenses you incur now that you don't expect to incur when you retire.

    1. Your current income from employment $_____

Add rise in expenses when you retire:

    2. Medical   _____

    3. Travel and leisure   _____

    4. Other: _____   _____

    5. Subtotal rising expenses (Lines 2 + 3 + 4) $_____

Deduct decline in expenses when you retire:

    6. Income taxes   (_____)

    7. Retirement plan contributions   (_____)

    8. Savings into nonretirement accounts   (_____)

    9. Job expenses   (_____)

    10. Mortgage   (_____)

    11. Tuition and other kid expenses   (_____)

    12. Other: _____   (_____)

    13. Subtotal declining expenses

        (Lines 6 + 7 + 8 + 9 + 10 + 11 + 12) $(_____)

    14. Estimated retirement budget

        (Line 1 + 5 − 13) $_____

Estimated retirement expenses as a percentage of your current income

(Line 14 divided by Line 1)   Line 14 / Line 1 = _____%

Notes:

Line 2: Medical expenses—Unless you're lucky enough to work for a company that pays lifetime health benefits, it's likely your medical expenses will rise at least somewhat when you're retired and may increase to the tune of several thousand dollars a year. It depends on your situation and a lot of uncertainty.

Line 3: Travel and leisure—The leisure afforded by the nonworking life isn't free. Unless you're already taking lavish vacations and indulging in expensive hobbies, be sure to factor some fun money into your retirement expense budget.

Line 6: Income taxes—Your income taxes will decline when you retire. For starters, you'll no longer have Social Security taxes taken out of your pay. This could reduce your expenses by almost 8 percent. On top of that, a lower retirement income will result in lower federal and state income taxes, and perhaps property taxes.

Lines 7 and 8: Retirement plan contributions—These will end when you retire, as well as most of any money you save in nonretirement accounts.

Line 9: Job expenses—Depending on your job situation, such expenses as commuting, lunches, and job attire will no longer be required. If you're married or partnered, you might even be able to off-load one car.

Line 10: Mortgage—If you pay off your mortgage (or, perhaps, just pay off a home equity loan) between now and the time you retire, this will be a whopping deduction.

Line 11: Tuition and other kid expenses—If you're currently saddled with tuition and kids at home, these not inconsiderable exactions will, hopefully, be substantially reduced when you retire. Prudence might dictate that all child-related expenses probably not be excised from your retirement budget, since children may always be somewhat needful of the parental purse.

SUCCESS STORY:
MOVING UP TO BIG-TIME SAVINGS

The success story of a recent retiree is by no means unique: "Up until about ten years ago, I had been saving only 2 percent of my income—enough to get the 401(k) match from my employer. I started planning for retirement and ran a retirement-planning program on one of the mutual fund companies, Web sites. It said that I should be saving 12 percent, which was a bit of a shocker. But I immediately went to personnel and upped my 401(k) contribution from 2 percent to 12 percent. That lasted two weeks. I couldn't afford the pay cut, so I went back to 2 percent thinking that I was going to have to retire on a park bench. But rather than continue feeling like a complete loser, I returned to personnel (I was on a first-name basis by then) and increased my contribution to 4 percent, a level I could easily handle. Six months later, I got a raise (and a tax refund) so I boosted the contribution to 8 percent. Within a year of that, I was at 12 percent, and really didn't miss the money all that much. Now I'm retired with a pretty healthy 401(k) account, thanks to my not giving up on my savings plan a decade ago."

You Can Do It!!

You'll find literally hundreds of tips and ideas designed just for you on the pages that follow. I'll help guide you through the important decisions that you'll need to make between now and the time you retire. Your generation is headed for the best retirement people have ever known. Whatever your current financial situation is, I want to help you achieve not just a comfortable retirement, not a good retirement, but a great retirement. It's within your grasp right now. *You can do it!*

CHAPTER 2

Success Secrets

You probably went through a stage in your younger years when you didn't trust older people. But now that you're an older person, at least from the perspective of a primary-school pupil, you may give more credence to the views of the older generation. This change in viewpoint was perhaps best articulated by Mark Twain: "When I was a boy of fourteen, my father was so ignorant I could hardly stand to have the old man around. But when I got to be twenty-one, I was astonished at how much the old man had learned in seven years."

For the past couple of years I have asked retirees to offer one piece of advice to baby boomers to help them better prepare for retirement or to describe the best thing they did for retirement. These reflections have been important in developing this book, and many of them are presented below. These thoughtful reflections will give you an early look at the important matters that are addressed hereafter.

Investment Diversification Is Essential

Investment diversification is fairly easy to understand and implement, but far too many people either don't pay enough or any attention to diversification. Lack of diversification can drag down investment returns just as surely as holding on to fetid investments. Chapter 3 will settle the diversification question once and for all.

There's strength in (investment) diversity. Even if investors understand the importance of diversification, that doesn't mean their investments are diversified. There's a big disconnect between theory and practice. Here's the advice of an investment veteran who understands the importance of putting theory into practice.

We are far from being investment experts, but we have been successful investors. Our success is not at all due to picking great investments. In fact, we rarely invested in individual stocks and bonds, preferring plain old mutual funds. Once we bought a fund, we tended to hold on to it for a long time, even though in hindsight we would have been better off replacing some of them. Why, you might ask, do we consider ourselves to be successful investors? In a word, diversification. By investing in a variety of different categories of stocks and bonds, we avoided the mistake of having a lot of money in a single category—technology stocks, for example. We've managed over the past twenty years to earn an average yearly rate of return of just about ten percent. That's not spectacular, but it has allowed us to increase our investments to the point that we don't have any financial concerns in retirement. The nice thing about diversification is that once you set your parameters, your various investments pretty much run on automatic. For us, diversification has been the key to our retirement success.

Stick to Investment Basics

Investing well isn't quantum physics. But by devoting a bit of time to selecting top-drawer investments and watching out for taxes, you can increase investment returns. In fact, as you'll find in chapter 5, you might even be able to double your investment income for retirement.

Retiree Reflections
"My Best Advice . . ."

Turn a lemon into lemonade. Sometimes adversity can throw a curve at our retirement plans, but it doesn't necessarily have to be a financial catastrophe. Insurance can provide some measure of protection, but sometimes insurance isn't enough. Here's the story of one woman's challenge.

> *My husband suffered from early-onset dementia in his early sixties. All of a sudden, I was responsible for our money, something I had never been at all involved with. I had to learn about investing for the first time. I joined an investment club, which was very helpful, and started to learn all I could about investing during my spare time. My advice is for both partners to understand and keep up-to-date with the family's finances. Also, don't be afraid to learn how to invest. I've quite enjoyed it in my retirement, and this knowledge allowed us to do okay financially in retirement.*

This woman, by the way, is modest about her investment acumen. She increased the value of their investments over tenfold in less than twenty years.

Retiree Reflections
"My Best Advice . . ."

Investing for the long term. No one can really predict short-term market movements.

> *After years of reacting to everything that happened in the stock and bond markets and buying the latest hot investment, with predictably dismal results, I finally came to the realization that trying to predict what was going to happen to my investments over the*

next week or next year, for that matter, was a zero-sum game. I wasn't going to need to access my investments for many years, so why should I fret over immediate matters? From that point forward, I would ask myself one question before making an investment: Will I be happy I made this investment five years from now? Since then, my investment gains both during my working years and in retirement, while not spectacular, have been a great deal higher than they were before when I obsessed over my investments. My advice to baby boomers is simple: Don't dwell on current conditions. Always take a long-term view.

Key Decisions Can Have a Big Effect on Your Financial Security

Many decisions that you make between now and the time you retire can have a lasting effect. Some, like taking out an annuity, are irreversible. Chapter 6 will help you make the correct choices on what may be some of the most important financial decisions of your life.

Retiree Reflections
"My Best Advice . . ."

Put your savings on automatic. Even though they didn't have access to the plenitude of easy ways to put money away that we enjoy today, our parents managed to succeed financially. Here are the observations of one recently retired couple:

We got married relatively late, in our forties. While my wife had a modest savings account, I had next to nothing, and this unhappy trend continued for our first few years of married life. We were excellent at spending everything we earned, but eventually our folly caught up with us when we couldn't even muster enough money to pay for a car repair. We knew then we had to change our ways. So we began to have money automatically taken out of our paychecks and put into a savings account, which for us was a lot safer than doing it ourselves. We didn't have the self-discipline. It worked, and over the years our employers and the financial companies made it even easier to put money away. There's no excuse these days not to take advantage of having money automatically moved from your paycheck or bank account into an investment account.

Retiree Reflections
"My Best Advice . . ."

Invest in your career. Baby boomers tend to be invested in their careers, but they may not realize that investing in those careers can be the single most important investment for achieving financial security. Here's how one person did it:

I spent my entire career as a teacher, or, more succinctly, in the education business. Education is hardly an occupation that provides grand riches, but I turned my first job as a primary-school teacher into a pretty well-paid career. After a few years teaching, I realized that I loved education, but didn't want to spend my life teaching, so I went back to school part-time for a master's degree. I steadily moved up the ranks in administrative capacities, took more course work, and attended lots of seminars. I was a principal at two different schools and eventually became superintendent of a school system. As my responsibilities grew, so did my income and pension. I retired from the system in my late fifties, but my experience was in great demand, so I consulted for several years thereafter. My experience is certainly not unique, but it is something that baby boomers in all occupations should consider. If you want to advance in your career and earn more money, do whatever's necessary to reach your goal—obtain more education, seek challenging assignments, change jobs, etc.

Retiree Reflections
"My Best Advice . . ."

Turn career setbacks into career success. Losing a job is inevitably expected to be a financial setback, if not a disaster. But, as the following reflection shows, in the words of industrial tycoon Henry Kaiser, "problems are only opportunities in work clothes."

> *I lost my job after twenty years, and at the time I thought both my work life and my finances were kaput. I feared losing the house and having to spend the retirement savings to buy food. Well, to make a long story short, that layoff was a turning point in my career. I had always thought of taking my experience in a different direction, and it worked out very well. If anything, my financial situation is even better. A lot of people are losing their jobs, and believe me, it's easy to get down on yourself. But use the experience as a time to shift gears if necessary. You just might find that the experience was a wake-up call to pursue your dreams.*

Timing (Your Retirement) Is Everything

Are you a member of the majority of baby boomers who want to continue working past the traditional retirement age? Or would you like to retire early? True to their independent spirit, no baby boomer seems to want to retire at age sixty-five. This is an important decision that brings together both financial and lifestyle considerations. Chapter 7 will help you navigate this important decision.

Retiree Reflections
"My Best Advice . . ."

Why retire at 65? Surveys indicate that the majority of boomers want to retire late, and while the debate over the "best" retirement age will rage on, here's a vote in favor of late retirement:

> *Here's my advice for working-age people: Think twice before retiring early. I was nowhere near ready for retirement when I was sixty-five—didn't know what I was going to do with all that free*

time. I also liked my job, and the company valued my knowledge and experience. When I did retire, I was much better prepared mentally, and I had a much larger income. Don't look at age sixty-five as some magic number when you have to leave the workforce. That may have worked for older generations, but sixty-five-year-olds today aren't necessarily ready for the rocking chair.

Retiree Reflections
"My Best Advice . . ."

Why wait until sixty-five to retire? As I said, opinions about when to retire vary. Here's a counterargument to the "retire late" contingent:

Retiring at sixty was the best decision we ever made. We had planned to do so for many years, reduced our standard of living, and were prepared to retire on less income in order to be able to enjoy those extra years of retirement. We've traveled a lot, spent the summers up North, and our golf handicaps are ten strokes lower than they were when we were working. If you can afford it, we heartily recommend early retirement.

Retiree Reflections
"My Best Advice . . ."

Don't get discouraged if you're a late starter. If you believe the media reports on baby boomer retirement preparedness, we're all in deep sneakers financially, but none so much as what is referred to as the proverbial "late starter." If baby boomers are in a dismal financial state, it follows that late starters are destined for destitution. At least that's how the media would have it. For another opinion, consider the reflections of this retired couple:

We'd like to address baby boomers who think that it's too late for them to start preparing financially for retirement. It's never too late, as we discovered. Imagine being fifty-eight-year-old renters with virtually no savings. Too late? That's what we thought, but did we have any choice but to try to do something to improve our circumstances? Through a combination of actions that involved saving, a bit of moonlighting, and delaying retirement until age sixty-seven, we're quite content with our lives. What a lot of people don't appreciate is how much Social Security can go toward your retirement expenses. Don't become discouraged. If we can do it, you can, too!

Are You Peripatetic or a Townie?

Just as important as when you're going to retire is where you're going to retire. Gone are the days where most retirees stayed put. Baby boomers are casting a wide—a worldwide—net in search of the ideal retirement locale. Chapter 9 will lay out the important criteria for deciding whether relocation is in your future.

Retiree Reflections
"My Best Advice . . ."
If you're going to relocate, stake out a place well ahead of time.

The best move we ever made in advance of retirement was to buy a second home in our fifties in a place where we were pretty confident we wanted to retire. We were able to spend quite a bit of time there over the years, and when we got ready to retire, we knew we had made the right decision. The sale of the big house provided us with a nice boost to our retirement savings. So our advice for baby boomers is to buy some real estate sooner, rather than later, if you're pretty certain you know where you want to retire. You can always change course later on, but having established roots in the new area made the transition to retirement a lot easier.

Retiree Reflections
"My Best Advice . . ."

Relocate and reduce. When they retire, baby boomers are expected to relocate in greater percentages than prior generations. Retiring to a more attractive locale, whether it's to a neighboring community, another state, or another country, can provide more opportunities to enjoy retirement. Moving to a lower-cost locale can work wonders on a retirement budget. Consider the following observations of a relocated retiree:

Moving from our high-cost, high-taxed state to a lower-cost state when we retired was the best financial decision we ever made. It cut our living costs almost by half. Moving to another locale is not something to be taken lightly. Expect family and friends to raise objections. But for us it was the right thing to do. We love our new home, new friends, and new activities. Our advice to baby boomers is, whether for financial reasons or simply to improve your quality of life, keep an open mind about relocating when you retire.

Making the Most of Your Abode

If most of your money is tied up in your home, you've got a lot of company amongst your fellow baby boomers. Decisions regarding your home can have a major bearing on your retirement prospects, as delineated in chapter 8.

Retiree Reflections
"My Best Advice . . ."

There's a lot to be said for trading in the old home for a new home. Downsizing has always made sense for many retirees, and baby boomers, always the trendsetters, are beginning to downsize well before they retire. But here's another reason to sell the old homestead:

We moved right after we retired. While the new place was a bit less expensive than what the old house fetched, our primary motivation was not financial. We wanted a place that wasn't going to require the work that a fifty-year-old home required. My husband and I aren't getting any younger, and we'd rather devote our time and money to travel rather than home repairs. It's the best retirement decision we made.

Preparing for the Unexpected and Unwelcome

Life is rife with perils and uncertainties, and you always need to defend yourself against unpleasant occurrences, many of which can be handled by having adequate insurance and keeping up-to-date wills and other estate-planning documents. Chapter 10 will provide guidance on dealing in advance with these problems so that most of them are just temporary annoyances.

Retiree Reflections
"My Best Advice . . ."

Don't let financial adversity discourage you. Few people get through their lives without suffering financial adversity. Even the legendary Donald Trump had to file business bankruptcy and was reported to be on the brink of personal bankruptcy, but he has done quite well since then, thank you very much. If you're ever in the throes of financial difficulty, take heart from this reflection by someone who has been in those shoes:

I'm amazed that I could ever retire, much less with the resources I have. I was close to destitute in my early fifties. I was laid up for months with medical problems and lost my job shortly after returning to work. I lost my condo and had to file for bankruptcy. But I got back on my feet, found a better job, and started anew. It wasn't easy, but my financial progress was steady. I bought a two-family house, and the rental income covers the majority of my housing expenses. A small inheritance went right into retirement savings. I'm retired now, and between the rental income, my retirement savings, and Social Security, I can live quite well. My advice for any baby boomers who find themselves in the same sinking boat is to pick yourself up and get back on track.

Good Wealth and Good Health Are a Family Matter

Achieving a great retirement is a family activity, and chapter 11 will review important financial and health matters that will benefit all family members throughout their lives.

Retiree Reflections
"My Best Advice . . ."

Don't keep up with the Joneses. Oh, the green-eyed monster, envy. Capitalism is a wonderful system, but one unfortunate by-product is that there are always people around who live a lifestyle we envy. But trying to keep up with these Joneses can be dangerous to your financial health. These retirees reflect on their years resisting financial temptation:

The best thing we ever did to attain financial security was actually something we didn't do. We didn't feel the need to live beyond our income. In fact, we became experts at stretching the family budget. We let our neighbors and friends support the economy through excessive spending. We didn't need a new car every few years or exotic vacations, or other symbols of the good life. Sure, we sometimes envied what others had, but we were actually very content with our life. I guess security was more important than owning whatever others owned. If spending is a problem for you, try to get off the "gotta have it" merry-go-round, as my husband and I call it. It's easier than you think, and the financial rewards are tremendous.

Retiree Reflections
"My Best Advice . . ."

Mind your health. According to the news reports, the baby boom generation wants to have it all. They want enough money to live well in retirement, and they want to enjoy good health so they can enjoy their wealth to the fullest. There's nothing wrong with that, so long as you pay attention to your physical as well as your financial health along the way.

Our recommendation for members of the baby boom generation is to develop good dietary and health habits. We both worked in the health-care business, so we can say firsthand that a small amount of effort keeping fit can pay many dividends later in life. Now that we're retired, we can see the difference. Some people are old at seventy-five while others are young at eighty-five. While there are no good health guarantees, you can most definitely stack the odds of a long, active, and healthy retirement in your favor by making good health a habit.

Retiree Reflections
"My Best Advice . . ."

Financially responsible kids = financially better off parents. What follows are some wise words from experienced parents.

The best thing we did for retirement might be a bit of a surprise, but it involved raising our kids to appreciate the value of a dollar. They've grown up to be reasonably good with money. That's not to say they don't have their faults. I think my son could actually survive without his boat. But the reason why I think helping children appreciate money and the value of work actually helps you in retirement is, quite simply, that if the kids are okay with money, then we don't have to shell out our retirement money to help support them (knock on wood). I can't begin to tell you how many of our acquaintances are having to scrimp in their retirement to help out their kids financially.

Retire with a Plan in Mind

Retirement planning isn't solely saving, investing, and number crunching. You also need to start thinking about what you want to do when you retire. There's nothing worse than an unplanned, boring retirement. Chapter 12 will help you plan what you're going to do when you retire. It's a pleasant process.

Retiree Reflections
"My Best Advice . . ."

Plan an active retirement. You may know some unfortunates who are miserable after they retire. Chances are they were either too invested in their careers or they didn't really give any thought to what they were going to do when they retired. Here are the sage thoughts of an ebullient duo who definitely like the retired life:

> We love retirement, but some retirees that we know are very unhappy. It's a shame to put in all that work and sacrifice only to end up at wit's end. We have a theory as to why this happens. They either never had any hobbies or interests when they were working, or they never planned any when they retired. So our advice to those who are thinking about retirement, even if it's ten or twenty years off, is to get a life outside your jobs. Then the transition to retirement will be very smooth. By the way, you've got to schedule in leisure time when you retire, because there are a lot of new, interesting, but unplanned activities that will arise. That was a bit of a problem for us early on. On the first anniversary of our retirement, my husband said that we'd been so busy over the past year that perhaps we should go back to work for a rest!

Retiree Reflections
"My Best Advice . . ."

Put training wheels on your retirement schedule. Retiring is a scary thought for many people. In the old days, those few people who survived to age sixty-five were usually so infirm that retirement was a relatively brief experience. But with so many people living into their nineties and beyond, the notion of retiring cold turkey and looking forward to (or dreading) twenty-five or more years of retirement is not something many people welcome. Add to that the need for many baby boomers to work a few years longer, and those who are contemplating retirement today are going to explore alternatives to outright retirement. They can continue to work full-time or they can taper down their work schedules by retiring gradually. Here's an endorsement from a gradual retiree:

> *I must confess that retirement was not something I looked forward to. My finances weren't in the best shape, and I just wasn't ready to retire. But I also wanted to leave my job at sixty-five. The idea of working part-time was appealing, so a couple of years before retirement I started planning and making inquiries about part-time job opportunities. This worked very well. I started working twenty-five hours a week, which sounds like a lot, but it was a welcomed reduction compared with the forty-hour week. I gradually reduced my work hours over the ensuing four years, but must admit that I still work about ten hours a week at age seventy-five. I just like the feeling of continuing to be productive. Financially, the extra income has been a big boost for me and has put me in a much better situation when I eventually retire completely.*

Changes Ahead at Retirement Time

As you approach retirement, you'll need to review each area of your financial planning to determine what, if any, changes need to be made. Chapter 13 takes a look at what's different in your investment and financial planning when you retire.

Retiree Reflections
"My Best Advice . . ."

Plan ahead for changes in your finances after you retire.

My best piece of advice is to think ahead about the changes you'll need to make in your finances when you retire. I waited too long and then hit the panic button the day after I retired, thinking I had to overhaul my investments, change my will and insurance policies. Had I thought about these things in advance and done a little homework, I would have avoided my uneasiness. It turned out that there weren't a whole lot of changes necessary, but those that were, were very important.

CHAPTER 3

The 60 Percent/40 Percent Diversification Solution

This and the two chapters that follow will help you dramatically improve your investment profits. This chapter deals with the key area of investment diversification. You undoubtedly have a variety of choices of places to invest for retirement. It's not easy getting an objective opinion about which are best for you, but the next chapter will set you straight once and for all. Chapter 5 will show you low-risk ways to maximize your investment returns. If you need a quick review of the basics of investing, including a primer on investment diversification and better understanding stocks, bonds, and mutual funds, visit Appendix II.

Double the income you receive from your investments. Depending on how you're currently investing, these easy-to-follow investment guidelines could easily *double* the amount of income you can withdraw from your investments throughout your retirement years, and achieving that lofty goal is well within your grasp. It doesn't involve high-risk investments or big bets on a particular investment sector. It won't require you to spend your evenings and weekends poring over investment information. It's an investment of perhaps a couple of hours each quarter. Think of it as a part-time job that pays hundreds, if not thousands, of dollars an hour in additional investment income.

Investing Made Easy

Most boomers have neither the time nor the inclination to devote a lot of time to studying the stock market and monitoring their holdings. Yet, you are at a stage in your life when investing wisely and well becomes crucially important, because ere long you're going to need this money to support you for decades. The older you get, the less time you have to make up for major investment errors. A boneheaded investment was a learning experience when you were twenty-five. A similar investment mistake can be a retirement setback at age fifty.

But sensible investing needn't be intimidating. As long as your money is well diversified, it's hard to go wrong. Depending on how much you want to be involved in your investing, here are two strategies for assembling and managing a sleep-tight investment portfolio:

✦ **Autopilot investing.** This is ideal for investors who would just as soon "set it and forget it." Simply divvy up your money according to your level of comfort with investment risk, identify the best possible investments for each account, and periodically review and rebalance your investment holdings.

✦ **Active investing.** If you like to actively manage your stash, a lot of sensible investing strategies will allow you to do your thing without taking undue risk. Once you set up your diversification parameters, refer to chapter 5 and Appendix III for some ideas for active investors.

The sections that follow will help you gain an understanding of how to structure your investments to avoid a common shortcoming—having too many retirement eggs in one basket. Here's what follows:

✦ **Building an investment foundation.** A strong investment foundation will allow you to invest in areas of greater growth potential without excessive risk.

✦ **There's nothing wrong with old-fashioned investing.** You don't need to venture outside the investment mainstream to capture eye-popping portfolio returns.

✦ **Diversification explained.** Diversification is a straightforward but often misunderstood axiom that you'll understand at last.

✦ **The 60 percent/40 percent solution.** The reason why a 60 percent stock and 40 percent bond allocation has benefited investors for generations.

✦ **Thou canst not predict the market.** Market timing is alluring. But no one can predict the near-term direction of the stock market or interest rates.

✦ **Rebalancing your holdings.** Periodically rebalancing your holdings will move you from being a merely outstanding investor to a truly great investor.

✦ **Maintaining the course, even during periods of maximum pessimism.** Why the temptation to change course amidst market turmoil is inevitably a losing gambit.

SUCCESS STORY: ATTENTION!!!!

"My biggest mistake in preparing for retirement in my forties was not paying attention to my investments. Fortunately, when I was in my early fifties, I began to take an interest in investing and vastly improved my returns, allowing me to retire two years earlier than I had originally planned."

Building an Investment Foundation

The great bull market of the 1990s caused a lot of people to think that diversifying your investments was no longer necessary, and that the more risk you take with your investments, the better they will perform. Some thought that a diversified portfolio consisted of one dot-com stock and one wireless-telecommunications stock. True, everyone needs to take risks with their investments, but there are different levels of risk. That's where building an investment foundation comes in. Think of all your investments as fitting into a pyramid, as depicted on page 36.

✦ At the highest level are the riskiest investments, including speculative stocks and sector funds.

✦ The middle level of the pyramid includes investments that are somewhat less risky, including small-company and international stock funds, which all investors should own, and junk bond funds that may be appealing when the economy is strong.

✦ Finally, and most important, is the lower level or foundation of your investment pyramid. It includes high-quality stocks and interest-earning securities or mutual funds that own these securities. Your entire investment portfolio is supported by the foundation.

What concerns me is that a lot of investors are still putting too much of their money into the top level of their investment pyramid and too little in the foundation. I urge you to evaluate where your investments fit in the pyramid, and to make sure you have a solid foundation. In fact, the stronger the foundation you build, the more risk you can assume at the two higher levels of your investment pyramid.

YOUR INVESTMENT PYRAMID

HIGHER-RISK
INVESTMENTS
$ Speculative stocks
$ Sector funds

MODERATE-RISK
INVESTMENTS

$ Small- and midsize-company stock funds
$ International stock funds
$ Junk bond funds

FOUNDATION
LOWER-RISK INVESTMENTS

$ High-quality stocks
$ Large-company stock funds
$ U.S. government bonds and bond funds
$ Higher-quality corporate and municipal bonds and bond funds

If most of those investment terms are unfamiliar, start by reviewing Appendix II, which describes the most common investment categories.

SUCCESS STORY: INVESTING CASH AT LAST

Whether out of fear or inertia, many savers haven't taken the next step toward becoming real investors. This is a success story shared by all of those who have taken the leap. "It's not like I didn't have any money invested in the stock market. Some of the money in my 401(k) was in stocks, and I had a couple of stock mutual funds in my IRA. But most of the money (over 80 percent, I found out) was sitting in bank savings accounts or the occasional CD. When I started hearing about how badly baby boomers were preparing for retirement, I figured it was time to do something about my money, despite the fact that the thought of losing money scares me. I wasn't about to sink all my savings into the stock market. So I started with 25 percent. It did okay, so I upped it very gradually over several years. Now I'm about 50 percent in stocks, which I think is a good level. The way I figure it, even if the stock market dives, I wouldn't be affected nearly as much as if I had a higher percentage in stocks. While some of the rest is still in savings accounts, most of it is earning a better rate of interest in U.S. Treasury notes, bond funds, and money market funds. I hate to think what kind of financial shape I'd be in if I had continued to let the money sit in low-interest accounts."

There's Nothing Wrong with Old-Fashioned Investing

Investing successfully is crucial to your financial future, but there is no mystery to it—just a lot of common sense applied to techniques that have been used by successful investors for decades. The following sections will lead you through the assembly of a diversified investment portfolio. You may be intimidated by the prospect of paying more attention to your investments. You may have been led to believe that investing is complicated and the average Joe and Jane are simply incapable of making sensible investment decisions. *Everyone* can be a successful investor, and the way to success is through old-fashioned, dull investments. Indeed, "happiness is a dull portfolio."

Many years ago, a photograph of me appeared in *The Boston Globe* above the caption: "Jonathan Pond advocates dullness and passivity." An acquaintance called my wife and read the caption, to which she responded, "Why is he telling the newspaper reporter about our love life?" Actually, I was warning about investors constantly buying and selling their investment holdings in the vain attempt to latch onto the next hot stock or market-leading mutual fund.

As mentioned above, diversification was discredited in the late 1990s when technology stocks were so hot that every other category of stocks paled in comparison. But the 1990s were followed by a big three-year downdraft (to put it mildly) that impaled technology stocks. Suddenly, investment diversification was back in vogue. But it had always been in vogue, because it was a lack of diversification that got all those tech-stock zealots in trouble. Diversification—in other words, spreading your money among several types of investments—accomplishes two crucial objectives:

1. You'll always have at least some of your money in investment areas that are thriving, and you'll never have too much money in an area that's diving.

2. Diversifying among various categories reduces overall investment risk while increasing investment returns. Lower risk with higher returns sounds too good to be true, but it is true.

There is a small price to pay for diversification. Because your money has been sown in many pastures, your investment returns are bound to underperform the leading performance benchmark—the one that gets all of the media attention. But you'll sleep like a rock.

INVESTMENT Q&A: WHY TAKE ANY RISK WITH MY INVESTMENTS WHEN I CAN EARN SOME PRETTY DECENT INCOME FROM NO-RISK INVESTMENTS?

Most of us are investing for the long term—unless you've just received a bad report from your doctor—and long-term investors should worry more about how their money will fare over the next five, ten, or twenty years rather than how it did last week or last quarter. Here's an example that illustrates my point: Had you put $100,000 into Treasury bills in 1996, you'd have about $150,000 in your kitty ten years later—not bad. But had you invested it in stocks—here I'm using the Standard & Poor's 500 Stock Index—you'd have about $260,000 over the same time period. That's over 70 percent more money, and keep in mind that the ten-year period includes the terrible three-year declining market from early 2000 through early 2003. Lesson: The biggest risk in investing is taking no risk at all, because it will then be well-nigh impossible to earn the kind of money on your investments necessary to reach your retirement goals. If you need more convincing that investment risk is actually your friend, not your enemy, please visit Appendix II.

HOW AGE INFLUENCES THE WAY YOU DIVERSIFY YOUR INVESTMENTS

Does age matter when it comes to investment diversification? Not as much as many boomers think. There are two phases of investing: the accumulation years, covering all of your working years, and the withdrawal years. The withdrawal years commence in retirement when you're going to need to gradually draw down on your resources to pay living expenses, assuming your children aren't going to step up and pay for your retirement. (Mine aren't.) There may be some portfolio tweaking just as you enter retirement, as discussed beginning on page 282. But so long as you're still working, there isn't a lot of difference as to how baby boomers should invest for retirement, no matter what their age. The primary way that age determines how you should invest is how long you'll need to rely on your nest egg to support you—your so-called investment horizon. Since it's prudent to plan on a life expectancy of at least age ninety, the oldest boomers who are now in their early sixties have an investment horizon of at least thirty years, while the youngest boomers have an investment horizon of about fifty years. In the milieu of investment diversification, there isn't a lot of difference between a thirty-year and a fifty-year time horizon.

MYTH DEBUNKER: WHEN BOOMERS RETIRE, THE STOCK MARKET WILL PLUMMET AS THEY ALL SELL STOCKS AT ONCE TO PAY LIVING EXPENSES

Sounds like a sound argument, but it doesn't wash. First, boomers won't be retiring en masse; rather, they will retire over a twentysome-year period. Second, affluent retirees—those who hold most of the stocks in the first instance—aren't going to be selling stocks in any great measure until much later in life, typically in their late seventies or early eighties. Until then, they'll actually be reinvesting their investment gains, rather than drawing them down. Finally, the younger boomers and the fifty-five million Generation Xers will pick up the slack as they enter their peak savings years.

The 60 Percent/40 Percent Solution

By this I mean investing 60 percent of your long-term investment money in stocks and 40 percent in bonds and other interest-earnings securities. As you grapple with how to structure your portfolio going forward, a little history lesson can be enlightening.

You're not too young to remember as far back as the 1980s—before the great bull market of the 1990s. Way back then, investors paid a lot of attention to the best ways to balance investment risk and return; in other words, how to earn attractive investment returns without taking too much risk. Of course, such concerns were of little import during the heady days of the 1990s, when everyone became obsessed with maximizing investment returns. Bonds were for sissies, as were Old Economy stocks. A New Economy had dawned, and risk was of little concern since all stocks were rising. The primary challenge was to make sure you invested in stocks that were growing the fastest, tech stocks in general, and dot-com stocks in particular. It was great fun while it lasted.

But now that investors have once again been reminded, albeit painfully, that stock price movements are not unidirectional, another look at history might again be illuminating. In the 1980s and before, most of the studies on asset allocation suggested that an investment mix of 60 percent stocks and 40 percent bonds was an optimal way for most investors to balance the two investment objectives of earning an inflation-beating return and not taking too much risk. Thus, it's no coincidence that "balanced" mutual funds (see page 56) almost always hew to a target allocation of 60 percent stocks and 40 percent bonds. If your investment diversification varies considerably from these parameters, you may be taking too much or too little risk.

A sleep-tight portfolio. *Bond,* like *risk,* is not a four-letter word in the Anglo-Saxon sense. While bond prices and stock prices don't always move in opposition to each other, bonds usually smooth out the volatility inherent in stock prices. Therefore, in bull markets, bonds reduce portfolio returns (hence, the aversion to bonds in the 1990s), but in bear markets, bonds can enhance portfolio returns, as has amply been demonstrated over 2000 to 2002. Stock devotees argue that since periods of rising stock prices are far longer in duration than periods of falling stock prices, a weighting in stocks heavier than a mere 60 percent is preferable. (Bonds, in the aggregate, gained 6.2 percent per annum over the past ten years, while the Standard & Poor's 500 Stock Index provided a 9.1 percent annualized return.) But most investors aren't willing to assume the risk inherent in an all-stock or heavy-stock investment allocation. Rather, they are willing to trade off the higher potential returns of a stock-heavy portfolio for the somewhat lower returns of a more balanced mix of stocks and bonds. Actually, the presence of bonds does not drag overall returns down as much as you might expect. That's because the assured interest paid by bonds and reinvested by retirement savers, while lower than bull-market stock gains, is nevertheless steadily adding to overall investment returns.

A 60 percent stock/40 percent bond investment allocation is not cast in concrete. Rather, consider it a benchmark around which you customize your own diversification strategy. One major ingredient in coming up with a diversification model that fits you is how comfortable you are with investment risk, which is next on the docket.

What kind of investor are you? If you're going to join the "sleep at night" investor fraternity, you have to decide how comfortable you are with investment risk. The investment community refers to this as your "risk profile," whatever that means. Basically, investors fall into one of three general categories depending on how well they can tolerate periodic dips in the value of their investments:

✦ An *aggressive investor* wants to achieve high long-term investment returns, even if that means that the investments will periodically experience heart-stopping short-term declines in value.

✦ A *moderate investor* wants to achieve a balance between earning attractive long-term investment returns and reducing periodic fluctuations in value.

✦ A *conservative investor* seeks stable growth in his or her investments, even if that means somewhat lower returns over time. A conservative investor is not as comfortable as other investors with the ups and downs of the stock market.

What's your preference? _____

Investment-diversification illustrations. Depending on whether you're a conservative, moderate, or aggressive investor, Table 3.1 shows examples of ways to diversify your investments. The essence of successful investing is divvying up your retirement money along the lines suggested in Table 3.1, putting the money into the most auspicious types of investment accounts (that's explained in the next chapter), buying the best investments you or your adviser can possibly identify (see page 94) and rebalancing your holdings periodically (explained on page 51). Sounds complicated and time consuming, but it isn't.

Why every well-diversified investment portfolio needs small- and midcap stocks in addition to large-cap stocks. Although the way you divvy up your investment money between stocks and bonds is important, that's only the first step in constructing an investment portfolio that will serve you well both during your remaining working years and when you're retired. You also need to spread your stock and bond money among the various categories of stocks and bonds. Many

TABLE 3.1
SUGGESTED INVESTMENT ALLOCATIONS
BY INVESTOR "RISK PROFILE"

	AGGRESSIVE	MODERATE	CONSERVATIVE
STOCKS/STOCK FUNDS			
Large company	30%	25%	20%
Midsize /			
small company	30	20	10
International company	20	15	10
Subtotal stock funds	*80*	*60*	*40*
BONDS/BOND FUNDS			
U.S. Government bond	5	15	40
Treasury inflation-			
protected securities			
(TIPS)	0	15	20
Corporate /			
municipal bonds	10	10	0
Foreign bonds	5	0	0
Subtotal bond funds	*20*	*40*	*60*
Total	100%	100%	100%

investors don't have much, if any, money invested in small- and mid-cap stocks. Ditto for many large financial institutions that manage individual portfolios, as noted on page 45. These institutions concentrate on what they research and know well—large-company stocks. While it may be comforting to invest in large, well-established companies, a stock portfolio consisting entirely of large-company stock shares is actually riskier than a portfolio that includes a serving of smaller-company stocks. Moreover, past performance indicates that midsize- and smaller-company stocks actually outperform their larger brethren, as Table 3.2 illustrates. (For a definition of large-cap, midcap, and small-cap stocks, see page 342.)

Lower your risk and increase your return. You or your financial adviser should take a close look at how well the stock portion of your investments is diversified. While you may be a bit reluctant to invest in small and midsize companies that aren't household names, investing in these stock categories should reduce overall risk in your stock portfolio while increasing investment returns. That's a pretty good combination!

w w w

Special note to investors whose money is being managed by large financial institutions. If your money is being managed by a big financial institution, such as a bank or brokerage firm, you may find that your investments are bereft of mid- and small-cap stocks. These firms usually specialize in large-company stocks, and they're often very good at what they do. But their expertise may not extend to small- and midsize company stocks, in which case you have three choices. First, you can maintain the status quo, but at the risk of lower returns and higher volatility from omitting smaller stocks from your portfolio. Second, you can ask the institution to add small- and midcap stocks to your portfolio, but be forewarned that they may do so by putting you into their proprietary mutual funds, which may be plodders. If so, ask your adviser to pick some better ones. A third choice would be to use money you have in other accounts, such as retirement accounts at work, to create your own small- and midcap stock portfolio—using mutual funds—to complement the large-company stocks being managed for you.

Foreign investments are crucial, too. There's always a bull market somewhere in the world, and it's frequently outside the United States. Just like mid- and small-cap stocks, international stocks add an important level of diversification. But investors have to be even more patient with their foreign stock investments than with their domestic

---

TABLE 3.2
SMALL- AND MIDCAP STOCKS
ADD SIZZLE TO A DIVERSIFIED PORTFOLIO

This table compares the performance of large-company stocks against the performance of mid- and small-company stocks using three Standard & Poor's indexes that track the performance of the three stock categories.

	ANNUALIZED RETURNS FOR PERIODS ENDING JUNE 30, 2006				
	1 YEAR	3 YEARS	5 YEARS	10 YEARS	15 YEARS
Large-cap stocks (S&P 500)	+9%	+11%	+2%	+8%	+11%
Midcap stocks (S&P 400)	+13	+18	+9	+14	+15
Small-cap stocks (S&P 600)	+14	+20	+11	+12	+14

---

stocks, because foreign stocks can perform poorly over long periods, with performance ranging anywhere from disappointing to downright awful, only to finally reward patient investors with quick and substantial gains. History has shown that international stocks can be particularly beneficial when U.S. stocks are struggling.

A complicated business. An international-stock investment manager must be on top of numerous bourses (a fancy word for "stock exchanges") from South Africa to Sweden, from China to the UK. At any time, some of these markets may be rising, while others are declining. But identifying propitious foreign markets is just part of the battle. Individual companies within these markets must be identified and monitored. The trouble is, most foreign stocks don't receive anywhere near the scrutiny that U.S. stocks do. That can be both a problem and an opportunity. The problem is simply finding these promising stocks. The opportunity is, since these stocks are not widely followed by the investment community, they may offer more growth potential than stocks with a wider following. Nevertheless, don't expect a smooth ride with foreign stocks.

You can opt for a variety of index funds and exchange-traded funds (ETFs) that invest in foreign stocks. (See page 113 for an explanation of index funds and ETFs.) While passive management can work well in several investment settings, the international stock arena is not one of them precisely because it comprises many stock markets, each with its own unique set of economic and investment conditions. At any one time, some bourses are probably best eschewed, while others are attractive. An unmanaged approach to international investing through index funds or ETFs means your money is invested in the good, the bad, and the ugly. Table 3.3 shows the performance difference between an international index and an average international mutual fund through mid-2006.

Mutual funds are preferable. You are well advised to employ the services of an investment professional with expertise in worldwide investing, one who has daily access to experts located in foreign countries who keep track of local market conditions and opportunities. Finally, the investment company should have experience in investing in foreign markets using foreign currency. How much will you need to invest to be able to hire such vast capabilities? A few million? Several hundred thousand? No, just a couple thousand dollars. That's how much it will cost you to secure the services of a

TABLE 3.3
THE CASE FOR INTERNATIONAL MUTUAL FUNDS

	3 YEARS	5 YEARS	10 YEARS	15 YEARS
MSCI EAFE Index*	+17%	+2%	+4%	+4%
Average International Stock Fund	+24	+11	+8	+9

*MSCI EAFE Index stands for a mouthful: Morgan Stanley Capital International Europe, Australasia, and Far East Index. It is widely considered the benchmark against which international-stock mutual funds are measured.

top-notch international or global mutual fund manager at a top-drawer investment company. **w w w**

Diversification notes. Here are some notes that will help you tailor your own diversification strategy to meet your unique situation:

✦ **Guidelines for all your investments.** These guidelines apply to all of your stock and bond investments—mutual funds as well as individual stocks and bonds. In addition to stocks and bonds, two other categories of investments are not considered herein, but that doesn't mean that they shouldn't necessarily play a role in your investing:

1. **Temporary investments,** such as money market funds, Treasury bills, and savings accounts are most appropriate to meet short-term investment needs. In other words, when you know you're going to need some money within the next year or two to pay for a home improvement, a new car, or your daughter's college tuition, for example. While temporary investments (also called short-term investments) usually pay only modest rates of interest, they also protect your principal—a judicious thing to do with money you know you're going to need soon (unless you're so flush that you can afford that risk). See page 117 for some guidance on making the most of your temporary investments.

2. **Real estate** is a fourth investment category, and an important category at that. If you invest in income-producing real estate or want to, some guidelines are presented beginning on page 362. If you're not all that anxious to become a landlord or landlady, you might consider a real estate mutual fund or individual stocks that invest in real estate, called real estate investment trusts, or REITs.

✦ **Combine all of your investment accounts.** If you have a 401(k) or similar plan where you work, remember to combine the money you're investing in that account, as well as all other investment accounts you might have, when deciding how to divvy up your money in a balanced and diversified fashion.

✦ **Be sure to hold "enough" stock.** You may think that the above percentages allocated to stocks are a bit weighty, particularly if you consider yourself a conservative investor and/or have otherwise been burned with stocks in the past. But every baby boomer needs a sizable helping of stocks to thrive in retirement. Hence, you should always have at least 40 percent of your retirement-earmarked money in stocks. That's the floor, not only for you, but also for septuagenarians and octogenarians, all of whom need a growth component in their portfolios.

✦ **Taxing matters.** The way you allocate your money in the bond categories depends on whether your investments are in tax-deferred retirement accounts and/or taxable accounts. Since the interest income from municipal bond funds is exempt from federal and, perhaps, state income taxes, you should invest in them only in a *taxable* investment account. Since the interest earned on corporate bond funds is subject to both federal and state income taxes, they are best suited for *retirement* accounts since the interest that would otherwise be heavily taxed is not subject to income taxes until you begin withdrawing. Tax-efficient investing, in other words, minimizing taxes on your investments, is further explained on page 106.

✦ **Treasury inflation-protected securities.** A definition is in order, because *Treasury inflation-protected securities* haven't yet been defined. TIPS, as they are affectionately called, are securities issued by the U.S. Treasury at a fixed rate of interest, but with principal adjusted every six months based on changes in the Consumer Price Index. TIPS offer a lower interest rate in exchange for the inflation protection. Also, the inflation adjustment is federally taxable annually, although not paid out until maturity or until you sell the individual bond or a TIPS mutual fund. Because you pay taxes on interest that you don't receive, TIPS are often better placed in a retirement account, since taxes aren't paid on the income until after retirement. All in all, TIPS are often a worthy addition to a retirement portfolio, offering the safety of a Treasury security with an inflation kicker, doubly important if you expect inflation to heat up in the future.

✦ **If you'll be receiving a pension . . .** When planning your investment portfolio diversification, count any expected pension benefits as a bond. This may argue for a higher percentage in stocks, particularly if your pension benefits are fixed or any increases may lag inflation. Having a somewhat higher percentage of your non-pension-plan investments in stocks will provide the growth you'll need to offset the declining purchasing power of a fixed pension. Remember also that Social Security retirement benefits are the equivalent of a bond as well, actually better than a bond because, as opposed to a bond's fixed-interest payments, Social Security benefits are adjusted annually for inflation.

✦ **If you use an investment adviser . . .** If you use an investment adviser, be sure to find out how your money is allocated. You may find out that it isn't well diversified, in which case ask your adviser to offer some suggestions for diversifying.

✦ **Why so much in small- and midcap stocks and international stocks?** You may be wondering why I'm recommending that you put half to 60 percent of your stock money in small- and midcap stocks and international stocks. Does it sound risky? It isn't, simply because spreading the money around among those categories simply adds to your overall diversification.

A WATCHED PORTFOLIO NEVER BOILS

I was giving a corporate seminar a while ago, and I asked members of the audience how often they checked their 401(k) plan investments. One wag proudly proclaimed, "Several times a day." My immediate reaction (not voiced) was that this employee should be fired. What could possibly be accomplished by checking your investments daily or even weekly? Do these people have a life? The problem with checking your investments incessantly is that you're likely to be motivated to *do something*. But when it comes to investing, often the best thing to do is nothing.

Rebalancing Your Investments — Icing on the Cake

If you parcel out your investment money, ipso facto you will achieve good investment results without subjecting your money to too much risk. But there's one further step in diversification. Periodically rebalancing your investment allocation should help you achieve even better results. It is so effective because it forces you to do the right thing, even if it requires you to go against the prevailing opinion of the Wall Street clique, which is often a good thing to do. **w w w**

Here's how rebalancing works. About every six months, summarize your investments to see how they're allocated. Be sure to combine all of your investment accounts. Rebalancing is a waste of time if you fail to consider all of the money you have available for investment. Figure out for your combined portfolios what the current percentages are in stocks and bonds. Chances are that you'll find that the percentages you now have in stocks and bonds vary a bit from the allocation you want, your "target allocation." That's because stock and bond values fluctuate. What rebalancing does is bring your investments back to your target-allocation percentages. Here's a brief example:

Reba Rebalance has a target allocation of 60 percent stocks and 40 percent bonds. But stock prices have declined over the past six months, so stocks now account for 54 percent of her portfolio's total value. What should Reba do? Rebalance by selling enough of her bond investments and using that money to add more to her stock investments so that she brings her portfolio back to her 60 percent stock and 40 percent bond target allocation. In selling bonds and buying stocks, Reba should try to adhere to her target percentage allocations within each of her various stock categories (e.g., large-cap, mid- and small-cap, and international) and bond categories (e.g., government bonds, corporate and/or municipal bonds).

In the above example, the stock market had declined rather sharply over the previous half year, and you're buying stocks after they have declined in value. Would this not be a good time to be buying a *small amount* of stock investments? If the market has declined sharply, the investment experts are flooding the airwaves with a dire outlook. You're probably buying some of your stocks at a time when the great majority of investors are selling. But that's okay. Rebalancing also forces you to sell some of your stock investments if the stock market has risen and add to bonds when interest rates have risen. Appendix II explains how bond prices change in reaction to changes in interest rates. By following this formula, you're buying cheap and selling dear, while avoiding making any major shifts in your investments. You're simply getting back to your target allocation. Rebalancing has and will continue to be icing on the cake for attentive (but not obsessive) well-diversified investors. There's also something gratifying about having the discipline to go against prevailing market wisdom, a trait shared by all of the world's greatest investors. Join that laudable crowd.

How often should you rebalance? You might be thinking that if rebalancing is such a great thing, you should do it all the time. It takes some time, and you don't want to burden yourself by doing it too often. While rebalancing once a year may be appropriate for many investors, my recommendation is to at least consider rebalancing about every six months, *unless* there has been a sudden and significant change in either stock prices or interest rates (which affect bond prices). Then, you might want to rebalance in less than six months.

Some important things to consider. Sometimes, the costs or inconvenience of rebalancing may outweigh the benefits.

+ **Taxes.** Before rebalancing, carefully analyze what, if any, tax consequences would result, and avoid making sales with costly tax consequences, particularly short-term capital gains, which are taxed more heavily than long-term gains. Instead, find alternatives that will result in your owing little or no taxes. Rebalancing in a retirement account is usually preferable since no taxes are owed until you start withdrawing money from the retirement account.

+ **Investment costs.** Also, be mindful of investment costs. The benefits of rebalancing can soon be lost if fees and commissions eat away at your portfolio. Rebalance through no-load funds or load fund families that allow no-cost switches within the fund family.

+ **De minimis amounts needed to rebalance.** Finally, you will often find that the necessary rebalancing involves such a small amount of money that it isn't worth your time and effort. Simply wait another six months before doing it. But you can't reach that conclusion without finding out exactly where your portfolio stands.

The Golden Rule of Investing: Thou Canst Not Predict the Market

The investment diversification and rebalancing guidelines described above are intended to take the guesswork out of investing. Nevertheless, you'll still have to cope with delusional people who actually think they can predict the near-term direction of the stock market and interest rates (interest-rate moves influence bond prices and short-term investment yields). The best analogy to market timing is natural family planning. As a conception (please excuse the pun), it certainly sounds doable. And as a short-term strategy, it may even work. But, over the long term, its failure will be announced with a lusty cry.

The allure of market timing is understandable. Long bull markets make investors skittish. Quick market downturns scare everyone. The notion that you or someone else can actually get out of the market just before it takes a dip and then get back into the market just before it rebounds is terribly attractive. I spent an inordinate amount of time in college trying to predict the market, and I had the grades to prove it. (While my friends were graduating cum laude, I graduated "thank you, laude.") Fortunately, my investment resources were modest, so I learned a not-too-expensive lesson.

The big challenge. The major challenge in trying to time the stock market is not so much getting out of the market before it drops as it is deciding when to get back in. Some investors manage to get out in time, but more often they get out in anticipation of a drop that doesn't occur. The real challenge is getting back in just before the inevitable rebound. Usually, stock prices surge quickly after a drop, and the jump occurs just when gloom and doom permeate Wall Street and Main Street. This reminds me of a caller on a radio talk show who told me he had gotten out of stocks entirely quite a while ago and was wondering if it was a good time to get back in. I gave him my Pavlovian response that any time is a good time for long-term investors to invest in stocks. But, since all of his money was on the sidelines, I encouraged him to reinvest the money gradually—over the next year or two. I then asked this chap when he got out of stocks. He said that it was right after a major stock decline many years prior, and since then the market had risen sharply, but he had just not been able to figure out when to get back in. While he was wondering when to reinvest, stocks had quadrupled!

The golden rule. Recognizing that you'll never be able to predict the near-term performance of the investment markets is epiphanic. Then you can confidently devise a diversified investment strategy and stick with it, even when you've lost money and the Wall Street pundits are spewing nothing but awful forecasts for stocks or bonds or both. Keep investing, using the power of dollar-cost averaging (investing relatively fixed amounts of money at regular intervals), which is precisely what most boomers are doing by contributing to their retirement savings plans and IRAs.

Maintain the course, even during periods of maximum pessimism. If you have the wisdom to devise and then stick with a sensible approach to investing, the biggest investment challenge you'll have to confront from here on out is avoiding the temptation to abandon your plan. The stock market has and will periodically scare the bejeepers out of you. You're also at an age when suffering losses is particularly anxiety-provoking. But the only worthwhile long-term investments will periodically lose value, including stocks, bonds, real estate, mutual funds, exchange-traded funds (ETFs; see page 113), and the like that hold those securities. They will temporarily lose value between now and the time you retire as well as after you retire. But patience is a virtue that should help you make up for lost ground—and then some. Consider Table 3.4, which chronicles all of the years since 1950 in which the Standard & Poor's 500 Stock Index has declined. The rightmost column shows the gain in the Standard & Poor's stocks during the subsequent year(s). Incidentally, the stock market crash of October 1987 didn't even make the list, because stocks were actually up for the year. FYI: Even though the following-year gains were usually greater than the losses, in some periods it was still not enough to recoup all of the losses. For example, if the stock market declines 20 percent, it would take a 25 percent gain from that level to get back to even. But the main purpose of this table is to show how dangerous it is to get out of stocks when you're losing money on them, no matter how painful that might be.

TABLE 3.4
IT'S ALWAYS DARKEST BEFORE THE DAWN

DOWN MARKET YEAR(S)	AMOUNT OF DECLINE	GAIN IN FOLLOWING YEAR(S)
1953	−1%	+53%
1957	−11	+43
1962	−9	+23
1966	−10	+24
1969	−9	+4
1973–74	−37	+70*
1977	−7	+7
1981	−5	+21
1990	−3	+31
2000–2002	−38	+50**

Gain over the two years following the two-year decline.

**Gain over the three years following the three-year decline.*

THE ONE FUND TO OWN IF YOU OWN
ONLY ONE FUND

If you have a small amount of money to invest or if you're setting up a small investment account for a younger-generation
family member, you can use a "balanced fund" to obtain instant diversification within a single investment. Balanced
funds maintain a "balanced" combination of stocks and bonds,
usually somewhere around 60 percent in stocks and 40 percent in bonds, an allocation that you know old Jonathan finds
quite attractive. One of the advantages of balanced funds
and a major reason they have done so well as long-term

investments is the forced discipline that they impose on the fund manager. As stock prices rise, the fund manager is forced to rebalance by selling stocks to bring the portfolio back into balance. Conversely, if stock prices decline, the fund manager will be purchasing stock to bring the fund back into balance. Thus, the manager is forced to "buy low" and "sell high." **w w w**

SUCCESS STORY: ROLLOVER MINEFIELD

Talk about bad timing. Andrew Lang moved to a new job, and in December 1999 his 401(k) was rolled over into an IRA. This was his largest investment account by far, and his friends were eager to help him. The most vociferous said that he'd lucked out, because his 401(k) plan didn't offer any technology stocks. "Now you can start to get some action in your IRA with some tech funds and dot-com stocks. After all, why settle for 15 percent on stock funds when you can at least double your money in technology?" Andrew was not convinced. He remembered his grandparents talking about the 1929 crash. So he resisted the advice and instead spread his money around among a variety of funds, putting only 10 percent into a tech fund. Well, the long and painful three-year bear market commenced almost immediately after he invested the IRA money. He ended up losing about 15 percent of the money, which looked pretty good compared to his technophile friend's 60 percent loss.

CHAPTER 4

The Best Ways to Invest for Retirement

Uncle Sam wants you—to save for retirement, and like any benevolent uncle, he's more than happy to assist you in planning your retirement. The federal government long ago concluded that it had two choices: Either provide incentives for people to save for retirement, or be prepared to use federal money to support retirees. In a rare moment of sagacity, the government concluded that foisting the burden of preparing financially for retirement on the working populace was better than having the government pick up the tab any more than it is already with the Social Security system. The incentives consist of tax breaks for retirement-plan participants. Of course, you'll end up paying Uncle back when you're retired and start withdrawing money from the plan, but, hey, that's off in the future. 'Tis much better to save a dollar in taxes this year in exchange for paying that dollar back ten, twenty, or thirty years from now.

Our collective uncle has been so eager to help us save for retirement that hardly a year goes by without the introduction of a new plan or a rules change that improves plans extant. This chapter will help you identify the best ways to invest for retirement, and since those depend in large measure on your own employment and financial circumstances, you'll find some checklists that will help you make these important decisions. Here's a rundown of the chapter:

+ **Selecting the best retirement investments.** Some plans are better than others, so it's important to know how the various plans stack up.

+ **Retirement-plan decision makers.** Depending on your employment situation, your decision maker will show you the best plans in which to participate.

+ **IRAs.** Regular IRA contributions are essential for most retirement savers, particularly boomers. Help on Roth IRA conversions is also provided.

+ **Evaluating your 401(k) and 403(b) plan choices.** Alas, far too many employee retirement savings plans offer an array of choices that range from below average to atrocious. This decision maker will help you make the most of your choices.

+ **IRA rollovers.** If you need help deciding whether to roll over an IRA from a previous employer's plan, this section will give you the information you'll need to make the right decision.

+ **Retirement plans for the self-employed.** If you currently have any income from self-employment or plan to in the future, you'll find out about two plans that allow you to put away stupefying amounts of money and deduct it all.

+ **Roth 401(k)s and 403(b)s.** You'll receive a heads-up on a new kind of workplace retirement savings plan that many employers will be rolling out.

+ **Life-cycle funds.** These funds, which include "lifestyle" and "target" funds, are becoming increasingly popular as a single place to invest retirement money, but are they right for you?

✦ **Simplifying your investment life.** If you have a surfeit of investment accounts, I'll give you some tips on paring down the number of accounts. Then you'll have more time to manage your exhausting baby boomer schedule!

Selecting the Best Retirement Investments

The primary motivational mechanisms created by our elected officials are tax breaks. By investing in the various retirement plans for which you qualify, you will enjoy at least one and possibly two of these tax-saving benefits:

1. **Tax deferral.** All retirement savings plans share one feature: the income you earn on investments inside these plans is not subject to taxes until you begin making withdrawals.

2. **Tax deduction.** Many retirement savings plans also allow you to take a tax deduction for money you put into the plan, or they allow you to reduce your salary by the amount of your contribution, which is the same as a tax deduction.

3. **Tax-free withdrawal.** In the case of the Roth IRA, the money you withdraw when you're retired is generally tax-free.

Table 4.1 summarizes the characteristics of the various retirement savings plans.

Which retirement plans are best? There's a lot of confusion about which retirement plans are preferable. Since most workers have at least a couple of choices, some guidance is in order. Almost all retirement plans are worthwhile, but some are better than others. Here's a hierarchy of retirement plans:

First, any plan where the employer matches your contribution is too good to pass up. After all, it's free money.

TABLE 4.1
TAX-ADVANTAGED RETIREMENT INVESTMENTS

CATEGORY	CONTRIBUTIONS	INVESTMENT EARNINGS	EXAMPLES
Deductible and tax-deferred	Deductible	Tax-deferred until withdrawal	Deductible IRA 401(k) 403(b) TSA SIMPLE IRA SEP IRA For self-employed: SIMPLE IRA SEP IRA Keogh Solo 401(k) Defined benefit
Nondeductible and tax-deferred	Not deductible	Tax-deferred	Nondeductible IRA
Nondeductible and withdrawals tax-free	Not deductible	All withdrawals tax-free	Roth IRA Roth 401(k) Roth 403(b)
Other tax-deferred investments	Not deductible	Tax-deferred	Individual stock and real estate investments Tax-deferred annuities

Second is any pretax plan such as a 401(k) plan, a tax-deductible self-employed plan, or a tax-deductible IRA, if you qualify. All reduce your current taxes.

Finally, a nondeductible plan will still grow in the future free of taxes. Of the available nondeductible plans, a Roth IRA is best if you qualify. In fact, a Roth IRA is so advantageous that it will probably be preferable to a tax-deductible IRA if you don't really need the deduction.

See the special reader Web site for an update on the rules surrounding the various retirement plans. **w w w**

BE CAREFUL ABOUT LEAVING A JOB WITH A PENSION PLAN

If you're fortunate enough to work for one of the dwindling number of employers who offers an old-fashioned pension plan, weigh carefully the financial implications of moving on to another employer. Traditional pension plans reward longevity—the more years you put in, the greater the benefits paid to you for the rest of your life. If you leave early, you may be sacrificing a lot of retirement income from the pension plan.

IS IT POSSIBLE TO ACCUMULATE TOO MUCH IN RETIREMENT PLANS?

In a word, no. Putting a lot of money into retirement plans used to be very taxing. There was a patently unfair 15 percent excise tax on "excess" retirement savings. There is no reason you shouldn't contribute to IRAs each year, even if you have $40 million in your IRA account.

Q&A: I'VE GOT CREDIT CARD LOANS. SHOULD I PAY THEM OFF BEFORE CONTRIBUTING TO A RETIREMENT PLAN?

The typical response is "Pay off your credit cards first to get rid of the high-interest debt." But I have a different take on this dilemma—one that has not been bereft of criticism. My suggestion is to put half the available money toward the credit card debt and the other half in a retirement plan—probably your plan at work. Yes, it will take you longer to pay off the credit card debt, but look at it this way: there's nothing uplifting about paying off credit cards, but there is when you're also putting money away for the future. Think of it as an investment in your mental health as well as your future financial health.

Retirement-Plan Decision Makers

Choosing the best tax-advantaged retirement investments can be confusing. But, depending on your circumstances, some tax-advantaged investments are superior to others. In general, any that permit you to contribute tax-deductible dollars are where your money should go first. If, on top of the tax deductibility going in, your employer offers a match, all the better. But after you've maxed out on all tax-deductible retirement-plan investments, you'll still probably want to contribute to other tax-advantaged investments if you can afford to. This is when the situation gets more complicated. The following decision-maker checklists will help you summarize and plan your participation in the various retirement plans for which you qualify. Use one of the following three checklists, depending on your sources of job income:

+ Use Table 4.2 if you are an employee and have no income from self-employment.

+ Use Table 4.3 if all of your job income is from self-employment.

✦ Use Table 4.4 if you are an employee who also has some income from self-employment (moonlighting or side business).

TABLE 4.2
RETIREMENT-PLAN PRIORITY CHECKLIST FOR EMPLOYEES

Note: Use this checklist if you are an employee and have no income from self-employment.

This checklist shows in order of priority the best retirement plans in which to participate. If you participate in a given plan, indicate whether you're currently contributing the maximum amount allowable. Refer to the comments beginning on page 65 for further information and explanations.

I QUALIFY AND PARTICIPATE		I QUALIFY BUT DON'T PARTICIPATE	I DON'T QUALIFY	TYPE OF PLAN
MAX	DON'T MAX			
❑	❑	❑	❑	401(k), 403(b), TSA, or SIMPLE
❑	❑	❑	❑	Roth IRA
❑	❑	❑	❑	Roth 401(k) or Roth 403(b)
❑	❑	❑	❑	Deductible traditional IRA
❑	❑	❑	❑	Nondeductible traditional IRA

Quick Takes on Available Retirement Plans and Investments

Here are some brief comments on the various retirement-plan and investment choices. ✶ ✶ ✶

Plans for Employees

✦ **401(k), 403(b), tax-sheltered annuity (TSA), or SIMPLE.** These plans top the priority list because of the tax savings. If an employer match is offered, so much the better—that's free retirement money.

✦ **Roth IRA.** If you qualify for a Roth IRA, the ability to make tax-free withdrawals at retirement means it is almost always

---

TABLE 4.3
RETIREMENT-PLAN PRIORITY CHECKLIST FOR PERSONS WHOSE JOB INCOME IS SOLELY FROM SELF-EMPLOYMENT

Note: Use this checklist if all your income is from self-employment.

This checklist shows in order of priority the best retirement plans in which to participate. If you participate in a given plan, indicate whether you're currently contributing the maximum amount allowable. Refer to the comments beginning on page 67 for further information and explanations.

I QUALIFY AND PARTICIPATE		I QUALIFY BUT DON'T PARTICIPATE	I DON'T QUALIFY	TYPE OF PLAN
MAX	DON'T MAX			
❑	❑	❑	❑	Keogh, SIMPLE, SEP, solo 401(k), or defined benefit
❑	❑	❑	❑	Roth IRA
❑	❑	❑	❑	Deductible traditional IRA
❑	❑	❑	❑	Nondeductible traditional IRA

TABLE 4.4
RETIREMENT-PLAN PRIORITY CHECKLIST FOR PERSONS WHO EARN INCOME BOTH AS EMPLOYEES AND FROM SELF-EMPLOYMENT

Note: Use this checklist if you are an employee who also has some income from self-employment.

This checklist shows in order of priority the best retirement plans in which to participate. If you participate in a given plan, indicate whether you're currently contributing the maximum amount allowable. Refer to the comments beginning on page 67 for further information and explanations.

I QUALIFY AND PARTICIPATE		I QUALIFY BUT DON'T PARTICIPATE	I DON'T QUALIFY	TYPE OF PLAN
MAX	DON'T MAX			
❑	❑	❑	❑	401(k), 403(b), TSA, or SIMPLE
❑	❑	❑	❑	Keogh, SEP, SIMPLE, solo 401(k), or defined benefit
❑	❑	❑	❑	Roth IRA
❑	❑	❑	❑	Roth 401(k) or Roth 403(b)
❑	❑	❑	❑	Deductible traditional IRA
❑	❑	❑	❑	Nondeductible traditional IRA

No matter if you're primarily a regular employee, self-employed, or a mix of both, there are other tax-advantaged ways you can save for retirement. Complete this checklist.

I PARTICIPATE		TYPE OF INVESTMENT
YES	NO	
❑	❑	Buying and holding tax-efficient investments such as individual stocks, index funds, ETFs, real estate, and municipal bonds
❑	❑	Deferred annuities

preferable to a nondeductible IRA and is usually preferable to a deductible IRA, unless you need the current tax deduction.

✦ **Roth 401(k).** Over the next few years, many companies will introduce a recent variation of the garden-variety 401(k) that allows you to put after-tax money into a separate Roth 401(k) account enabling tax-free withdrawals at retirement. See page 83 for more information on the Roth 401(k).

✦ **Deductible traditional IRA.** If you need the current tax deduction and qualify for a deductible IRA, that's fine. Otherwise, it's usually better to give up the current deduction and enjoy the long-term tax benefits of a Roth later on.

✦ **Nondeductible traditional IRA.** A lot of baby boomers who don't qualify for either a Roth or a deductible IRA eschew a nondeductible IRA. (See page 72.) That's shortsighted, because you will still enjoy tax-free growth from your nondeductible IRA.

Plans for Those Who Have Full- or Part-Time Income from Self-Employment

✦ **Keogh, SEP, solo 401(k), or defined benefit.** All of these plans are deductible against any income from self-employment, so it's a matter of selecting the one that best fits your own situation. If you currently have a plan, it may not be the best one for you, but dropping one plan and going to another is usually, though not always, easy to do. **w w w** If you're looking for:

- ❑ **Simplicity.** A SEP-IRA plan, which stands for "simplified employee pension" plan, is the easiest to set up and maintain.

- ❑ **Higher contribution levels.** The solo 401(k) requires a bit more paperwork to set up and maintain, but it permits higher tax-deductible contributions. For more details on the solo 401(k), see page 81. A Keogh plan could also be considered, but the contribution level is lower than the solo 401(k).

- ❑ **Gargantuan contribution levels.** A defined benefit (DB) plan for the self-employed (see page 81) permits contributions that are breathtaking for those who have a high income. Deductible contributions of $200,000 or more are possible, which may be particularly useful for older baby boomers who have a lot of self-employment income but haven't yet put a lot of money into retirement plans. DB plans are more costly to set up and maintain than the other self-employed plans.

Remember that if you have employees, the regulations generally require that you make contributions to these plans on their behalf as well.

Other tax-advantaged investments that might be useful for boomers who are saving for retirement. While participating to the max in the above-described retirement plans is usually a prerequisite, the following investments also offer tax advantages for retirement savers.

- ✦ **Tax-efficient investments in taxable brokerage accounts.** You can invest in several types of securities outside of retirement plans while still enjoying the benefits of tax deferral. This includes buying and holding individual stocks, index funds, or exchange-traded funds. "Tax-managed" mutual funds are managed to minimize the annual tax bite. Buying and holding investment real estate (see page 362), like stocks, is a tax-favored investment since you owe no capital gains so long as you hold on to the property.

✦ **Deferred annuities.** Last but not necessarily least are deferred annuities, which are described on page 145. Those who are in a position to put a sizable chunk of money away for retirement and are prepared to keep the money intact for many years might benefit from a deferred annuity. But deferred annuity money should almost never be put inside an IRA account (since an IRA account is already tax-deferred), and a deferred annuity should never be purchased unless you have already maximized your retirement-plan contributions and expect to be able to do so in the future.

Use it or lose it. One of the most important things you can do now, whether you're just a couple of years or a couple of decades from retirement, is to contribute as much as you possibly can to every plan for which you qualify, starting with the highest-priority plan and working down from there. Contributing to retirement plans is a "use it or lose it" proposition. Since every plan has a maximum allowable contribution level, each year you forgo making a contribution is a year you can't make up for in the future. Of course, it's not possible for most people to contribute to the max every year, but you should contribute to the best of your ability—this year and every year thereafter.

Retirement-plan contributions first, then college savings and mortgage prepayment. Elsewhere in these pages I extol the virtues of saving for college and, particularly, paying down the mortgage. But as enthusiastic as I get about those strategies, don't put large amounts away for college, don't make sizable payments against your mortgage, unless you're making the maximum contributions to every available retirement plan, including an IRA. The reasons are simple. First, retirement plan contributions offer more tax advantages than extra mortgage payments or 529 plan contributions. Second, you can always overcome the burden of paying for college or paying off the mortgage later on. But it's a lot tougher to overcome years of niggling retirement-plan contributions.

SUCCESS STORY: STARTING SMALL

"On my forty-fifth birthday, it hit me like a ton of bricks. I was a single mother with two kids, and as if that weren't challenging enough, retirement was twenty years away. At least I hoped I could retire in twenty years. At the time, I was pretty much living from paycheck to paycheck and hadn't paid any attention to retirement. I didn't want to wait another twenty years to do something about it, though. So I started putting away just 2 percent of my pay into the 403(b) plan at work. I really didn't miss the money—it was only $15 a week, but it was a start. That got me looking for ways to cut back on our spending. It took a while, but I'm now putting 10 percent into the 403(b) and feel a lot better about being able to retire. If I can do it, anyone can do it."

NEED SOME MONEY FAST?

If, or more likely when, some unexpected emergency expense arises that exceeds your ready resources, there's an easy way to get some money on the quick if you have an IRA account. Once a year, you can withdraw money from one of

> your IRA accounts, use the proceeds for any purpose, and
> you will not be subject to taxes or penalties on the withdrawal
> so long as you repay the same amount to any of your IRA ac-
> counts within sixty days. This once-per-year privilege applies
> to each IRA account if you have more than one. If you don't
> replenish your IRA coffers within the sixty-day limit, you'll pay
> taxes on the distribution and, unless you're over age 59½, the
> unrequited withdrawal will also probably fall victim to a 10
> percent penalty.

IRAs—Your Retirement Nest Egg Trump Card

A plenitude of baby boomers think they don't qualify for an IRA contribution. All but a smidgen are wrong, wrong, wrong. If you have
income from a job or your spouse has job income, you qualify for an
IRA. Bill Gates qualifies for an IRA, as do people of lesser means,
such as Katie Couric, as well as those of far lesser means, such as you
and me. Yet less than one in five of us who are eligible to contribute
are doing so.

There's too much confusion about IRA contribution eligibility
even though the rules are reasonably straightforward, which is a lot
better than with most tax regulations. Perhaps the cause of the confusion is that highly paid workers earn too much to qualify for either
a *taxdeductible traditional* or *Roth IRA*. But they still qualify for a
nondeductible traditional IRA, which still offers the benefit of tax
deferral. Anyway, here's a checklist that should clarify these matters
so that you can find out where you fit:

❑ You can contribute to a *traditional IRA* if you or your spouse received taxable job income. Only one spouse has to receive income. Since you're a baby boomer, you don't have to worry about
age restrictions, but suffice it to say that someone doesn't qualify

to make a traditional IRA contribution if he or she will be age 70½ or better by the end of the tax year.

❑ If neither spouse was covered for any part of the year by an employer retirement plan, you can deduct the entire allowable *traditional IRA* contribution.

❑ If either spouse was covered by a plan, certain income limits dictate whether the *traditional IRA* contribution is fully or partially deductible or wholly nondeductible.

❑ *Roth IRA* contributions can be made if you qualify based upon income limitations.

❑ A person over age 70½ can continue a *Roth IRA* if he or she meets the income limitations.

There you have it. Contrary to popular opinion, or popular excuses, every baby boomer who works or who has a spouse who works can and should make an IRA contribution. Here's the IRA contribution two-step:

1. If you qualify for either a Roth or a deductible traditional IRA, choose the Roth unless you need the tax deduction.

2. If you only qualify for a nondeductible IRA, do it anyway. You'll thank me twenty years from now.

IRA contributions may seem trivial and annoying, but over the years, these contributions do add up to some welcome extra retirement income. **w w w**

TABLE 4.5
IRA=IMPROVE RETIREMENT ASPIRATIONS

A little extra can go a long way. This table shows how much your annual income will increase if you:

1. Put $4,000 into an IRA each year until you retire. You probably qualify for a larger contribution, and, like ice cream, more is better.
2. Let the money sit in the IRA for five more years after you retire.
3. Withdraw equal amounts over the next twenty years.

The annual income from the IRA account is 7 percent.

SAVE $4,000 PER YEAR IN AN IRA FOR: →	LET THE MONEY SIT IN THE IRA FOR 5 MORE YEARS =	ADDITIONAL ANNUAL INCOME FOR NEXT 20 YEARS
5 years		$3,100
10 years		7,300
15 years		13,300
20 years		21,700

LET THE IRS HELP YOU BANKROLL INCREASES IN YOUR RETIREMENT SAVINGS

Have you been getting a refund each April from the IRS, maybe because your retirement contributions lower your taxable income? Rather than waiting until you file your tax return to get the fat refund, simply ask your payroll department to give you IRS Form W-4, Employee's Withholding Allowance Certificate. It contains a work sheet that will help you figure out how many additional withholding allowances to claim. The payroll department might also be able to help you. Shortly after you complete Form W-4, reflecting the higher withholding allowances, your take-home pay will increase, thus helping you more easily afford your loftier retirement-plan contributions.

Consider a Roth IRA Conversion If You Qualify

The Roth IRA received a lot of attention when it was first made available several years ago. But now, a lot of investors who should be converting their traditional IRAs into Roth IRAs aren't doing so. To refresh your memory, if you meet the income requirements, you can convert money that is in a traditional IRA into a Roth. While you have to pay taxes to do so, the advantage is that subsequent withdrawals from a Roth IRA will probably be tax-free. ♥ ♥ ♥

Roth IRA conversion Decision Maker. Here is a quick Decision Maker to help you decide on a Roth IRA conversion if you qualify now or in the future:

Yes *No*

☐ ☐ **1. Can you afford to pay the taxes due on the conversion out of nonretirement money?** If you will need to tap into retirement-account assets to pay the taxes, you shouldn't do the conversion. Paying taxes and, perhaps, penalties to use retirement money to pay the taxes on the conversion doesn't make financial sense.

☐ ☐ **2. Do you expect to be in the same or a higher income tax bracket during your retirement years?** If you anticipate being in a lower tax bracket, you're better off avoiding the taxes due on the conversion now—when you're in a higher bracket—and paying the taxes on IRA withdrawals at a lower rate when you're retired.

☐ ☐ **3. Will you be able to wait at least ten years before withdrawing money from the converted Roth?** The longer you allow the money to grow tax-free, the better, but in no case should you plan to withdraw money within the first ten years after the conversion.

If you answered yes to all three of the above questions—and you qualify—you should definitely consider the Roth IRA conversion.

Getting Friendly with Your Retirement Savings Plan at Work

Your company retirement savings plan may be your largest single investment account, although if it's not, you still need to become familiar with the available choices. Even if you have an investment adviser, chances are you're pretty much on your own when investing in your workplace retirement savings plans, including 401(k), 403(b), and supplemental retirement plans like TSAs.

Work Sheet for Analyzing Your Employee Retirement-Plan Choices

Far too many employee retirement savings plans—401(k) plans, 403(b) plans, etc.—offer a limited number of choices, some or many of which are detestable. If you're in that boat, use this work sheet to summarize the choices so that you can concentrate your plan investments in the better choices. Performance information is available from your plan administrator. Pay particular attention to how each fund's performance compares with its benchmark index, information that should be provided by your plan administrator. Also, find out how well or how badly each fund is ranked by the likes of Morningstar (Morningstar.com) and Reuters (Reuters.com). If the choices are really putrid, work with some of your coworkers to encourage your employer to either change the choices or switch to a better plan.

PERFORMANCE

STOCK FUND CHOICES	GOOD	FAIR	STINKS	PERCENTAGE CONTRIBUTION LEVEL
Large Company				
_____	❑	❑	❑	____%
_____	❑	❑	❑	____
Midsize Company				
_____	❑	❑	❑	____
_____	❑	❑	❑	____
Small Company				
_____	❑	❑	❑	____
_____	❑	❑	❑	____
International				
_____	❑	❑	❑	____
_____	❑	❑	❑	____
Other (e.g., target or balanced)				
_____	❑	❑	❑	____
_____	❑	❑	❑	____
BOND FUND CHOICES				
U.S. Government Bond				
_____	❑	❑	❑	____
_____	❑	❑	❑	____
Corporate Bond				
_____	❑	❑	❑	____
_____	❑	❑	❑	____
Other (e.g., stable value or international bond)				
_____	❑	❑	❑	____
_____	❑	❑	❑	____
				100%

Suggestions:

1. If you currently have any money invested in mediocre funds, move the money out of those funds into better performers within your plan.

2. Concentrate your company retirement plan investments in the better choices. Fill in any gaps by emphasizing those categories in your other retirement or investment accounts. For example, if your plan has a pathetic choice of small-company funds, don't waste your money investing in that fund. Rather, invest in a top-notch small-cap fund or ETF outside the company plan, for example, in your IRA account. Refer to chapter 3 for help on diversifying all of your investments, including your plans at work.

There's a case study in the **You Can Do It!** reader Web site that illustrates how you can make the most of your workplace plan choices and round out your diversified portfolio with investments outside your employer's plan. **w w w**

DO YOU HAVE TOO MUCH OF YOUR OWN COMPANY'S STOCK IN YOUR 401(K) PLAN?

If you work for a big corporation, you may hold some of its stock in your 401(k) plan account. It's not unusual for 401(k) participants to be overinvested in their own company's stock, which is too risky. Too many 401(k) plan participants have had years of savings wiped out within months, if not days. Think Conseco, Enron, HealthSouth, Kmart, WorldCom, not to mention many of the airline stocks. Your retirement money is too important to risk on the price fluctuations of a single stock.

And do you really want to depend on one company for both your career and your retirement income?

As optimistic as you might be about your company's future, you never know. I don't think you should invest any of your 401(k) money in your employer's stock, and certainly no more than 10 percent. If the company offers a stock purchase plan, buy the stock through that plan—not through the 401(k). In fact, if the stock purchase plan offers the stock at a discount, you're crazy not to participate. But if you start to accumulate a lot of company stock through the stock purchase plan or through stock options, sell some of it. There are a lot worse things in life than paying capital gains tax—such as wallpapering your family room with worthless stock certificates.

ALERT: YOU MAY BE ABLE TO GET OUT OF A LOUSY 401(K) PLAN

It's really a shame how many workers are stuck with a pitiful 401(k) plan. Sadly, several of the financial services companies that most aggressively solicit 401(k) plans to smaller and medium-size companies offer abysmal investment choices. If you're stuck with a mediocre 401(k) plan, there may be a glimmer of hope. Many, but by no means all, plans allow workers who are age 59½ or over to roll their 401(k) plan investments into an IRA of the employee's choosing while continuing to participate in their company's 401(k) plan. So if you're over age 59½, you're unhappy with your plan choices, and you're comfortable with the greater individual choice offered by an IRA, ask your plan administrator if you can do an IRA rollover.

Decisions, Decisions: Should You Leave Retirement Money in a Former Employer's Savings Plan?

A surprisingly large percentage of individuals who change jobs leave their retirement-plan money—401(k), 403(b), 457 plans—with their former employer. This is surprising because most such plans offer a very limited range of investment choices, and as noted earlier, many plan investment choices range from undistinguished to pathetic. Nevertheless, in some circumstances, if it's feasible, keeping your money in a former employer's plan may be okay. This Decision Maker will help you decide:

Employer Retirement Savings Plan Rollover Decision Maker

Yes *No*

☐ ☐ **1. Are you comfortable managing your investments on your own or through your financial adviser?** If yes, an IRA rollover may be preferable to keeping the money in the plan.

☐ ☐ **2. Are there only a small number of fund choices available in the plan?** If yes, consider the rollover, so long as you're okay choosing among literally thousands of alternatives available in many IRA accounts. Some would prefer to stick with a smaller universe of choices.

☐ ☐ **3. Are the investment choices in the plan by and large average performers or worse?** A "yes" response to this should set off a rollover alarm bell. There's no reason to let money languish in subpar investments when you can move it out. Even if you're not inclined to invest on your own or through an adviser,

Yes   *No*

roll the money over into an IRA and put it into a few index funds. You'll probably do better than the status quo.

❏   ❏   **4. Is your former employer in financial trouble?** Even though your money is probably not at risk with a financially struggling former employer, why worry about it? Move the money into a safer house.

❏   ❏   **5. Does your new employer offer attractive 401(k) plan options?** If your new employer's 401(k) offers some splendid choices, a rollover from your former plan to your new company's plan may be the ticket, particularly if you'd rather not manage your own IRA (or pay someone to manage it).

If you decide to do a rollover, make sure the money is transferred directly from the former employer to the new financial institution. If the transfer check is made out to you, taxes will be withheld on the transfer, and it's a major annoyance getting the tax money back.

Two Great Retirement Plans for the Self-Employed

If you have income from self-employment—either full- or part-time—you're probably aware of the many retirement plans available to people of your ilk. But you may not be aware of two relatively new, rocket-propelled plans that could permit you to sock major money away for retirement. This may be particularly propitious now or in the future for those many baby boomers who intend to work for themselves, perhaps as part of a gradual retirement strategy (see page 172).

The Solo 401(k) Plan for Those Who Work Solo

The solo 401(k), also called the self-employed 401(k), is a recently introduced retirement savings plans for the self-employed that allows you to put more money into the plan than you could in either a Keogh Plan or a Simplifed Employee Pension (SEP) Plan.

Annual contributions consist of two parts: First, the plan owner can contribute up to 100 percent of the first $15,000 of compensation or self-employment income. Plan owners age fifty or over can contribute $20,000. Second, additional contributions of up to 25 percent of compensation income or 20 percent of self-employment income are permitted up to certain limits. Solo 401(k) plans are not efficacious if you have or contemplate having any employees other than family members. Plans must be set up, but not necessarily funded, by December 31 of the tax year in which contributions are to be made. Annual contributions are not required, and when contributions are made, they can be at any affordable amount, up to the specified maximum. Many financial services firms offer solo 401(k) plans at little or no cost. Another advantage of solo 401(k) plans is that loans from the plan are permitted. The following table provides an example of a solo 401(k) contribution for a fifty-year-old self-employed person whose net business profits are $100,000.

If the self-employed person is under age fifty, the allowable contribution would be $5,000 less, or $33,587. Oh, the disadvantages of youth.

Self-Employed Defined Benefit Plans Offer High-Octane Retirement Contributions

The old-fashioned defined benefit (DB) pension plan may be an endangered species in large corporations, but higher-income self-employed persons are finding DB plans to be an excellent way to sock away a lot of money for retirement while saving mucho taxes to boot. Depending on age and how the plan is designed, a self-employed person could

CONTRIBUTION LIMITS	EXAMPLE
Tax-deductible contribution (up to 25 percent of compensation, not to exceed $44,000)	$18,587*
Elective deferral (up to 100 percent of compensation, not to exceed $15,000)	15,000
Catch-up deferral (if age fifty or older, not to exceed $5,000)	5,000
Total contribution	$38,587

Don't even try to figure out this calculation unless you have a master's degree in taxation. But, for the curious, here's how the amount is derived: Subtract one-half of the self-employment tax deduction, $7,065, from the $100,000, leaving $92,935. Multiply that amount by 20 percent (rather than 25 percent) since the allowable deduction is based on 25 percent of net income after the solo 401(k) deduction. So $92,935 times 20 percent equals $18,587.

contribute and deduct from income taxes as much as $200,000 a year or more. These plans work best if you have no employees, but they can work if there are just a few employees, particularly if some or, better yet, all are family members.

Defined benefit plans are particularly appropriate for:

✦ Self-employed people over age fifty, because with a defined benefit plan, the older you are, the more you can contribute to your DB plan.

✦ High-income earners who can afford to contribute a substantial amount to their plans.

✦ Those who expect their income to remain high for at least a few years.

But there's a price to pay for the generous benefits. The plans cost money to set up and maintain, including annual tax filings. If you're interested, ask an attorney, accountant, or your investment adviser to steer you to someone who can set up a plan. An increasing number of the big financial institutions are geared up to provide defined benefit plans.

Roth 401(k) and 403(b) Plans May Be on Your Investment Horizon

Because our elected officials in Washington, God bless them, are always looking for ways to encourage workers to save more for their retirements, beginning in 2006 a new generation of 401(k) and 403(b) plans—the Roth 401(k) and Roth 403(b)—was introduced. While employers have been slow to offer them, you may become eligible at some point, in which case you've got yet another decision to make. That decision is whether to stick with the old, reliable 401(k) or 403(b) or switch to the new models.

Here are the differences between the two:

	TRADITIONAL 401(K)/403(B)	ROTH 401(K)/403(B)
Contributions	☺Pretax	After-tax
Withdrawals	Taxable	☺Tax-free

The crux of the decision is whether to take the tax break now in the form of, in effect, a tax deduction for your contribution, or to forgo today's tax break in exchange for being able to withdraw the money tax-free when you're retired. While most of us like immediate gratification, postponing the joy of avoiding taxes may be more advantageous.

Roth 401(k) and 403(b) Decision Maker

Yes *No*

☐   ☐   **Do you expect to be in a lower tax bracket when you retire?** The prevailing wisdom is to take the tax break now with a traditional 401(k) or 403(b) if you expect to be in a lower tax bracket when you retire. But before eschewing the Roth alternative on that basis, take heed that you may well not be in a lower tax bracket when you retire, and even if you are, unless it's dramatically lower, the tax benefits and security of enjoying tax-free income during retirement may outweigh the benefit of taking the tax break now.

☐   ☐   **Do you need the immediate tax break from a traditional 401(k) or 403(b) so as to afford the contribution?** If you need the tax break now in order to make your planned contribution, you should probably stick with the traditional alternative. But here's a homework assignment: plan now to get into a position where you can make a similarly generous contribution to a Roth next year.

☐   ☐   **Will you be able to wait at least five years and until you're at least age 59½ before making withdrawals from a Roth 401(k) or 403(b)?** I hope the answer to this is yes, because that's the time you need to wait to beat Uncle Sam out of any taxes or penalties from your luscious Roth 401(k) or 403(b).

Additional considerations. Some points in considering a Roth 401(k) or 403(b) contribution:

✦ **Much larger contribution limits than Roth IRA.** If you like the Roth IRA, you'll adore the Roth 401(k)/403(b) because the annual contribution limits are much higher.

✦ **No income limits.** Has your income been too high to qualify for a Roth IRA? There's good news: there are no income limits for making contributions to Roth 401(k) or 403(b) plans.

✦ **Employer match doesn't qualify.** But all of the news isn't good. You can't put any employer matching contributions into the Roth. The match can still be put in a traditional 401(k), so you don't lose it, but later withdrawals will be taxable.

✦ **Roll over to a Roth when you leave your job.** You can roll your Roth 401(k)/403(b) account into a Roth IRA when you change jobs or when you retire.

✦ **Favorable distribution rules.** In addition to the primary allure of a Roth—the ability to withdraw money tax-free—you won't have to make minimum distributions beginning at age 70½, as with a traditional 401(k), so the tax-deferral and estate-planning advantages can be enormous.

MYTH DEBUNKER: "I NEED TO PUT SOME MONEY AWAY IN A SAFE PLACE FOR AN EMERGENCY FUND."

True, we do need some funds that are readily available in the event that some unexpected financial emergency arises. But don't let the need for some emergency money dissuade you from putting as much as possible into retirement accounts. Free sources of emergency money include unused credit-card balances, unused home-equity credit lines, and the cash value of life insurance policies. These sources cost you nothing unless and until you use them. Finally, you can also borrow from each of your IRA accounts once per year without penalty as long as you redeposit the borrowed money within sixty days (see page 70). By the way, speaking of financial emergencies, if something you really want to buy goes on sale, that does not constitute a financial emergency.

Taxes are too often overlooked when planning for retirement. You work hard, put money away for retirement, and then—*boom*—you're socked with taxes on your retirement-plan withdrawals, not to mention on just about everything else. The hidden beauty of the Roth 401(k) and Roth 403(b) is that you add a degree of certainty to your postretirement tax situation by protecting yourself at least somewhat from high taxes when you can least afford the financial shock.

Finally, if your employer doesn't yet offer a Roth 401(k) or 403(b), make a polite request and encourage your like-minded coworkers to do the same. These plans can make a big difference in your retirement prosperity.

Are Life-Cycle Funds the Wave of the Future?

"Life-cycle funds" are attracting a lot of investor attention and money. Many fund families have introduced a stable of life-cycle funds. They are becoming particularly popular among the 401(k) and 403(b) plan crowd, who are attracted to the simplicity of a single all-purpose fund rather than having to pick from among a long list of retirement savings plan choices. But while life-cycle funds do offer simplicity, they may not be suitable for all investors. Our research has found a bewildering variation in how these funds invest. One fund family's growth-oriented fund may be very different from other families'.

Two different species. There are two different kinds of life-cycle funds:

+ **Lifestyle funds.** These are the older siblings and consist of funds that take a different and pretty consistent approach to the way the money in the fund is invested. Lifestyle funds are usually offered as a series of mutual funds under such names as *conservative, income, balanced, growth,* and *aggressive.* Each individual fund is managed as a particular mix of stocks, bonds, and cash. For example, a "growth" fund would hold a much higher percentage of stocks than a "conservative" fund, which would be heavily invested in bonds. Lifestyle funds hold either mutual funds or individual securities.

✦ **Target funds.** Target funds are designed to take the mystery out of age-based investment diversification. All you need to do is guesstimate your retirement date, select a target fund that's nearest the date, and the mutual fund company will gradually change the allocation over the years. Target funds are easy to identify because they have the target dates in their names: 2015, 2020, 2025, for example. These "funds of funds" typically hold several different stock and bond funds within a single fund family in various proportions to suit an investor who is at a specific stage in life (e.g., a younger person with decades to invest, a pre-retiree who desires to invest a bit more conservatively, or a retiree who needs investment income). While target funds have been around for quite a while, investors have been confused about how and when to shift money among the various lifestyle funds as they get nearer or enter retirement.

How target funds work. The manager of a target fund will gradually reduce stock exposure and increase bond exposure as the years pass. One potential drawback is that someone who intends to retire at roughly the time the fund "matures" may not be well served by staying in such a fund. While the fund will likely have eliminated a good deal of investment risk by its end date, that may not be the right way to handle your investment allocation. Most new retirees need at least as much of a growth component as an income component in their portfolios because retirement is not an "end date." Rather, it's the beginning of a time over which the investments must not only provide income, but also growth of principal—a period that will likely span decades. For example, one target fund dated 2000 contained 25 percent stocks, 30 percent bonds, and 45 percent cash, which, in the opinion of your steadfast author, is way too conservative for a nascent retiree. So a few words to the wise: before investing in a target fund, make sure you thoroughly understand how the money will be invested over the years, and that the fund's investment philosophy is congruent with your own, particularly since companies differ in how they allocate investor money. A comparison of four 2015 target funds found stock allocations ranging from 50 percent to 75 percent, for example.

If you're considering investing in a target fund through your retirement savings plan at work or in one of your other accounts, a Target Fund Decision Maker appears on the special reader Web site. **w w w**

Life Is Too Short to Be Chockablock with Investment Accounts

Do you have a gaggle of IRA accounts? Or a plenitude of brokerage accounts, many of which have small balances? If so, consider combining these accounts, which will, at a minimum, save a tree or two, and might also save some of those annoying annual account fees. You probably don't need so many accounts, particularly if you have or can open up accounts in the large financial supermarkets that allow stocks, bonds, as well as mutual funds from many different mutual fund companies in a single account. These tips will help you consolidate your accounts. **w w w**

Taxable Accounts

✦ A single or joint brokerage account should be all you need. (If marital bliss is enhanced by having two individual accounts rather than a joint account, so be it, but make sure it's okay to have a joint account from an estate-planning standpoint. The attorney who drew up your will can advise.)

Retirement Accounts

✦ With respect to IRAs, you should be able to combine all of your traditional IRAs, including contributory and rollover accounts, into a single account. Roth IRAs require a separate Roth IRA account.

✦ Spouses can't combine IRA or other retirement accounts with the other spouse's accounts.

Self-Employed Retirement Accounts

✦ If you have set up retirement accounts for contributions based on your self-employment income, you generally need only a single account for the type of account you have established—a SEP-IRA or Keogh plan, for example.

✦ Many self-employed people switch to another plan somewhere along the line. If, for example, you've moved from a Keogh plan to a defined benefit plan, you can usually terminate the previous plan and roll it over into your traditional IRA account.

CHAPTER 5

Doubling Your Retirement Income

D o you like to dabble more actively in your investing? Good for you. After all, it's your money and your future. While there's certainly nothing wrong with using a financial professional to help you with your investments, the more you understand about investing, the better the relationship you'll have with your investment adviser.

If you invest on your own (which is almost certainly the case with at least some of your money, including your retirement savings plans at work), keeping up to date on what's going on in the investment markets, periodically monitoring your diversification, and evaluating the performance of your individual investments are essential. This need not become a second job. In fact, it needn't consume more than a few hours each quarter to stay on top of your investments. But if you do, you could enjoy twice as much income from your investments when you retire compared with your recalcitrant fellow baby boomers.

What's Your Number?

A lot of attention is being paid these days to your "number," in other words, the magic amount that you'll need to have when you retire to sustain you throughout your retirement. It's easy for the media and the financial services industry to come up with a number that's frighteningly high—the press usually starts at $1 million and works up from there. One article indicated that if you have a mere $5 million, you're only "beer and pretzels rich."

But life's not that simple, particularly when dealing with something as complex as a financial projection that could span as many as forty years for older baby boomers to almost sixty years for younger boomers. The best-run corporations in the world don't do much forecasting beyond the ensuing few years.

Rather than becoming obsessed—and upset—by your number, focus instead on how you can control the various factors that ultimately boil down to your number:

- ✦ The money you save for retirement.

- ✦ How much, if any, of your total retirement-income needs Social Security and pension benefits will cover.

- ✦ How much income you'll need when you retire.

- ✦ Your age when you retire.

- ✦ How well you invest your retirement resources.

One person's $1 million number is another person's $200,000 number. The number varies a great deal, and a lot of decisions you make between now and the time you retire and after your retirement will have an enormous bearing on your number.

The importance of investment returns. The focus of this chapter is on how well you invest your retirement resources, arguably one of the most important, if not the most important, factor in determining your number. Other important number considerations are dealt with elsewhere herein, including Social Security benefits on page 134, how much income you'll need when you retire on page 290, and when you retire in Chapter 7.

Here's a rundown of this chapter:

✦ **The 9 Percent Solution.** Inattention to the performance of your investments (by you and/or your investment adviser) can result in far lower investment returns than you could earn by spending some time identifying top-drawer investments. You'll soon learn how.

✦ **Taxwise investing.** Unless you feel an obligation to pay more taxes on your investments than you have to, you'll find straightforward ways to reduce your investment tax bite and, hence, further increase your investment returns.

✦ **Using exchange-traded funds (ETFs) and index funds.** Minimizing investment expenses is yet another smart way to increase your investment returns, which in turn boosts the amount of retirement income you'll be able to enjoy. ETFs and index funds are a low-cost and, in many instances, a tax-friendly way to reach your retirement expectations.

✦ **Maximizing returns on temporary investments.** While temporary investments don't usually comprise a large portion of your total investments, there's no reason not to maximize the interest you can earn on them.

Doubling your retirement income? If you're like most investors, whose investment returns are best characterized as middling, following the advice in the following pages will substantially increase the money you earn on your investments, which could as much as *double* the amount of income you can enjoy in retirement.

SAVVY INVESTORS THINK LONG TERM

The great economist John Maynard Keynes noted, "Very few American investors buy any stock for the sake of something that is going to happen more than six months hence, even though this probability is exceedingly high; and it is out of taking advantage of this psychological peculiarity of theirs that most money is made." True to his economic roots, this statement is not a paragon of clarity, so let me edify: "Invest for the long term." Let the denizens of Wall Street and most individual investors worry about what's going to happen to their money over the next six months. The advantage of figuring out how best to diversify your money and filling up the various "slots" (for example, big-cap, international, government bonds, etc.) with excellent mutual funds and/or individual securities is that you don't really have to worry about what's going to happen in the short run, because you know you'll do just fine in the long run.

The 9 Percent Solution

A lot of studies and articles aim to help baby boomers figure out how much they're going to need to accumulate for retirement and how much they can safely withdraw. The one thing they have in common is that they're based on *average* investment performance. Another commonality is the focus on certain flawed indexes to derive average performance, notably Standard & Poor's 500 Stock Index. It, like most other stock indexes, is "market-weighted," which means the bigger a stock's total value on the stock exchange, the more it influences the movement of the average. Some people have noted that the fifty largest companies in the S&P 500 so dominate the index that it should really be called the S&P 50 Stock Index. Another flaw is that small- and midsize-company stocks and foreign stocks are generally ignored in most, but not all, of these studies. So, in essence, forecasts of future investment performance and retirement withdrawal rates are based heavily on the fortunes of just a handful of stocks, and a group of relatively uninspiring stocks to boot. No wonder these retirement studies and forecasts come up with such depressing scenarios!

Why settle for average? Are you happy to settle for average investment results? Most investors don't even earn average investment returns because their timing is atrocious. They tend to get into promising investments only after most of the gains (that produce the average) have been earned. I had just enough statistics courses in my checkered academic past to learn that many investors nevertheless earn above-average investment returns. If you can do the same, your financial future gets a lot brighter than the prevailing forecasts portray. Consider Table 5.1, which shows how much you would be able to withdraw from a $500,000 retirement fund over thirty years. Incidentally, research has shown that the typical investor who doesn't pay much attention to diversification and investment performance can expect to earn about 4 percent. This results in a far lower retirement income than for those who invest more successfully.

Hopefully, Table 5.1 will persuade you of the merits of being an above-average investor.

How to Identify Great Mutual Funds

There are a lot of approaches to identifying great mutual funds, and I've experimented with all of them over the past twenty years. The method that appeals to most investors is also one of the least effective—investing in funds highlighted in the financial press. Alas, these funds all too often disappoint after making the headlines. Here's a strategy for selecting excellent funds—ones that should continue to be excellent—that doesn't involve elaborate computer models or laborious analysis. Rather than focusing on hot-performing funds,

TABLE 5.1
HOW INVESTMENT RETURNS INFLUENCE YOUR RETIREMENT WITHDRAWALS

This table shows approximately how much you could withdraw from a $500,000 nest egg in your first year of retirement, increasing the withdrawals by 3 percent per year each year thereafter, depending on the size of your annual investment returns. The money will last thirty years.

ANNUAL INVESTMENT RETURNS	FIRST-YEAR WITHDRAWAL
3%	$15,000
4	18,000
5	22,000
6	25,000
7	28,000
8	32,000
9	36,000
10	39,000

it adheres to your diversification model developed in chapter 3 by identifying the best funds in each investment category. So you can enjoy great investment performance within the parameters of sensible diversification.

Here's the way for you or your investment adviser to find great investment candidates among the many thousands of available mutual funds:

Identify funds that have ranked in the top 25 percent (the top quartile) compared with their peer group for the past one, three, and five years.

A strict screening process. Lots of funds—in fact, between four thousand and five thousand funds—rank in the top quartile of their peer groups over one of those periods, and the ads for such funds are quick to point that out. But only a select few are consistent enough to outperform three-fourths of their competitors over all three periods.

✦ Be sure you're comparing apples to apples (e.g., a small-company growth fund versus all small-company growth funds).

✦ Beating 75 percent or more of a peer group over three time periods is indeed a stringent test of a fund manager's skill. Yet, still, a lot of funds fit the "all-star" bill. Here's how many funds met the test in selected investment categories in early 2006:

128 large-cap funds
247 mid-cap funds
123 small-cap funds
 40 international stock funds
 27 multisector bond bunds
 62 intermediate-term government bond funds
 82 intermediate-term corporate bond funds

Including all fund categories, over sixteen hundred funds beat their respective peer groups over the past one, three, and five years, so there's no dearth of excellent choices, whether you invest on your own or through an adviser. For help on identifying great funds, visit the special reader Web site. w w w

✦ While-top quartile funds are more likely to perform well compared with their lower-ranked brethren, they might falter later on, so you need to check up on them periodically. See page 100 for guidelines.

> ## Q&A: I HAVEN'T MADE ANYWHERE NEAR 9 PERCENT PER YEAR OVER THE PAST DECADE. ARE THOSE KINDS OF RETURNS REALLY POSSIBLE?
>
> While most investors don't enjoy that level of return, it's certainly attainable, without having to take undue risk. First, devise a diversification model that's comfortable for you (as described in chapter 3) and don't deviate from it. Second, pick the best investment choices that are available in your company savings plans, and in your other accounts where you have much broader choices, select top-quartile mutual funds—the best of the best. How tough is it to earn 9 percent a year on average? Balanced mutual funds, which generally invest about 60 percent of investor money in large-cap stocks and the rest in bonds (described in more detail on page 56), are a case in point. While they don't usually dabble in small-cap and international stocks, which add a lot of sizzle to portfolio returns, these funds are otherwise nicely diversified. Despite that shortcoming, over the past decade, twenty-four balanced funds produced average returns in excess of 9 percent. Ten of those had average annual returns over 10 percent! So, yes, a 9 percent return on a diversified portfolio is well within your grasp.

Case Study: Tom Timid, Irene Indifferent, and Victor Vigilant

The following case study, involving three different investors, shows how important investment returns can be to your retirement well-being.

✦ **Tom Timid.** Tom Timid lost a lot of money in the early part of this decade, so he wants to preserve what's left, plus his additional savings, by investing only in ultrasafe securities, such as savings accounts and CDs. Tom is not alone in sticking with no-risk investments, but as we'll soon see, he'll be paying a big price for his conservative investments when he retires. His average investment returns have been running around 3 percent.

✦ **Irene Indifferent.** Irene, like many baby boomers, has her money all over the place and doesn't really pay much attention to the individual holdings. She's happy to see the value of her many accounts rise when the stock market is strong, so she's content to leave things alone. Irene has enjoyed investment returns over the past decade averaging about 6 percent per year.

✦ **Victor Vigilant.** Victor is a careful investor who regularly evaluates his overall investment diversification as well as his individual holdings. He identifies outstanding investments, primarily mutual funds and ETFs, and he doesn't hesitate to jettison any lagging investments in favor of more promising securities. His investment performance befits his diligence with average annual returns of 9 percent.

3 percent, 6 percent, 9 percent. This might not seem like much of a difference in returns, but even these "small" changes in investment returns make an enormous difference in the amount of wealth you accumulate over your remaining working years and the lifestyle you can enjoy throughout your retirement years. We will make the following assumptions:

✦ **Current retirement investments:** $250,000.

✦ **Annual savings until retirement:** $10,000 per year.

✦ **Length of time money will last after retirement:** Thirty years.

✦ **Increases for inflation:** The amount of income in the first year of retirement can be increased 3 percent per year over the thirty years to pay for rising living expenses.

The following table shows just how significant investment returns will be on your retirement income.

SAVVY INVESTORS REAP REWARDS IN RETIREMENT

INVESTMENT RETURN	INCOME FROM SAVINGS IN FIRST YEAR OF RETIREMENT*
IF YOU PLAN TO RETIRE IN 5 YEARS . . .	
3%	$10,000
6	16,800
9	26,300
IF YOU PLAN TO RETIRE IN 10 YEARS . . .	
3%	$12,000
6	22,000
9	39,000
IF YOU PLAN TO RETIRE IN 15 YEARS . . .	
3%	$13,000
6	28,000
9	56,000
IF YOU PLAN TO RETIRE IN 20 YEARS . . .	
3%	$15,000
6	35,000
9	78,000

. . . and be able to increase your withdrawal by 3 percent each year thereafter to keep up with rising living costs.

* These amounts are expressed in current dollars (as opposed to future, inflated dollars) so you can compare the amount of expected retirement income to your current spending level. Also, add Social Security and, if applicable, any pension benefits to these amounts to derive your total expected retirement income.

For additional illustrations of how much your investment success will mean to your retirement lifestyle, visit the *You Can Do It!* Web site. **w w w**

A few important words to the wise. The 9 Percent Solution shows the dramatic impact of earning higher investment returns than the typical investor, both on the amount of investments you accumulate during your working years and, more delectably, the amount of income you can withdraw from your retirement funds throughout your retirement. Caution is advised, however. No one can predict the future of the investment markets, and while an average investment return of 9 percent has been achievable in the past, as is so often said, "Past performance is no guarantee of future performance." You may not be comfortable withdrawing the entire amount indicated in the above table, instead choosing to hold some back in case future investment returns disappoint. By keeping some money in reserve, all of your future financial surprises will be pleasant ones. Also, if you assume an average investment return greater than 6 percent, you should be prepared to pare back your spending in case your investments don't achieve the returns originally assumed.

Q&A: CAN I ACHIEVE A 9 PERCENT RETURN IF I BUY MUTUAL FUNDS THROUGH A STOCKBROKER?

Yes, you can. Over five hundred of the all-star funds that have posted top-quartile returns over the past one, three, and five years are broker-sold funds.

Is It Time for a Portfolio Housecleaning?

When was the last time you reviewed the performance of your investments? Investors tend to fall into two categories: those who constantly review their investments, and those who rarely, if ever, review their investments. One important ingredient to being a sagacious investor is reviewing regularly extant holdings and getting rid of any underperformers that show little hope of improving their (and hence your) fortunes. It must be human nature, but most of us hold on to really lousy stocks or mutual funds in the vain hope that they may rebound. Or, you simply may not know how bad some of your investments are.

How bad is it? Recalcitrance can be a costly investment habit. Here's an example: A search was conducted of mutual funds that have ranked in the bottom quartile compared with their peers (i.e., similar funds in their category) over the past one, three, and five years. That's pretty bad. But over a thousand mutual funds qualify for this Hall of Shame. There's little or no reason for anyone to put money into these funds, unless, I guess, you have a close relative who is managing the fund. Even more shocking is how much money investors have put into these funds: $120,000,000,000. (Looks to me like the cost of a three-bedroom home in California.) If you're a mathematically challenged classics major, that amount expressed in words is $120 billion, which works out to an average of over $1,000 per U.S. household. Here's hoping that based on the law of averages, your neighbor is holding $2,000 of these dogs and you're holding none.

Evaluating mutual funds. Most mutual funds are bought because they have had a good track record. If a fund begins to disappoint, as some inevitably do, smart investors will give the manager some time to get back on track. My rule of thumb for jettisoning a mutual fund is that it has to underperform the average for its category (in other words, for similar mutual funds) for two consecutive years. Why wait so long? Because top fund managers will return to glory within two years, so the last thing you want to do is dump the fund just before it comes roaring back. The importance of always comparing a fund with its category average can't be overemphasized. A mutual fund (or a stock, for that matter) that is down, say, 10 percent may be better (in its category) than one in a completely different category that is up 15 percent, if the former beat its category average while the latter lagged its peer group. You wisely want to continue investing in the category that's doing so "poorly," in order to maintain your diversification benchmark.

Evaluating stocks. Evaluating a stock is trickier than evaluating a mutual fund. A mutual fund's performance is largely a reflection of its manager, who may be on or off his/her investment game. Certainly, a stock's performance is at least partially a reflection of its management, but the vagaries of the stock market, the economy, and conditions within its industry—beyond the direct control of management—also influence stock performance. But, as with mutual funds, comparing how a stock is performing against the average of stocks in its industry will give you an indication of how in or out of favor a particular stock holding is.

In addition, the opinion of stock analysts is often important in deciding what to do with a stock that has been warming neither your soul nor your wallet. *The Value Line Investment Survey* has a well-earned reputation for offering objective opinions on many stocks. It's available at most libraries. One often-cited, but perhaps a bit overly simplistic, rule of thumb for holding or selling a stock is: if you wouldn't buy more of it, then sell what you own. After all, there are probably stocks that you would like to buy, so free up some money by selling what you don't want more of.

The most successful investors impose on their holdings a disciplined approach to selling. For example, if a stock is down, say, more than 20 percent over a six- or twelve-month period or is down way more than its peer group, the stock is sold. After all, these disciplinarians opine, a stock that has deteriorated rather quickly is more likely to continue its sad trend than it is to suddenly reverse course. Limit orders on stocks you own, which are described on page 352, may help you avoid holding on to a stock that is taking a swan dive.

A special note for bottom-fishers. I don't want my suggestions on stock selling to offend a savvy subset of successful investors, sometimes styled "bottom-fishers." These stalwart souls look upon the same dogs that most of us would be happy to get rid of as buying opportunities. After all, some stocks are only temporarily in the dog-house, and it's just a matter of time before they regain their former glory, potentially rewarding investors with substantial gains. So before you sell a disappointing holding, keep in mind that someone is buying the stock you're selling. If the company is strong but has recently been going through a rough patch, you may want to hold on. The emphasis here is on the word *strong*—a company that is dominant in its industry.

When is a good time for an investment review? The end of the year is a particularly auspicious time to cull out losing investments in any of your taxable investment accounts. Since that's also when stock mutual funds may pass on hefty capital gains, any losses that are harvested by selling losers held in taxable brokerage accounts can be used to reduce capital gains taxes. Be that as it may, any time is a good time to evaluate your investments. That said, there's usually no reason to review your investments more than once a quarter, and doing so a couple of times a year (once a year *at least*) should suffice. Since you should be rebalancing your investments every six months or so anyway (see page 51), why not get it all done at once?

Steps in your investment analysis. The following procedures help you evaluate your mutual fund and other investment holdings consistent with the tenets of the "9 Percent Solution" described on page 93.

First. To get your investments on the right track, first analyze all of the mutual funds that you hold in retirement accounts, brokerage accounts, everywhere. As noted above, you can get performance information from a variety of Web sites. An up-to-date list can be found on the special reader Web site. **w w w**

Table 5.2 will help you summarize and evaluate your mutual fund holdings.

TABLE 5.2
ANALYSIS OF YOUR CURRENT MUTUAL FUND HOLDINGS

FUND NAME	INVESTMENT CATEGORY	PERCENTILE RANK VS. PEER			OKAY	SO-SO	GHASTLY
		1 YR.	3 YRS.	5 YRS.			
_____	_____	___	___	___	❏	❏	❏
_____	_____	___	___	___	❏	❏	❏
_____	_____	___	___	___	❏	❏	❏
_____	_____	___	___	___	❏	❏	❏
_____	_____	___	___	___	❏	❏	❏
_____	_____	___	___	___	❏	❏	❏
_____	_____	___	___	___	❏	❏	❏
_____	_____	___	___	___	❏	❏	❏
_____	_____	___	___	___	❏	❏	❏
_____	_____	___	___	___	❏	❏	❏
_____	_____	___	___	___	❏	❏	❏
_____	_____	___	___	___	❏	❏	❏
_____	_____	___	___	___	❏	❏	❏
_____	_____	___	___	___	❏	❏	❏
_____	_____	___	___	___	❏	❏	❏
_____	_____	___	___	___	❏	❏	❏

Here are some suggestions to help you decide what to do with the mutual funds you now hold:

✦ If a fund ranks in the top quarter for at least two of the three time periods, it's definitely a keeper.

✦ If a fund ranks in the top half for performance (fiftieth percentile or lower) over all three periods, it's worth holding on to, although you should keep an eye on it every quarter to make sure it doesn't slip. However, if you or your investment adviser uncovers a fund in the same category that's consistently ranked higher, replacing the current fund may be in order.

✦ If a fund ranks in the bottom half compared with its peers (higher than the fiftieth percentile) over both the past three and five years, it's not helping your financial future and should be replaced.

✦ If a fund has slumped over the past year to the bottom half, but its three- and five-year rankings are strong, you may want to keep it. Many otherwise excellent funds periodically slump, but more often than not they rebound smartly soon thereafter. Keep a watchful eye on it, though.

Second. Identify some excellent mutual funds to replace any laggards or to invest in anew. The best way to do so is outlined on page 94. Also, check the *You Can Do It!* special reader Web site for a select list of all-star mutual funds that pass this top-quartile test. **w w w** If you use an investment adviser, ask him or her to recommend some funds that satisfy this test.

SUCCESS STORY: INVESTMENT TURNAROUND

For more years than one investor cares to remember, whenever he read an article on hot mutual funds or skyrocketing stocks, he was smitten. "It wasn't unusual for me to buy one supposedly great fund only to sell it a couple of months later to buy another. I paid zero attention to how my money was diversified, so I ended up in late 1999 with most of my money in technology stocks and tech funds—the hottest performers at the time. But I didn't make a lot of money even during the tech-stock boom because I was always getting in too late.

Did I ever get hammered when tech stocks collapsed. During that dismal time, nothing was hot, so I spent some time studying how the great investors managed to survive past market debacles. In addition to diversifying, something I had never worried about, they emphasized investments that they could hold on to for years—companies or mutual funds that may not do so well over the next year, but had strong long-term prospects. In essence, they were value stock investors, the diametric opposite of the growth stocks I had been chasing. So I adopted a new mantra: diversify and buy value. It has worked very well in both up and down markets. I only wish I had done it a decade earlier."

Taxwise Investing

Are you interested in adding 1 to 3 percent per year to your investment returns with little or no effort? No, this is not a get-rich-quick pitch, but it does mean that to earn those extra returns, someone else will be out the money. It's not your mother. It's not even coming out of your mother-in-law's hide. The loser in this is your grumpy Uncle Sam. Sadly, scant attention is paid to how investments are taxed. Even many investment advisers are guilty of this omission. Minimizing current income taxes incurred on investments is called tax-efficient investing, and you don't have to be a CPA to master many of the straightforward strategies for doing so. Studies have shown that taking simple steps to minimize taxes on investments can add anywhere from 1 to 3 percent to the after-tax return, which, over the years and decades, can substantially add to your wealth.

Strategies to minimize taxes on investments. The current tax structure, which favors dividends over taxable interest and long-term over short-term capital gains, makes tax-efficient investing all the more important. You can use a variety of strategies to save taxes on your investments.

✦ **Maximize contributions to retirement plans.** In almost all cases, contributing as much money as possible to retirement plans will allow working-age people to take maximum advantage of the tax-deferral feature inherent in retirement-plan holdings, even if the initial contribution is not tax-deductible.

✦ **Emphasize lower-taxed investments in taxable investment accounts.** Within your various investment accounts, the essence of tax-efficient investing (one that is too often overlooked) is quite straightforward: emphasize lower-taxed (tax-efficient) investments in taxable accounts and place tax-inefficient investments into retirement and other tax-deferred accounts. Examples of tax-efficient investments include:

Exchange-traded funds and index funds
Tax-managed mutual funds
Low-turnover mutual funds
Municipal bonds and municipal bond funds
Individual stocks

Please keep in mind that there are exceptions to the above list. For example, some index funds and exchange-traded funds are not particularly tax-efficient. Individual stock holdings are not tax-efficient if you or your adviser trades them frequently, incurring short-term capital gains.

As I mentioned above, tax-inefficient investments are best placed in retirement and other tax-deferred accounts since no taxes are payable on any gains or income within the account until withdrawals commence. The primary tax-inefficient investments include high-turnover stock funds that tend to pass on considerable short-term capital gains, and corporate and government bond funds whose interest is subject to both federal and state income taxes.

Here are some other ways to save taxes on your investments:

✦ **Manage the timing of capital gains recognition.** Within your taxable brokerage accounts, tax efficiency can be enhanced through the judicious timing of capital gain and loss recognition. Avoiding short-term capital gains, which are subject to much higher taxes than long-term capital gains, will reduce taxes, as will realizing capital losses—in other words, selling investments in which you have a loss, to offset capital gains.

✦ **Donate appreciated securities.** Capital gains taxes on appreciated securities can be avoided by donating same to a charity outright. Or they can be postponed by making a deferred gift of appreciated securities through a charitable gift annuity or, for those who can afford a sizable transfer, a charitable remainder trust. See page 110 for information on deferred-income charitable gift annuities, which are becoming a popular way for baby boomers to lock in a lifetime income after they retire.

✦ **Avoid late-year mutual fund purchases in taxable accounts.** Many investors unwittingly buy an unnecessary capital gain by purchasing a mutual fund for a taxable account shortly before it distributes its realized capital gains, typically late in the year. Postponing the purchase until immediately after the distribution will avoid unwanted tax consequences.

✦ **Delay withdrawals from tax-deferred accounts.** Once you retire, keep in mind that current tax regulations are quite favorable for retirees who can afford to make only the minimum required distributions from their retirement accounts, or, in the case of a Roth IRA, no distributions at all. By so doing, taxes on retirement-plan withdrawals, which are subject to regular income tax rates, will be minimized. In fact, it's often better to invade principal in taxable accounts to meet retirement living expenses in your early years of retirement, thus paying nominal taxes on the withdrawals, in order to let the retirement-plan assets continue to grow tax-deferred.

If the above discussion on ways to minimize taxes on your investments piques your interest, the special reader Web site has more guidance and a case study to help you reduce taxes to the bare minimum. **w w w**

HOW THE RICH GET RICHER

The rich get richer by buying and holding individual stocks (or real estate), letting them appreciate in value throughout their lifetimes, then passing them on to their ill-deserving heirs, who inherit the stocks not at the price their ancestors paid for them, but rather at the price of the asset when the dearly departed departed. Now, you might think, these people must have been pretty rich if they didn't have to sell any stock along the way. Well, they may have lived off the dividends, which probably increased at a rate greater than inflation over the years. The beauty of individual stocks is that you aren't having to pay capital gains every year as you would with most stock mutual funds. In short, owning individual stocks is a taxwise way to invest in your taxable investment accounts. Of course, if you (or a parent) eventually do sell a stock that you've owned a long time, your investments won't be decimated because long-term capital gains rates are quite low. In fact, given the recent tendency for some long-revered stocks to take it on the chin, you're a lot better off paying a 15 percent federal capital gains tax than incurring a 50 percent loss on a flopping blue-chip stock. That's where limit orders on stocks that you own can save you from your natural tendency to hold on to a stock that's been with you for a long time. Limit orders are explained on page 352.

DEFERRED-PAYMENT CHARITABLE GIFT ANNUITY: HAVING YOUR CAKE AND EATING IT, TOO

Speaking of taxwise investing, if you're charitably inclined, are looking for a nice tax break this year, and would like to earn a lifetime income for you and, if applicable, your spouse or partner, a charitable gift annuity is worth considering. The usual charitable gift annuity commences payments immediately after the contribution is made, but baby boomers who can afford the largesse (these usually require minimum contributions of at least $10,000) are setting up "deferred-payment charitable gift annuities." These are particularly well suited to a younger donor who needs an immediate tax deduction but not additional income at this time. Here's how it works: You make a gift today and choose a future year (between one and thirty years) in which to begin to receive payments. You may fund a deferred gift annuity with cash, but if you fund the annuity with appreciated stock, you will avoid the capital gains tax on a significant portion of the appreciation. While charitable gift annuities are usually a pretty good financial deal, you can probably do a bit better by holding on to the money and investing it yourself, because with the gift annuity, it's only fair that the charity ends up with a goodly portion of your contribution.

The table below illustrates the potential benefits for a $50,000 gift of cash for a deferred charitable gift annuity. Your particular benefits will depend on the age(s) of the income recipient(s), the date you make your gift, the number of years in which payments are deferred, and the gift amount.

AGE AT DONATION	AGE AT FIRST PAYMENT	ANNUAL PAYMENT RATE	ONE-TIME TAX DEDUCTION
45	60	12.8%	$7,100
45	65	17.3	11,100
50	60	9.9	8,800
55	60	7.7	9,900
55	65	10.4	13,600
60	65	8.0	14,300
60	70	11.0	19,000

The payment rate (expressed as a percentage of the amount of the donation) and the charitable-contribution income tax deduction will change according to prevailing interest rates.

Deferred income charitable gift annuities are a wonderful way to set yourself up for a lifetime income when you retire while receiving tax breaks and, of course, supporting a favorite charity. The best way to find out the details is to contact said charity.

IT'S VITAL TO KEEP YOUR INVESTMENT EXPENSES IN CHECK

Lofty investment expenses will drag down your returns, possibly way below the 9 percent target level. Here are some tips for keeping your investment expenses in check:

+ **If you make your own investment decisions.** First, avoid trading too frequently, which will drive up your expenses. Keep in mind that many mutual funds assess a fee if you sell the fund shortly after you buy it. Also, use discount brokers and no-load mutual funds, perhaps including some ETFs and index funds to cut fees to the bone. These are discussed in the next section.

+ **If you use an investment adviser.** Be sure you understand how your investment adviser is compensated, and don't be reluctant to ask for a discount on commissions if you have quite a bit of money with a brokerage firm. Also, if you buy mutual funds through a broker, make sure the fund's share class—A class, C class, etc.—is consistent with your investment goals, and that the class is most beneficial for you, not the broker.

+ **If you have a 401(k) or 403(b) plan.** While most plans, particularly those offered by larger companies, assess reasonable fees, some are intemperately high. While many plans are quite adept at hiding their fees, it's your right to know. If the fees are indeed gluttonous, which may also signal lousy fund performance, you and your coworkers might gently convey your displeasure to management. I wouldn't suggest that you threaten to quit if management doesn't make a change, but many employees have reported to me that management did replace an awful plan after hearing complaints from enough employees.

Using Exchange-Traded Funds (ETFs) and Index Funds

Index funds and, particularly, exchange-traded funds (ETFs) are giving traditional actively managed mutual funds a run for their money. Since the majority of mutual funds aren't able to keep pace with the stock indexes, legions of investors are discovering that attaining "average" investment returns isn't so bad. In case you're not familiar with ETFs, here's a primer.

ETF 101. In essence, ETFs are like mutual funds in that they hold a bunch of individual stocks or bonds, but they are bought and sold on the stock exchange, rather than from a mutual fund company. Most ETFs are passively managed and are designed to achieve the returns of a particular stock index, although a newer iteration of ETFs involves some active management, a variation that your devoted author views with some skepticism. All you need to buy and hold an ETF is a brokerage or an IRA or other retirement account where you can hold stocks. An index fund is similar to an ETF in operation. The primary difference is that you buy an index fund from a mutual fund company and an ETF on the stock exchange.

Proponents of indexing argue that it is futile for mutual funds to try to beat the market. Studies show that few experienced investment managers consistently beat the market indexes. So, the argument goes, why pay a manager when simply buying a fund that equals the market average will work just as well—if not better? On the other hand, some funds, including the top-quartile funds discussed on page 94, pretty consistently outperform the index funds.

Advantages of ETFs and index funds. ETFs and index funds offer a number of advantages, particularly low expenses. Because they are usually passively managed, there is no need to pay expensive analysts or managers to do research. The computer buys and sells the fund holdings instead, and it does a pretty good job to boot. The annual expenses for an index fund and ETF are usually, but not always, much lower than those of actively managed funds. Investors may also find the up-front cost of buying an ETF to be lower than the cost of a mutual fund with an initial load (commission). Index funds are broadly diversified across many industries. For investors with a limited amount of money to invest, ETFs and index funds can be an excellent way to achieve diversification. Finally, index funds can be tax-friendly in that they tend to distribute low capital gains compared with actively managed funds. Therefore, ETFs and index funds are particularly efficacious for your taxable brokerage accounts, although they can also work well in retirement accounts.

Limitations. With all the compelling advantages of indexing, however, it is not the magic solution to all of your investment needs. For example, you must be happy to achieve average market returns, even in declining markets, because that is the best an index fund or ETF can do. Fund managers are usually prohibited from using any defensive measures, such as moving out of stocks if the manager thinks stock prices are going to decline. So ETFs and index funds will not be able to protect your investment in the event of a market downturn. Thus, in comparison with some actively managed stock funds that periodically take defensive measures when the market turns down, ETFs and index funds tend to be more volatile. These funds are available in a host of flavors. In addition to the better-known U.S. and foreign indexes, ETFs and index funds are available in many more specialized areas, including energy, health, and real estate, and single-country or single-region foreign funds (but always beware of buying into the "hot" sector of the moment). Note that newer ETFs are emerging that attempt to employ more active management—it's best to avoid these and stick with regular mutual funds if you want active management.

How to Use ETFs and Index Funds in Your Investing

ETFs and index funds can play a role in any investment program. In fact, many, if not most, of the massive institutional investment portfolios, such as college endowments and state retirement plans, make generous use of these investments.

If you don't really want to pay any attention to your investments, these types of investments will assure that none of your investments will do any worse than the market as a whole. Simply slot these passive investments into your diversification framework and periodically rebalance as described in chapter 3.

More active investors can also benefit from ETFs and index funds. They can build a sound foundation to your investment pyramid (see page 36), allowing you to take more risk with the investments at the middle and top of your pyramid.

Example. E. T. Fund has had great success investing in both ETFs and traditional mutual funds. Here's how he has put together his portfolio:

20 percent total U.S. market ETF

10 percent international ETF

10 percent multisector bond ETF

The remaining 60 percent of E. T.'s holdings are in actively managed mutual funds with a smattering of individual stocks.

Q&A: CAN THE 9 PERCENT SOLUTION WORK IF I INVEST IN EXCHANGE-TRADED FUNDS AND INDEX FUNDS?

It can work, but the funds that consistently rank in the top quarter of their peer groups usually outperform like-minded ETFs. As I've said before and will no doubt say again, nothing in your financial life is "either/or," so a good solution if you like ETFs and index funds is to put some of your money in them and the rest in the all-star mutual funds.

WHAT ABOUT GOLD?

Gold and other precious metals are certainly a legitimate investment, so long as you don't sink too much money into them. Holding gold bullion or other precious metals is a hassle, and buying gold coins can be a sucker's bet, so the best way to play this market is usually through a precious-metals mutual fund. These funds typically own mining companies throughout the world, but may also hold the metals themselves. Don't succumb to the pitches from the gold dealers who usually come out of the woodwork during those times when gold is on the rise. In fact, despite the recent sharp rise in the price of gold, it has been one of the worst-performing investments, if not the worst, over the past twenty-five years. A mid-2006 news report noted that gold has risen to the highest level since 1981. A less-than-sage investor might think that gold must be a great investment. But a more scrupulous reflection of the facts would be "If you had held gold over the past twenty-five years, you would have made no money."

Temporary Investments

If you're going to need money in the near future, temporary investments are the most sensible place to put those dollars. In the parlance of the investment community, temporary investments are "cash equivalents" or just plain "cash." Others may refer to them as "short-term investments." When you hear some despondent investment manager saying, "I'd recommend that investors pull back and put some money in cash," that doesn't mean take it out of your investment accounts and store the currency in a plastic bag under your bed. But too many investors don't do much better with their cash, putting it into low-interest savings accounts or, worse, no-interest checking accounts. Cash-equivalent investments are safe investments that can easily be converted into cash. The price you pay for safety and liquidity is a lower rate of interest than on bonds and other longer-term investments. And while cash-equivalent investments hardly offer breathtaking returns, you might as well earn as much as you can on them.

When cash is a sensible investment. While you benefit from taking a long-term view when selecting and managing your investments, at times you will need to tap into some money in just a few months or in a year or two without risking a large loss in principal. You might want to keep some money in cash-equivalent investments to:

✦ Meet foreseeable short-term cash needs, such as college tuition, home improvements, an imminent first or second home purchase, or another big-ticket item.

✦ Have some money on the sidelines in case an interesting investment opportunity arises (TV infomercial "opportunities" don't qualify).

✦ Safely and gradually invest a substantial amount of money resulting from a financial windfall—an inheritance, for example.

✦ Temporarily take some money off the stock and bond table if the markets are scaring you. (But deviating from your sensible investment plan is a risky countermeasure that, if done in a big way or frequently, smacks of market timing, which doesn't work.)

When you retire, you might also want to switch some of your retirement investments into cash to assure being able to meet your living expenses over the ensuing six months or year without having to sell into a down market.

Finding the best returns on temporary investments. As opposed to stocks and bonds, temporary investments are pretty straightforward. With a little bit of effort, however, you can make the most of these otherwise mundane investments. The keys to maximizing the interest you'll fetch are:

✦ **Ascertaining the current average interest rates and top yielding interest rates paid by various categories of temporary investments.** This information can easily be found by accessing any number of Web sites, such as Bankrate.com, that show average and top interest rates. Also, the financial pages of most newspapers regularly show the interest being paid on most types of temporary investments, including rates offered by local banks. Now this may strike you as a time-consuming process that will only net you a few cents more interest. Not so. You can substantially increase your temporary investment interest and, over the years, that can add up. The table on page 120 shows just how beneficial comparison shopping can be.

✦ **Comparing after-tax yields to find the temporary investment with the best return—after taxes are taken out.** Once you've determined the interest that's being paid on the various temporary investments, the next step is to find out which pays the most after taxes are factored in, assuming, as is usually the case, the temporary investments are being held in a taxable account. If they're being held in a retirement account, taxes don't matter (yet), so pick the temporary investment with the highest yield. Table 5.3 on page 121 summarizes the way temporary investments are taxed. The trick here is simply to do some ciphering to determine how much taxes would reduce the investment return, based on your tax bracket. Even though the stated interest rate on a particular cash-equivalent investment may be lower, it's how much you get to keep after taxes that counts.

Other tips for selecting temporary investments. Here are a few other suggestions to help you make the most from your temporary investments:

✦ **If you're in the market for a CD,** a little shopping around— even outside your hometown—could reap rewards. First compare rates among banks in town; banks are in hot competition with each other. If you have a broker, check with him or her about CD offerings that the brokerage firm may have. Finally, check the Web for the highest-yielding CDs in the country. Remember, as long as the issuing bank is FDIC insured, you shouldn't really care where your CD comes from.

✦ **If you have an account with a mutual fund or a broker offering several different kinds of money market funds,** be sure to compare yields to make sure the one you select offers the best after-tax return. This may require you to periodically compare the returns among various money market funds, but, what the hey, if you can improve your return by periodically switching among money market funds, it's more money in your pocket.

It Pays to Comparison Shop

Here are some comparisons between the average yield on various cash-equivalent investments and the top yields offered by major financial institutions. This comparison was made in mid-2006, but it's representative of the benefits of comparison shopping in any interest-rate environment. **w w w**

CASH-EQUIVALENT INVESTMENT	NATIONAL AVERAGE YIELD	TOP YIELD
Bank money market deposit account	0.8%	5.0%
Taxable money market mutual fund	4.7	5.1
Tax-exempt money market mutual fund	3.0	3.4
Six-month CD	4.6	5.4
Twelve-month CD	5.0	5.5

PROFITING FROM SIGNALS SENT BY INVESTMENT ADVERTISEMENTS

Whenever the investment markets are suffering, purveyors of dubious investment products step up their advertising on the theory that beleaguered investors are so desperate for something that purports to make money that they will jump at the chance. Dealers of gold coins fill the airwaves during such times or during those times when gold is actually doing well. Whatever the price of gold might be, the ads will say it's poised to double. Then there are my personal favorite ads that appear only when virtually every investment category is suffering and investors are desperate for moneymaking opportunities. Judging from the ads, llama farming is *the* place to be for the investment cognoscenti. Were you aware of the profit potential from raising llamas? If you're looking for a surefire contrarian investment signal, when you start to see llama-farming ads, rest assured that the stock market has bottomed out and is headed for a rebound.

TABLE 5.3
SUMMARY OF HOW TEMPORARY INVESTMENTS ARE TAXED

TYPE OF TEMPORARY INVESTMENT	INTEREST INCOME IS SUBJECT TO:	
	FEDERAL INCOME TAXES	STATE INCOME TAXES
Available through banks:		
Savings accounts	Yes	Yes
Money market deposit accounts	Yes	Yes
Available through mutual funds or brokers:		
General money market funds	Yes	Yes
U.S. Treasury money market funds	Yes	No
Tax-exempt money market funds	No	Yes
Single-state tax-exempt money market funds	No	No
Available through banks or brokers:		
U.S. Treasury bills	Yes	No
Short-term CDs	Yes	Yes

CHAPTER 6

The Most Important Financial Decisions of Your Life

There are only a handful of watershed moments in our lives, most of which heretofore have entailed large outlays of money, such as weddings, college graduation, buying a home, the birth of a child—days we'll never forget. As baby boomers approach retirement, some more watershed moments—decisions—will likely influence how well you will enjoy retirement, financially and psychically.

Planning your financial future involves a lot of decisions, but some are more important than others. The closer you get to retirement, the more critical they become, but even if retirement is a decade or two away, the sooner you start thinking about these critical decisions, the better prepared you will be to make the "right" decisions. The world of retirees is rife with those who made unsound decisions to their eternal regret.

These decisions are best classified according to how difficult they are to undo once the decision is made.

Three Critical Decisions

How much it's going to cost you to live when you retire. While human nature prevents many baby boomers from wanting to figure out how much retirement living expenses are likely to be, this calculation is nevertheless essential. You may be pleasantly surprised to discover that it will cost you a lot less to retire in style than the scary amounts that are commonly proffered in the media.

When to commence Social Security retirement benefits. Most people think that the best decision is to collect Social Security benefits at the earliest possible time, and it may well be. But many considerations should enter into the decision, which, once made, you'll have to live with the rest of your life.

Whether to purchase an annuity. Income annuities—those that pay a lifetime income—are becoming popular among retirees, but investing in one is a move that is best considered well before you retire. After all, it, too, is an irreversible decision. The advantages and drawbacks of annuities and alternatives to annuities will be described to help you make a smart decision about if and when you should purchase an annuity.

These three weighty matters are the subject of this chapter, but other crucial decisions that you will be making are unpleasant to reverse and are discussed elsewhere.

Big Decisions That Are Costly or Painful to Undo

When to retire. If the surveys are to be believed, baby boomers aren't in any hurry to retire. Perhaps it's because they worry about not having enough money or becoming bored. But in matters of retirement planning, imprecision is unwise. Chapter 7 will help you consider the effect of retiring early or later. If you're still desirous of retiring later, you will be pleasantly surprised, if not astounded, at how much more income you'll be able to enjoy in retirement.

Where to retire. Do you want to stay put, sell the family homestead but stay in the same locale, move to another area of the country, or move to a foreign realm? As never before, baby boomers are considering a wide range of relocation options, and many would-be nomads are planning to move well before retirement age. Help with this big decision can be found in chapter 9.

Nothing in Your Financial Life Is "Either/Or"

A lot of people think that most of their financial decisions are "either/or"—they must either take one course of action or the other. But most *financial* decisions don't require you to do *either* one thing *or* the other. Often, a combination is more appropriate. Examples abound:

✦ If you can't decide whether to sell an investment you own, you can always sell half. That's what a lot of professional investors have always done when unloading a holding.

✦ If you're trying to decide between using a full-service broker or a low-commission broker and no-load mutual fund company, why not use the low-commission broker and/or no-load fund company for your own investment decisions, and the full-service broker for investment guidance and recommendations?

✦ If you're trying to decide whether term insurance or cash value insurance is better, try getting part cash value and part term insurance.

✦ Owners of traditional IRAs who qualify are often in a quandary as to whether they should convert them to Roth IRAs. Perhaps converting part of the IRA money to the Roth is the answer. You could always convert the rest later.

✦ Compromise may be advisable with long-term-care insurance policies. Either you get the coverage with all the expensive bells and whistles or you go naked (that's insurance jargon), right? A compromise might be to obtain a basic policy that offers considerable protection but won't bankrupt you with gargantuan premiums.

✦ Some baby boomers think they must either take a lump-sum payout from their company retirement savings plan or put the money into an income annuity. But again, perhaps a combination of a lump sum and an annuity is the better course of action.

So always keep in mind that very little in your financial life involves an either/or decision. Realizing this will help you take better control of your financial future; one absolute certainty is that you are your own best financial planner, whether you rely on financial planners or do it yourself.

SUCCESS STORY: MARITAL DISCORD DEFLECTED

Shortly before they retired, this couple was in a real quandary, to put it politely. "Fortunately, we agreed on most matters pertaining to our retirement finances, including the need to receive regular income from our retirement savings to supplement Social Security. The problem—a contentious one—involved how we would receive the income. He was hell-bent on going out and getting an annuity. This is what his parents had done, and it really saved them since they're both still alive—in their nineties. On the other hand, I'm not a big fan of insurance companies, and the notion of handing over most of our money—which took decades to accumulate—to an insurance company was, to say the least, uncomfortable. After some rather animated 'discussions,' we came up with a compromise that has worked out pretty well so far. We divided our retirement savings into thirds. One-third was put into an annuity. We are taking out monthly payments from the second third. So if we die within a few years, the kids will still be able to receive most of the money in that account. We refer to the final third of our money as the 'inflation' account. This money will be tapped into later on to help us keep up with inflation and also pay for any big expenses we have. Our initial plan is to take out only the income and capital gains from the third account, leaving the principal intact in case we need to tap into it in our old age. Anyway, our plan has worked well so far, and best of all, we both think we won the original argument."

Figuring Out How Much It's Going to Cost You When You Retire

It's always important to estimate what your living expenses will be when you retire, because this amount, above all, will influence what you'll need to do between now and retirement time to accumulate the resources necessary to meet those expenses. You may think it's too early to prepare a retirement expense budget if you're a boomer of relatively more tender years (i.e., in your forties). But the further you are away from retirement, the more time you have to do the necessaries to achieve what you want to financially in retirement.

What's your percentage? Everyone planning for retirement worries about their *percentage*, in other words, what percentage of my preretirement income will I need to support me (or us) once retired? Eighty percent is commonly used, but I've seen as much as 110 percent. These are scary amounts, but what else is new in the prevailing genre of scaring the hell out of baby boomers? Many boomers can live on quite a bit less than 80 percent of their preretirement income, and I'm not just talking about rich folk.

Why you may be able to retire well on less than you think. Here's a way to get a preliminary idea of how much it will cost you to retire in comparison with what you're currently spending. These are expense items that will probably decrease when you retire, including estimates of the percentage ranges of income that baby boomers are currently spending on each. You'll be able to make your own estimates of how these various expenses might change when you retire on the Expense Change Work Sheet on page 132. Also check the special reader Web site for tips on preparing retirement budgets on the web. **w w w**

EXPENSE ITEM	TYPICAL BOOMER SPENDING LEVEL
Savings	5 to 20% of income
Work expenses	3 to 5%
Social Security (FICA) taxes	6 to 8%
Expense reductions at retirement	14 to 33%
Reduced income taxes*	7 to 10%
Expense and income tax reductions at retirement	21 to 43%

* The average retiree pays about 7 to 10 percent less in income taxes compared with preretirement taxes due to reduced income and favorable taxation of Social Security benefits.

Through the magic of subtraction, these expense and income tax reductions suggest that a boomer could expect to retire on roughly—very roughly—between 57 percent and 79 percent of preretirement spending.

While these expense reductions are typical of most retirees, you may be incurring additional expenses now that could possibly be eliminated by the time you retire, which would further increase the above expense reductions, including:

Mortgage	15 to 20%
Children	10 to 20%

Whatever your situation, you may be delighted to find that your ability to retire in comfort will require quite a bit less than the pundits have been opining. It's time to look at your own situation, where you can evaluate both the expected reductions and the increases (health care, for example) in your retirement budget.

Retirement budget smorgasbord. Depending on the extent to which you want to delve into retirement expense budgeting, you have three choices of how to proceed:

1. **Bang-up job.** The retirement expense budgets in Appendix I, combined with the remarks presented below, will help you prepare a pretty detailed estimate.

2. **Quick-and-dirty forecast.** A very simple estimate can be penciled in on the work sheet on page 14. Again, the commentary below can provide some ideas about how your retirement expenses are likely to change once you retire.

3. **Just thinking about it.** If you loathe putting numbers on a budget form (hopefully this is not a permanent aversion), please at least read the following comments to get you thinking about areas where your retirement spending may decline or increase.

Be realistic. Whatever course you choose, be realistic, particularly when you are within a few years of retirement. The cost of understatement can be onerous. Curtailing spending after retirement can be quite difficult and is psychologically as well as financially distressing.

Review of Living Expenses
That May Change When You Retire

The following comments will help you get an idea of which of your expenses are likely to decrease or increase when you retire. You can guesstimate the amount of each change using the Expense Change Work Sheet on page 132.

Expenses That May Decline or Be Eliminated When You Retire

1. **Savings, including retirement-plan contributions.** You *will* probably need to continue reinvesting some of your income in order to keep up with the relentless rise in the cost of living, but it will probably not be anywhere near the percentage you had been putting away for retirement during your latter working years.

2. **Mortgage and other housing costs.** As you will soon surmise in chapter 8, I can't disguise my passion for trying to pay off the mortgage before you retire, or within a few years after you retire. Downsizing is another way to dramatically reduce your retirement costs. If you relocate to a lower-cost locale, housing costs will likely decline, as will many other items in your retirement budget.

3. **Loan and credit card payments.** If you're currently saddled with debt but plan to pay it off or at least reduce the burden, that will translate into lower expenses after you retire.

4. **Clothing.** Unless you plan to be a dance host on a cruise line (not at all a bad idea), you may save on clothing after you retire, particularly if you had to dress up for work or had to pay for uniforms.

5. **Transportation.** Many, if not all, retirees will find that transportation costs will be lower, and if you're a multicar family, you might be able to get by with just one car after retirement, although that may be too much to ask of a relationship.

6. **Professional and business expenses.** The money you might save on job-related expenses depends on what can be avoided in retirement. If you went out for breakfast and lunch at work, many of these costs may be avoided.

7. **Child care.** Hopefully, all or most of these expenses will go by the wayside by the time you retire.

8. **Alimony and child support payments.** If applicable and depending on the agreement, let's hope that these costs are gone or are reduced by the time you retire.

9. **Tuition and education.** With any luck, expenses you're now paying related to the younger generation's schooling will be kaput by the time you retire.

10. **Life insurance.** Your life insurance needs often decrease after you retire. (See page 232.) You might also be able to save on other insurance categories as well.

11. **Income taxes.** Your income taxes are probably going to decline, since, if you have lower income, you'll almost always pay lower income taxes. Also, your share of Social Security withholding taxes, amounting to about 8 percent for most of us, will no longer be paid once your job income ceases. Imagine that. After decades of paying into Social Security, you'll be on the receiving end at last!

Expenses That May Rise When You Retire

12. **Medical care and medicine.** It's no secret that health-care costs rise steeply after retirement, and further advances in health care, particularly pharmaceuticals, will surely add to the burden. How much more medical care and drugs will cost depends on how much you're paying now. Don't be chary in estimating your health-care costs; it's one expense area that retirees commonly underestimate.

13. **Medical insurance.** Medical insurance, including Medicare, Medicare Drug, and Medicare Supplemental coverage, needs to be included in your retirement estimate, as well as long-term-care insurance, if you have or will obtain that coverage.

14. **Recreation and travel.** If these costs are likely to be higher than they were during your working years, they should be added to your budget. After all, you'll have plenty of time to recreate and take trips.

15. **Hobbies.** If you've longed to enjoy a particular hobby or other leisure-time activity, this needs to be reflected in your budget, particularly if it's something along the lines of restoring vintage Rolls-Royces.

EXPENSE CHANGE WORK SHEET

Use this checklist to estimate areas where your retirement living expenses may change. The preceding comments on each line item will help you prepare your estimate. Once you have completed this work sheet, you're ready to prepare either the quick-and-dirty retirement-expense forecaster on page 14 or—and you'll make me so happy if you do—the detailed work sheets beginning on page 315.

	NO CHANGE	DECREASE ↓ AMOUNT	INCREASE ↑ AMOUNT
Annual expenses that may decline when you retire:			
1. Savings and retirement-plan contributions	❏	❏ –	❏ +
2. Mortgage	❏	❏ –	❏ +
3. Loan and credit card payments	❏	❏ –	❏ +
4. Clothing	❏	❏ –	❏ +
5. Transportation	❏	❏ –	❏ +
6. Professional and business expenses	❏	❏ –	❏ +
7. Child care	❏	❏ –	❏ +
8. Alimony and child support payments	❏	❏ –	❏ +
9. Tuition and education	❏	❏ –	❏ +
10. Life insurance	❏	❏ –	❏ +
11. Income taxes	❏	❏ –	❏ +
Expenses that may rise when you retire:			
12. Medical care and medicine	❏	❏ –	❏ +
13. Medical insurance	❏	❏ –	❏ +
14. Recreation and travel	❏	❏ –	❏ +

	NO CHANGE	DECREASE ↓AMOUNT	INCREASE ↑AMOUNT
15. Hobbies	❑	❑ – _____	❑ + _____
16. Other changes			
_____	❑	❑ – _____	❑ + _____

Total decreases and increases $_____ $_____

Net change in retirement spending

(Total increases minus total decreases) $_____

Case Study—Retirement Budgeting for Young Boomers

Bertha and Bert Boomer, age forty-two, are smartly beginning to look at how much they'll need to spend when they retire, even though it's twenty years away. They summarized their current income and expense situation in the chart below. Because they want to retire early, Bertha and Bert realize they have to set ambitious goals that include:

1. Paying off their mortgage before retirement

2. Saving half of their future raises and putting same into retirement plans

	CURRENT STATUS AT AGE 42		FORECAST AT AGE 62	
	%	$	%	$
Income:				
(4% annual raises)		$80,000		$175,000
Expenses:				
Mortgage	20%	16,000	–	(paid off)
Social Security taxes	8	6,000	8%	14,000
Retirement savings	12	10,000	31	55,000
All other stuff	60	48,000	61	106,000
Total expenses	100%	$80,000	100%	$175,000

In this example, if Bertha and Bert Boomer retire at age sixty-two, they should be able to live off 61 percent of their preretirement income ("all other stuff"), although that amount may be somewhat higher with extra retiree expenses, such as medical costs and travel. On the other hand, "all other stuff" expenses include income taxes based on their current income, which would certainly decline once they retire on a lower income. Incidentally, if their savings rate of 31 percent at age sixty-two seems high, one comprehensive study of boomer savings rates put the average savings rate at 20 percent for fifty-year-olds. Also, the Boomers' plan involves gradual increases in their savings from their current rate of 12 percent.

When Should You Begin Collecting Social Security Retirement Benefits?

When should you start collecting your Social Security retirement benefits? If ever a question riles people up, that's the one. I should show you the mail I received after I suggested on a national television program that collecting Social Security benefits early may not be a wise thing to do. I received a plethora of responses ranging from those saying I was nuts all the way to suggesting that I do something to myself that is anatomically impossible. I'm quite sure that all of my detractors were early collectors of Social Security, so I can understand their ire at my suggestion that they may have made a bad decision. After all, this is an irrevocable decision, and no one likes to be second-guessed on a decision that you'll have to live with for the rest of your life. How important is it? Social Security benefits could be your most important source of retirement income, and one that rises with inflation to boot. Social Security typically replaces from 35 percent to over 50 percent of average preretirement earnings.

So allow me to go through the various matters to weigh in making this important decision. You *could* be better off collecting Social Security benefits early, like about 75 percent of retirees. Some are doing the right thing, but I fear that many are not. Rather than relying on the advice of your friends and the pundits, spend a few minutes evaluating your own situation.

First things first. Let's first review three key dates that dictate the level of benefits you'll receive:

1. **Early retirement.** You can begin collecting benefits as early as age sixty-two, but if you do, your benefits will permanently be reduced. How much they'll be reduced depends on when you were born. Table 6.1 shows the percentage benefit reduction based upon your birth year. If you retire sometime between age sixty-two and full retirement age, your benefit level will increase gradually each month you delay commencing benefits after sixty-two.

2. **"Full" retirement.** Full retirement age used to be sixty-five, but it is now being gradually increased for baby boomers depending on your natal year. Table 6.1 will also give you the bad news about when you attain full retirement age, which could be as high as sixty-seven.

3. **Delayed retirement.** Those who delay collecting benefits after full retirement age will receive a benefit increase for each year after full retirement age until, but not after, age seventy. For those born in 1943 or later (i.e., all members of the baby boom generation), the increase is a hefty 8 percent per year.

Based on those three dates, there are five different time periods to consider in this important decision:

1. **Age sixty-two.** Take the money and run. Widely recommended, even by many counselors at the local SSA offices. Detractors like to say, "Once a lower check, always a lower check."

2. **Sometime between sixty-two and full retirement age.** Sensible if you're going to continue to earn enough income after age sixty-two to otherwise sacrifice benefits. Keep in mind that

additional income will not impair benefits after you reach full retirement age.

3. **Full retirement age.** This is when our forebears began collecting benefits, and it isn't necessarily such a bad time to do so, although only about one-quarter of our elders wait this long nowadays.

4. **Sometime between full retirement age and age seventy.** Takes advantage of 8 percent per annum increase in full-retirement-age benefits. This may be particularly beneficial if you're still working and you'll rely on Social Security for the lion's share of your income. Also, if you or your spouse will rely primarily on the Social Security benefits of one spouse, delaying collection will help assure that the spouse with the low earnings record will receive an adequate retirement benefit if the higher-earning spouse predeceases.

5. **Age seventy.** There's no reason to wait beyond age seventy to collect benefits, unless you feel guilty about collecting them at all. If you feel guilty, may I suggest that you collect them anyway and send the checks to my kids' college funds or give them to some other worthy charity?

Can you count on Social Security? It has long been fashionable for boomers to say, "I'd better not count on Social Security in my retirement planning, because the Social Security system is going bankrupt." I beg to differ. Certainly, it's easy to be cynical. Projections differ as to when the system is likely to encounter problems meeting its obligations to the growing number of retirees. But if you think our elected officials are going to curtail, much less eliminate, Social Security, start by asking your representatives in Washington if they envision voting for such legislation. It's hard for me to imagine that Washington would even tinker with the benefit levels. This could certainly be done a variety of ways, however:

- **Reduce overall benefit levels for future retirees.**
  Not likely to happen.
- **Reduce benefits for affluent retirees.** A means-based test for Social Security benefits has been suggested, particularly by some filthy rich senators. There's nothing like $5 million of trust fund income to enable you to suggest that rich people can afford to forgo $20,000 in Social Security benefits. The trouble is that our members of Congress have always defined "rich" as anyone who makes a few dollars more than the average salary of a member of Congress, which affects a lot more people than the trust fund set.
- **Eliminate the cap on Social Security tax withholdings.** Social Security has always had a cap on the level of job income that is subject to Social Security taxes. More than scant attention has been paid to the idea of eliminating the cap so that higher-income earners pay more into the system. This would presumably be attractive to the majority of workers whose earnings don't exceed the cap. That is to be understood, because any tax that someone doesn't have to pay is a fair tax. But I still think eliminating the Social Security income cap is a long shot. The Social Security retirement system is a defined benefit plan. The more you contribute to the system over your working life, the greater the benefits to which you are entitled. If the cap is removed, either the benefits accruing to richer workers will be increased, thereby limiting the impact of the removal on the financial health of the system, or, if benefits are not increased, then this simply amounts to a transfer of wealth from

the well-to-do to those of lesser means. Again, this could be an attractive partial system fix, but one that Congress might not rush to enact, since many of their major campaign contributors are likely to be those who would be socked with a permanent tax increase for the rest of their working years.

- **Further delay full retirement age.** While this approach has some merit, given increasing life expectancies, there's little likelihood that this will be imposed anytime in the near future. There is a social cost to motivating workers to further delay retirement, since, all other things being equal, the longer people work, the fewer the number of jobs opening up for younger workers. Even if, in Social Security parlance, "normal retirement age" and/or the minimum age to collect benefits is increased, it's unlikely to have any impact on the benefits received by older boomers, and it will only have a nominally deleterious effect on younger boomers as any delays will most likely be gradually implemented, as was the case with the first round of age advancement that we're now in the midst of.

- **Change the formula used to calculate annual inflation adjustments.** This notion has been bandied about as a way to apply a Band-Aid for looming Social Security shortfalls. But again, any such change is not likely to be implemented anytime soon.

All that said, as in all matters related to federal laws and regulations, it's best to assume in your planning that the status quo will continue indefinitely. If you're more comfortable leaving Social Security benefits out of your retirement-income forecast, that's fine. Indeed, if you can thrive in retirement without Social Security, we admire and envy you.

TABLE 6.1
FULL RETIREMENT AGE AND BENEFIT
DEDUCTIONS FOR EARLY RETIREES

YEAR OF BIRTH	FULL RETIREMENT AGE	REDUCTION IF COLLECTING BENEFITS BEGINNING AT AGE 62
1943–54	66	25.0%
1955	66 and two months	25.8
1956	66 and four months	26.7
1957	66 and six months	27.5
1958	66 and eight months	28.3
1959	66 and 10 months	29.2
1960 and later	67	30.0

Please note that if you were born on January 1 of any year, you can use the previous year in the chart.

It's not such an easy decision. While there is no magic formula for determining the "right" time, some matters to consider include:

+ **Don't collect before full retirement age if you're still working.** The shocking thing to me about the 75 percent who are collecting early is that a good portion of these people are still working, and they're therefore likely to be sacrificing benefits because benefits are reduced if job income exceeds a fairly modest level. What are these people thinking? Not only are they receiving slimmed-down benefits by collecting early, they're not even entitled to receive all of their already reduced benefits.

+ **You won't sacrifice benefits if you work after full retirement age while collecting benefits.** Those still working after reaching full retirement age will no longer have their benefits reduced by the SSA. The majority of baby boomers currently intend to work after full retirement age, and they are probably well advised to begin collecting benefits at full retirement age, even though they continue toiling. There are important exceptions to this rule of thumb, however, which are described below.

✦ **Collecting early to pay your living expenses is often a danger sign.** Opting to collect benefits early because you need the money to pay bills is often a danger sign that you can't really afford to retire. It is important to realize that most financial arguments that urge early benefit collection assume that the retiree saves, rather than spends, the benefits, which for many is simply not the case.

✦ **Your health and likely life expectancy may be an important consideration.** Your and your family's health history can be an important determinant of many later-life decisions, including when to begin collecting retirement benefits. Those in poor health or with a family history of shorter life expectancies may want to begin collecting early, while those who enjoy both good health and good genes may want to wait until attaining full retirement age or even later.

NORMAN NOTSOBRIGHT IS NOT SO BRIGHT

One of the biggest risks of collecting Social Security benefits early when you expect to continue working until reaching full retirement age is that your benefits will be reduced by one dollar for every two dollars you earn over a specified level ($12,480 in 2006).

Example. Norman Notsobright heeded the clarion call from all of his acquaintances to collect Social Security benefits as soon as possible. So he started collecting a benefit of $15,000 when he turned sixty-two in 2006. But he also earned over $42,480 that year, thus losing all of his benefits. If the high earnings continue, he won't be entitled to benefits until he reaches full retirement age sixty-six, when job income is no longer an impediment to collecting benefits.

Social Security Decision Maker
Crucial Considerations for a Crucial Decision

I really want to help you make the right decision if, for no other reason, I can avoid invoking your wrath later on. Even if you're a decade or more from retirement, you should begin to think about when you'll probably begin to collect Social Security, because it will need to be incorporated into your retirement planning and financial projections. Here are the important matters to evaluate. "Yes" responses may suggest postponing the collection of benefits.

Yes   *No*

❑   ❑   **1. Are you likely to earn more than a minimal amount of income before you reach full retirement age?** If you earn more than the allowable minimum income of about $13,000, your benefits will be reduced and could be eliminated altogether until you reach full retirement age. If there's even a slight possibility that you'll return to work, consider the possible effect it could have on your benefits.

❑   ❑   **2. Do you have an irregular earnings history?** Social Security benefits are based on your earnings history. The way the SSA calculates the benefits would make an MIT professor's head spin, but if your earnings history includes years when you made little or nothing, delaying benefits and working between age sixty-two

Yes   No

and full retirement—or later—can significantly increase your benefits.

☐   ☐   **3. Will Social Security benefits comprise a major portion of your retirement income?** If you expect that Social Security benefits will comprise half or more of your total retirement income, delaying the collection of same will result in a higher lifetime check, substantially higher if you take advantage of the 8 percent annual increase offered to those who postpone collection after full retirement age.

☐   ☐   **4. Will your spouse need to rely on your Social Security retirement benefits?** If either you or your spouse hasn't contributed much to Social Security, it will probably be worthwhile for the spouse with the greater earnings record to wait until full retirement age or later. This will provide additional income for the lower- or non-earning spouse at retirement. More important, if the higher-earning spouse predeceases, the surviving spouse is entitled to the deceased spouse's full benefit.

☐   ☐   **5. Are you in good health?** The whole argument surrounding when to collect benefits is based on a "break-even" point that, depending on how it's calculated, generally ranges from eleven to seventeen years. If you're in pretty good health, you have a good chance of living well beyond the break-even point, which argues for postponing benefits. It's rather unpleasant making bets on how long you'll live, but, just as in baseball, it's best to "play the percentages," and a soon-to-be retiree with no significant health problems has a good chance of outliving the break-even. That said, the most important thing that you can do is live each day as if it's your last. Someday, you'll be right.

Yes   No

❏   ❏   **6. Have your ancestors, particularly your parents and grandparents, enjoyed long lives?** If your ancestors, particularly your parents and grandparents, survived into their eighties and nineties, like it or not, you've got a better-than-average chance of living that long or longer, which could make you glad you delayed collecting Social Security benefits.

Generating Income When You Retire

Is it better to self-manage your retirement money or to take an annuity? The answer is anything but simple, the ramifications can be huge, and it is made even more perplexing by the conflicting and often biased advice on the subject. True, some pension plans make it easy: they don't give you a choice, requiring you to take an annuity when you retire, period. On the other hand, many company-funded plans allow you the option of taking a lump-sum payout.

If you're one of the majority of workers whose employers don't offer a traditional pension plan, you still can make the same choice—managing the funds or annuitizing the funds for any retirement plans that you have contributed to, such as 401(k) and 403(b) plans and IRAs, as well as any other nonretirement money that's lying around.

Key considerations. Here are the key considerations when making the manage-it-yourself versus annuity decision:

1. **Investment risk.** If you decide to manage the money yourself, what happens to it is your business. If you lose it through unwise investments—or even "wise" ones that go sour—there's no recourse but to suffer in silence and, perhaps, cut your spending. Unless you are confident of your investment abilities—or those of a competent adviser—you may be better off taking the annuity.

2. **Liability risk.** Money that you are investing on your own is usually not protected from liability. These funds have to be used up to pay major medical (or other) expenses, including nursing home costs, if you exhaust other resources. In many cases, though, annuities are not subject to this liability.

3. **Inflation risk.** While some annuity plans are adjusted (at least partly) to offset the effects of inflation, most are not. The reality of a fixed-payout annuity is a steady loss of purchasing power. If you invest the money on your own, you have a good, but by no means assured, chance of investing it so that it will keep up with inflation.

4. **Anticipated income.** Generally, annuity payouts give you less income than you could make if you were investing the money on your own. *Reason:* The payout schedules tend to be figured conservatively to minimize the annuity company's future financial risks. In plain English, this means that the company is betting you'll live to two hundred. Find out the exact monthly or quarterly stipend you'd receive from an annuity and compare this figure to your anticipated rate of return if you were investing the money on your own.

5. **Mortality risk.** Traditionally, annuity payments cease when you do. Consequently, if you die prematurely, your estate is considerably poorer than it would have been if you'd taken a lump sum. Note, though, that many annuity plans—both the corporate type and the kind you buy on your own—offer some sort of provision for this event, although at a price. Typically, it's a continuation of some lesser stream of payments for the benefit of a surviving spouse, or the option of receiving a lump-sum payout of a portion of the money that was originally put into the annuity.

Each payout method has advantages and disadvantages, and no financial decision is "either/or." (See page 124.) Many retirees will benefit from taking an annuity for part of the money and investing the rest. If you do decide on an annuity, be sure to shop around. Don't assume that the first annuity you come across or your company annuity is the best. Chances are, it isn't.

Annuities Explained

Before delving into a discussion of annuities, let me first explain the various permutations and combinations of annuities. While the subject here is income annuities, the following primer covers both income and deferred annuities. For some information on deferred annuities, see page 155.

Annuity primer. Everyone's heard about annuities, but your eyes may glaze over when trying to figure them out. Here's a quick explanation of four characteristics of annuities:

✦ An **income** annuity (synonymous with "immediate" annuity) begins making regular payments to you as soon as you put money into it.

✦ With a **deferred** annuity, you invest your money now, let it grow inside the annuity tax-deferred, and later withdraw it in a lump sum, by receiving regular payments until the money runs out, or by rolling the money into an income annuity for lifetime income.

✦ A **fixed** annuity grows or makes payments at a fixed rate of return.

✦ A **variable** annuity invests the annuity money in a variety of mutual funds of your choosing.

Therefore, there are actually four kinds of annuities based upon these characteristics:

TABLE 6.2
HOW ANNUITIES WORK

	DEFERRED	**INCOME**
FIXED	Accumulates value based on a predetermined interest rate	Fixed payments received for life or a fixed period
VARIABLE	Increase in value based upon performance of selected mutual funds	Payments vary based upon performance of selected mutual funds

Thanks to the ingenuity of the insurance industry, not to mention its desire to sell more annuities, all manner of variations of the above taxonomy are offered. For example, immediate fixed annuities may include an inflation kicker, and deferred variable annuities may have features that allow you to periodically lock in investment gains. Whether any of these additional bells and whistles are appropriate for you depends on your circumstances. But the best course of action, as with most financial products, is to stick with the basics. There's more competition among the insurance companies for the basic policies, which often helps keep costs down. Also, the newfangled policies are more difficult to evaluate and compare, and many experts in the field fear that there's less than meets the eye with a "new and improved" type of annuity.

Income annuities are hot. Income annuities have been receiving a lot of attention in recent years, primarily because of losses sustained during the three-year bear market from 2000 to 2002. Stories of people nearing or in retirement who lost substantial portions of their nest eggs during that awful period have given new credence to the relative safety of an income annuity. This despite a time of low interest rates. Generally, the higher current prevailing interest rates are, the greater the annuity payout.

Making a Smart Income Annuity Decision

Reasons for choosing an income annuity:

✦ You're entering retirement or are already retired.

✦ You have retirement resources (pension distributions, retirement accounts, brokerage accounts) that you want to convert into an income stream.

✦ You're concerned about outliving your income.

✦ You want a guaranteed source of income in retirement.

✦ You have other retirement investments that can be invested for growth to offset the loss in purchasing power of a fixed annuity later in your retirement.

Despite their increasing popularity, these annuity arrangements have some nagging drawbacks. Nevertheless, with careful planning, the drawbacks can be ameliorated.

✦ **Income annuity drawback #1: your early demise.** This is the income annuity horror story. Some poor sap signs up for an annuity, receives a couple of monthly payments, and then has the audacity to die. And the winner is—the insurance company.

Solution. Consider an annuity that guarantees payments for at least a set number of years. Then, if you die before that set number of years, there will be something left for your survivors. Of course, payments will be reduced somewhat to account for a guaranteed number of payments.

✦ **Income annuity drawback #2: the annuitant predeceases some other needful soul.** If you have someone who would suffer financially (as well as, we hope, emotionally) if you're first in line for the grim reaper, a single-life annuity is probably a bad idea.

Solution. The obvious solution is a joint and survivor annuity that will continue payments to a survivor. Of course, this will reduce the initial payments, but this may be a small price to pay in exchange for both of you receiving payments for life.

✦ **Income annuity drawback #3: inflation ravages the annuity's purchasing power.** Inflation can wreak havoc on a fixed annuity. In short, while $1,500 per month in annuity income, in addition to your Social Security and other stuff, could look mighty appealing now, when you retire, you're quite likely to see the purchasing power of that $1,500 chopped by half or more, even if inflation stays relatively low. At a 3 percent annual rate of inflation, the buying power of that $1,500 will shrink to just $817 in twenty years.

Solution. Fear of loss in purchasing power has not been overlooked by our beloved insurance industry. They're more than happy to sell you an annuity with an inflation kicker. However, compared with a fixed annuity without the inflation kicker, you'll receive a considerably reduced initial payment. For example, if a sixty-five-year-old male buys a $100,000 annuity, his annual emolument goes down from $7,851 for a fixed annuity to $5,865 if he adds an inflation kicker. However, if you've got longevity in the family, you may find comfort in either an annuity that increases payments in accordance with the actual rate of inflation (as measured by the Consumer Price Index) or one that rises by a fixed percentage each year (choose *at least* 2 percent; 3 percent would be better). Finally, you might consider taking a fixed annuity, but reinvesting enough of each payment to allow you to keep up with inflation later on. This is further explained on page 150 and illustrated in Table 6.3.

✦ **Annuity drawback #4: the insurance company dies before you do.** The likelihood of an insurance company bellying up is low. But the last thing you want to do during your retirement is lose sleep over some insurance company's financial travails.

Solution. The strategy here is to make sure the insurance company with whom you are contracting for your annuity is in tip-top financial shape, as evidenced by its readings from the various insurance company ratings agencies. Even if you can get a better deal from a lower-rated company (i.e., one whose ratings grades look like my grammar-school report cards), don't be penny-wise and pound-foolish.

✦ **Annuity drawback #5: it's an irreversible financial commitment.** After considering all of the above-described drawbacks, you may still be uneasy with what is, after all, a major financial commitment that can't be undone.

Solution. Annuities are by no means an essential retirement-income tool. If you simply are turned off by any annuity at all, fine. There are many ways to generate needed retirement income. For example, you can create your own income annuity by investing in dividend-paying stocks, bonds, and other interest-earning securities. Alternatively, you could give an income annuity a test run by initially investing only a portion of the money you might ultimately put into annuities and then deciding later on if you want to purchase more.

Income annuity rule #1—gradual is the byword. Such a "staged" approach to income annuities has other advantages in addition to reducing an initial investment in an annuity. By waiting to commit additional money to an annuity, you can increase your income considerably. A male purchaser of a $100,000 fixed-payment annuity would receive $7,851 if he bought it at age sixty-five, $8,942 at age seventy, and $10,448 at age seventy-five. Also, purchasing more than one annuity allows you to spread your money out among different insurance companies in the unlikely, but not inconceivable, case that one of the companies goes under. Delaying an annuity purchase can also be advantageous if current interest rates are low. Since fixed annuity payouts are partially tied to the interest rates prevailing at the time the annuity is taken out, waiting until interest rates have risen can make good sense.

Shop till you drop. If and when you're ever in the market for an income annuity, shop for the best return so long as you entrust your money to a financially strong insurance company. Shopping for the best return is particularly important because, once you sign up, there's usually no turning back. You're in it for life, so you'd hate to end up with an annuity that pays quite a bit less than others that were available. Check out the special reader Web site for additional annuity examples and illustrations. **w w w**

Loss of purchasing power. This is a major concern of fixed-income annuities. Rather than settling for a much lower payment from an inflation-adjusted income annuity, you might consider:

1. Opting for a higher fixed annuity benefit.

2. Saving a portion of each payment.

3. Using those savings to keep up with inflation later on.

Here is an example of a fixed annuity with lifetime payments of $18,000 per annum. By saving $3,000 per year, the annuitant can add 3 percent per year to spending and keep up with that inflation kicker for thirty years.

Forgoing $3,000 out of an $18,000 payment is a small price for turning your fixed, eroded-by-inflation annuity into one that rises with inflation. Another advantage of your personal inflation-adjusted annuity is that if you live beyond thirty years, not all is lost. You'll still receive $18,000 per annum for the rest of your life. Also, if you die

TABLE 6.3
YOUR PERSONAL INFLATION-ADJUSTED ANNUITY

YEAR	ANNUITY INCOME	SAVINGS	SPENDING
1	$18,000	$3,000	$15,000
2	18,000	3,000	15,450
3	18,000	3,000	15,900
4	18,000	3,000	16,400
5	18,000	3,000	16,900
10	18,000	3,000	19,600
15	18,000	3,000	22,700
20	18,000	3,000	26,300
25	18,000	3,000	30,500
30	18,000	3,000	35,300

before thirty years (perish the thought), you'll have something left over from your savings for your kids or other heirs.

Other Ways to Derive Retirement Income

Creating your own annuity with SWPs. If you're leery about committing to a lifetime annuity, you could create your own annuity, albeit with more risk. This strategy is known as a SWP ("swip"), which stands for "systematic withdrawal plan." You simply instruct the financial institutions that are holding your investments to automatically transfer money from your investment account to your checking account by electronic funds transfer. You can even elect to have taxes withheld, which may be particularly useful if the money is coming out of a retirement account whose withdrawals are entirely or mostly taxable. Unless you're Johnny on the Spot with your quarterly estimated tax installments, earmarking a percentage of your regular SWPs to income taxes could avoid some nasty tax surprises later on.

The appeal of systematic withdrawal plans is that you remain in control of the money rather than ceding it to the insurance company. If the investment gods shine on your money, you might be able to increase your yearly SWP transfers to help you keep up with inflation. So what's the downside? You could still run out of money or run so low that you'd have to reduce your withdrawals later on. A lifetime annuity *guarantees* payments over your lifetime, even if you end up shafting the insurance company by living a lot longer than their actuaries thought you would.

For your own low-cost, inflation-adjusted annuity, delay collecting Social Security. Here's a strategy for creating an inflation-adjusted annuity at much lower cost than buying one from an insurance company. Simply spend your own money from age sixty-two until you become eligible for full retirement benefits. If you want to supercharge your "maximized Social Security benefits" delay benefits until after full retirement age—this can increase your benefits by a third or more. If you work the numbers, you'll probably find that you're financially better off following this strategy compared with purchasing the income annuity. By so doing, you'll enjoy a considerably higher lifetime Social Security benefit that's inflation-adjusted to boot.

www

NEW DEVELOPMENTS IN ANNUITIES

The insurance industry is introducing a range of products that better meet the demands of the baby boom generation. These new annuity programs replace the old complex and

rigid arrangements with simpler and more flexible ones. If it's
at least a few years before you retire, it behooves you to consider the ever-widening range of annuity products. Just keep
in mind that "new and improved" doesn't necessarily mean
"improved." **w w w**

Income Annuity Decision Maker

This Decision Maker will help you decide whether an income annuity should be part of your financial planning.

Yes   *No*

❑   ❑   **1. Are you uncomfortable investing your retirement savings in the stock market?** Fixed-income
annuities and inflation-adjusted income annuities alleviate any concerns about possibly losing money on your
investments, although fixed-income annuities will lose
ground to inflation. If you are comfortable with the
stock market, you could consider a variable-income annuity whose value fluctuates according to the performance of the annuity's underlying mutual funds, or
simply invest the money on your own without an annuity.

❑   ❑   **2. Will your retirement income consist entirely
or almost entirely of Social Security and withdrawals from your contemplated annuities?** If
resources available to invest for growth are small or
nonexistent, inflation-adjusted annuities may be preferable to minimize the risk of losing out to inflation.
Where other resources can be invested for growth, a
fixed-income annuity might be preferable.

Yes   *No*

❏   ❏   **3. Are you and, if applicable, your spouse or part-ner in good health?** The better your health, the more efficacious a lifetime annuity. Those in poorer health should usually opt for annuities with a mini-mum or fixed guaranteed payment period.

❏   ❏   **4. Have your ancestors lived long enough to make the Social Security Administration cringe?** Again, long life expectancies bode well for the an-nuitant and bode ill for the insurance company. What a shame.

❏   ❏   **5. If you are married, are you concerned that years of nursing home expenses could impover-ish the other spouse?** If so, an annuity can provide a measure of protection for each spouse since the an-nuity is not subject to forfeiture to pay nursing home or other care costs. Should other assets have to be spent down, a lifetime annuity will continue to pay for the remainder of the surviving spouse's life.

Still More Annuity Decisions

Like the knife salesperson on TV infomercials, I'm afraid I have to say, "But wait, there's more." In this case, it's not knives, but it's a couple of other important annuity decisions that you may need to make.

1. **Selecting an annuity survivor benefit.** If you have a spouse or other dependent family member, you need to decide which survivor option to take on the distributions—100 percent, or 50 percent, for example. You can find an Annuity Distribution Decision Maker on the *You Can Do It!* reader Web site. **w w w**

2. **Considering and evaluating a deferred annuity.** In some cases, deferred annuities can play a role for baby boomers who have significant resources outside their retirement plans that they can afford to set aside for many years until they begin making withdrawals in retirement. The special reader Web site offers tips for deciding on both variable and fixed deferred annuities. **w w w**

CHAPTER 7

Deciding When to Retire

Here's a common baby boomer question: What's so sacrosanct about retiring at sixty-five? A short history lesson might show why this is such an important question. Apparently, the notion of retiring at age sixty-five originated in Europe around the turn of the twentieth century. While the details are murky, I'll reconstruct a likely scenario. As best as I can imagine, and assuming such a corporate function existed in the early 1900s, some enlightened human resources department manager reviewed personnel records and discovered a startling fact. Few employees even made it to age sixty-five, and those who did died fairly soon thereafter. (Life expectancy at the dawn of the twentieth century was around forty-seven.) So this foresighted manager went before the board of directors and said, "Few of our employees are surviving to age sixty-five. So I'm recommending that the company let them 'retire' at that age so they can spend a few months relaxing before they die."

But what a difference a century makes! Baby boomers who retire at sixty-five have a good chance of living until ninety, and many will live well beyond ninety. Only about a third of the baby boom generation wants to retire early or at normal retirement age. There's no reason to consider sixty-five the "normal" retirement age anyway, given longer

life expectancies and the mental and physical abilities of this generation to work well beyond age sixty-five. While the primary incentive
for delaying retirement is psychological (boomers are so invested in
their careers, the idea of retiring is abhorrent to many), delaying retirement can have some rather significant and positive financial implications as well. I'll focus on the money aspects and let the psychologists
explain the touchy-feely reasons why boomers want to postpone retirement. My initial academic training as an accountant was heavy on
practicality and bereft of developing people skills. As you may know
from any interactions you've had with accountants, most of us are de-
void of emotion, so I'm incapable of dealing with any matters involving
feelings and relationships.

What's your plan? The notion of retiring at normal retirement age is
so . . . well, normal . . . that few baby boomers, a fiercely independent lot, even give it a thought. So in this chapter I'll pretty much
assume that you're planning to retire at some time other than the
customary age sixty-five. Here's the rundown:

+ **Retiring early.** While the majority of baby boomers seem to
  disdain the notion of retiring early, it's nice to be in a position
  where you can, given job uncertainty and the possibility of poor
  health disrupting your plans to work indefinitely.

+ **Winning the retirement catch-up game.** While the majority of
  baby boomers are on track to achieve a decent retirement, nowhere near all are happy with their progress. This section will
  provide you with a lot of not-very-painful ways to improve your
  prospects, no matter how near or far you are from retirement age.

+ **Delaying retirement.** This seems to be the wont of your generation, and for those who haven't made the financial progress
  that they'd like, delaying retirement can result in a whopping
  increase in their retirement income. Late retirement needn't require you to stay with your old job. Many boomers will find that

retiring gradually, taking less-stressful jobs and working fewer hours, is all that's needed to provide both psychological and financial benefits.

Retiring Early

Baby boomers will redefine the retirement landscape. It's not just the baby boomers who are rejecting early retirement. Some demographers are predicting that early retirement will not be as popular among baby boomers as many think, reflecting a trend away from early retirement over the past several years. A number of factors in the retirement landscape will influence how boomers approach retirement, many of which render early retirement less appealing, such as the shift away from pension plans to contribution plans such as 401(k)s, longer life expectancies, cutbacks to retiree health insurance, and more.

Despite these factors, however, early retirement is still on the docket of many baby boomers. In fact, every worker should consider early retirement, because not all early retirements are voluntary.

Why workers retire early. Early retirement isn't necessarily the culmination of a long-term plan. People who retire early pretty much fit into one of four groups:

1. Workers who decided themselves that they wanted to retire early.

2. Workers who were compelled to retire early because of such circumstances as health problems or the need to care for a family member.

3. Workers who retired as a result of an employer incentive offer.

4. Workers who had to retire, most commonly as a result of a layoff with slim chances of finding a suitable alternative job.

Whether or not you are an aspiring early retiree, your retirement planning should consider the possibility that the other three reasons for early retirement may arise. In fact, 40 percent of retirees say they left the workplace earlier than originally planned, often because of illness, disability, or layoffs.

Throughout your working years, everything you do with your financial planning and your career is geared toward an overriding objective—to be able to retire comfortably. The more diligent you are in these endeavors, the better able you will be to cope with an "involuntary" early retirement.

SUCCESS STORY: UNINTENDED EARLY RETIREMENT

Many baby boomers will retire early for reasons beyond their control, but that need not mean lifetime financial setback. "I left work several years earlier than planned because of my wife's serious illness. It's one of those things that we thought only happened to other families. The financial impact wasn't as severe as we had originally feared, thanks to health insurance and our savings. Looking back on this ten years later, my leaving work early was important, and while it resulted in a somewhat lower standard of living, I'm really surprised at how well we can live despite the disruption in our financial and retirement plans."

Keys to a successful early retirement. If you want to or might have to retire early, take heed. If there's one common characteristic of people who can afford to retire early, it is sacrifice. This is how they do it:

✦ **They plan early.** Unless you're already blessed with prodigious resources, you probably can't decide when you're fifty that you want to retire at fifty-five. It takes many years of planning. Successful early retirees often work for companies with generous pension plans and avoid hopping jobs so that they can accrue substantial benefits. Some couples decide not to have children so they won't incur the astronomical (this adjective based on my personal experience) expenses of raising them. Many live in low-cost cities and towns.

✦ **They sacrifice during their working years.** Successful early retirees have high savings rates. They often live in inexpensive housing, and they become experts at keeping their living expenses low. Those who own homes get out from under their mortgage as soon as they can—certainly no later than when they plan to retire.

✦ **They sacrifice after their working years.** Even though they have spent many years living modestly, successful early retirees may cut back even further when they retire. They realize how much money they will have to continue saving to make ends meet thirty or forty years hence. They relocate to low-cost areas of the United States. A steadily increasing number even move out of the United States to settle in countries whose living costs are lower.

The above is not meant to dissuade you if you desire an early retirement, but it does reflect how past early retirees have surmounted the challenge. If your financial situation is similar to the average baby boomer's, which is far better than that of previous generations, your prospects for successfully retiring early are far better as well. But the key things to keep in mind are that retiring early does require more advance planning and, almost certainly, some sacrifice.

SUCCESS STORY: LOWER RETIREMENT LIVING EXPENSES = EARLIER RETIREMENT

"I'm going to retire next year, which is actually two years earlier than I had planned. I had always heard that retirees will spend almost as much to live as they did during their working years. But that's certainly not going to be the case with me. If you're planning your retirement, be sure to calculate just how much income you're going to need when you retire. I'll bet you'll find out that it's quite a bit less than you think, particularly if you curtail some of your spending excesses before you retire."

Early Retirement Decision Maker

If you're considering early retirement, this Decision Maker will help you achieve this ambitious goal. Even if you're many years away from an early retirement, these questions will help you identify important considerations that will help you reach your goal.

Yes   *No*

❑   ❑   **1. Are you convinced that early retirement is a good idea?** Has your career provided you with a sense of personal worth and fulfillment that may be hard to replicate in retirement? Just because people have enough money to retire doesn't mean they're emotionally ready. On the other hand, it's hard to find financially well-prepared early retirees who regret the decision.

❑   ❑   **2. Have you carefully analyzed your financial preparedness at the time you'd like to retire, using a realistic life expectancy?** Find out what you'll need to accumulate by regularly running a retirement income and expense forecast. **w w w**

❑   ❑   **3. If you plan to retire before age fifty-nine, will you have sufficient money in nonretirement accounts to be able to support yourself until age 59½, when you can begin withdrawing from**

Yes   *No*

retirement plans without penalty? If not, you may have to pay an early-withdrawal penalty to tap into retirement accounts. If you're under age 59½, there is an exception to the usual 10 percent early-withdrawal penalty if you agree to take a predetermined amount of money from your IRA each year. There are several methods for calculating this, but you'll probably need a tax professional to help you figure out how. That loophole aside, here's a fundamental question if you're planning to take money out of retirement accounts before 59½: Are you sure you have enough money in these accounts to last what could be a forty-year retirement?

❑   ❑   **4. Will health insurance be continued or be readily obtainable until Medicare commences?** If employer-provided health insurance will cease before you become eligible for Medicare, will privately purchased health insurance be available and affordable until you qualify for Medicare? Preexisting health conditions can be problematic.

❑   ❑   **5. Will major obligations (mortgages, credit cards, and other loans, education costs, needed home improvements, etc.) be paid off when you retire?** If not, will you be able to continue to meet these obligations after retirement?

❑   ❑   **6. Have you determined how your Social Security retirement benefits will be affected by early retirement?** Social Security benefits are based on the average of your best thirty-five years of work, adjusted for inflation. In some circumstances, if your early retirement will include years when your income was low or nil, your eventual Social Security benefits could be disappointingly low. It's best to find out now what the deleterious effect, if any, will be. **w w w**

❏   ❏   **7. If you have a pension plan and retire early, have you decided how you're going to take the distribution?** If you have the choice between taking an annuity or a lump sum, this is a complicated decision that may require some professional help. Annuities guarantee that you'll have a lifetime income, but they may lose a lot of purchasing power thanks to inflation. If you can take a lump sum, you have more control over the money, but may risk exhausting it over a long retirement. See page 143.

❏   ❏   **8. If you will be receiving payments from a pension plan, have you determined how to receive the payments?** This is an important decision that will affect you for the rest of your life. See page 154 for more direction.

❏   ❏   **9. Have you evaluated the advantages and drawbacks of collecting Social Security benefits before normal retirement age?** While most early retirees collect Social Security early, this may not be the most prudent decision. See the Social Security Decision Maker on page 141.

❏   ❏   **10. Have you been offered an early-retirement incentive plan?** If so, evaluate it carefully with the help of the checklist on page 165.

❏   ❏   **11. If your early-retirement plans include beginning a second career or working part-time, have you lined up opportunities, or are you confident of your ability to find such employment?** If you're

Yes   No

going to need job income after taking early retirement, it's important to realistically assess your chances
of finding meaningful work. A recent study suggested
that a large percentage of early retirees had more difficulty obtaining worthwhile work than they had anticipated.

❑   ❑   **12. Have you figured out what you're going to do
when you retire?** This is particularly important for
early retirees, because many people who have worked
hard and sacrificed to be able to retire early have
done little during their working years to develop hobbies and cultivate other pastimes. Lack of leisure activities can be a real shocker when they retire and
wonder what they're going to do over the next forty
years. See chapter 12.

SUCCESS STORY: WHY WE SHOULD ALWAYS CONSIDER OUR PARENTS' FINANCIAL ADVICE

"My parents gave us some simple advice that has benefited
me for decades. Buy a home and pay off the mortgage in less
than thirty years. Save 10 percent of your before-tax income
in your thirties and gradually increase that savings percentage
by 5 percent each succeeding decade: 15 percent in your forties and 20 percent in your fifties. We're in our late fifties and
could retire now, but we're putting it off awhile. Incidentally,
my parents were good spenders as well as good savers, as
evidenced by the tiny inheritance passed on to their children.
But their advice thirty years ago was better than any inheritance."

Evaluating an Early-Retirement Incentive Plan

Early-retirement incentive plans are a popular way for a company or nonprofit organization to achieve a reduction in workforce, whether due to mergers, takeovers, or downsizing. These efforts are often directed toward higher-paid mid- and late-career employees, so baby boomers are and will continue to be the focus of many early-retirement plans.

Retirement incentive plans may sound particularly appealing to you if times are tough at your company and you feel there are no guarantees that you'll be able to keep your job if you don't accept the offer. The plan may seem fairly compelling, but many of them offer a lot less than meets the eye. For example, even a beefed-up early-retirement pension is likely to be considerably smaller than the pension you could expect if you continued to work.

Here's a checklist for evaluating any early-retirement incentive plan that you are offered:

❑ 1. Compare the package to the retirement benefits you would receive if you continued to work—not those you would receive if you retired immediately without the package.

❑ 2. Consider how happy you are with your job and think about whether you would prefer to continue working. If you do in fact retire, would you enjoy the leisure of retirement or would you feel bored and restless?

❑ 3. Project your retirement expenses and income until age ninety-five. The retirement benefits that look so generous now will look a lot different thirty or more years hence unless the benefits are adjusted for inflation.

❑ 4. Determine how long any severance benefits and personal resources will last to make sure you avoid penalties for early withdrawal of retirement-plan money.

❑ 5. Realistically examine prospects for finding other work. If you have sufficient time to seek out other opportunities before making the decision, by all means do so. If you've already been seeking a job or career change, the early-retirement plan may turn out to be a blessing.

Winning the Retirement Catch-Up Game

Do you worry that you haven't made enough progress financially to afford to retire at seventy-five, much less sixty-five? It's easy to feel that way, thanks to the barrage of media reports suggesting that most boomers are headed for a retirement of deprivation. Serious research on the subject suggests that a healthy majority of boomers are on track for a pretty good retirement. But many others still have their work cut out for them. If you think you're one of them, I'll offer some suggestions for closing the gap between what you have now and what you'll need when you retire. Much of this advice will also help you if you think you're in pretty good shape but wouldn't object to an even richer retirement.

A dozen ways to play catch-up with your retirement planning. The challenges confronting those who haven't yet made the kind of progress toward retirement that they would like really boil down to two matters:

✦ How much should be saved between now and retirement?

✦ Are there other ways to close the gap between what is needed at retirement and what has been accumulated so far?

It may also be helpful here to mention the ways in which the above-mentioned gap can be closed.

1. Put your spending on a diet, both now and in retirement.

2. Fatten up your income during your working years and, perhaps, in the early years of your retirement.

But beyond the obvious, here are a dozen ways to play catch-up with your retirement planning. Some are straightforward while others entail significant life changes. While all of them will help you achieve your retirement goals, some can have a major impact. Like all things financial, you can't do everything, but do check off the ones that make sense for you so that you can make your own retirement success story.

		Tough to Do
Can Do	*Might Do*	*or Not Applicable*
❑	❑	❑

1. Increase your savings. Start with a small increase that you can easily afford and move up from there. Save a sizable portion of any future raises. Since the money you're saving is earmarked for retirement, put it into retirement plans at work and into IRAs to take advantage of the tax breaks available for retirement savers. The tax savings allow you to contribute even more. For suggestions on the best places to put your retirement money, see chapter 4.

❑   ❑   ❑   **2. Reduce your living expenses.** Bifurcate your living expenses between those that are essential (your mortgage or rent, for example) and those that can be reduced (for example, meals at restaurants). Pay particular attention to daily expenses that may seem trivial but can add up to big money over a year. The budget work sheets in Appendix I can help you identify areas where you can cut back with the least pain.

❑   ❑   ❑   **3. Control the costs of big-ticket items.** Major expenses, notably college costs and cars, can derail your retirement saving. With respect to college, if it boils down to cutting back on retirement contributions or taking out student loans, take the loans. Having to repay student loans will provide additional incentive for your college student to seek gainful employment upon graduation, which will most certainly reduce *your* living expenses. Cars are a major financial drain that can be stanched by simply keeping your car longer. Page 266 will show you how much that can save.

Can Do	Might Do	Tough to Do or Not Applicable

❑   ❑   ❑   **4. Reduce debt.** Add up your monthly debt payments and imagine for a moment how much your retirement budget would be reduced if they're paid off by the time you retire. Start modestly paying more than the minimum and gradually raise your debt payments. Just as important, minimize your use of credit cards, and if you refinance your home to take advantage of lower interest rates, never refinance for a longer maturity, and try to shorten the maturity.

❑   ❑   ❑   **5. Invest for growth.** Many people think they should invest more conservatively if their retirement resources are limited, but the opposite is true. You need to take more risk with your investments, which should provide you with higher returns. Emphasize stocks while still diversifying within several different stock categories, large company, small company, international, etc. Chapter 3 shows you how to diversify.

❑   ❑   ❑   **6. Work for companies with pension plans.** While pension plans are becoming an endangered species, particularly in the private sector, if you or your spouse or partner can work a sufficient number of years to earn at least a modest pension, this will certainly help if you're playing catch-up. If you work for an employer that provides a pension, don't quit without taking a careful look at what that would cost you in pension benefits. Most pension plans are heavily skewed to favor worker longevity.

		Tough to Do
Can Do	*Might Do*	*or Not Applicable*
❑	❑	❑ **7. Moonlight.**

7. Moonlight. Working part-time has a profusion of advantages; for one, the additional earnings can be added to retirement savings and/or reduce debt. If you toil as an independent contractor rather than as an employee, you can set up a self-employed retirement plan (see page 67) and take other tax deductions for your business-related expenses. Your part-time work may help you hone your career skills and could ease the transition from full-time employment to part-time employment if you opt to retire gradually, as explained on page 172. One big caveat to moonlighting: Don't commit a lot of your own money to starting a business or buying a franchise. Spending a lot to set up shop is risky, particularly for those who are playing catch-up with their retirement. Be cautious of getting into a business in an area completely unrelated to your career.

❑   ❑   ❑   **8. Delay retirement.** Many baby boomers plan to work beyond normal retirement age, for both financial and lifestyle reasons. Delaying retirement has a number of financial advantages. You can make your money last anywhere from seven to ten years longer by working an extra three years. Delaying retirement can add 10 percent to your retirement income for each year you delay retirement. Why? The longer you work, the more time you have to (1) add to your savings, (2) let your savings grow, and (3) increase your Social Security (8 percent per year after full retirement age) and, if you qualify, other pension plan income. See page 173 to gauge the financial impact of delaying retirement.

❑   ❑   ❑   **9. Retire gradually.** Gradual retirement will be a popular strategy for the baby boom generation, many of whom are torn between the conflicting desires to continue working (the money certainly helps) and to start slowing down from a frenetic work life. Just earning enough to pay your living expenses will work wonders on your future retirement income as illustrated on page 172. Employers, perhaps your own employer, will welcome part-time veteran workers. American industry forecasts a serious shortage of qualified workers as the baby boom generation retires.

Can Do	Might Do	Tough to Do or Not Applicable	
❑	❑	❑	**10. Reduce retirement expenses.**

Throw out the conventional rules of thumb about the percentage of preretirement income needed to sustain you in retirement—80 percent, 90 percent, even 110 percent have been estimated by the "experts." You'll either find that your needs are a lot less or that you can find ways to reduce your retirement expenses (see page 126). In fact, the good habits you develop now to reduce your spending and boost your savings will help you better control your retirement budget as well. But don't wait until just before retirement to look for ways to pare your retirement spending. The sooner you take a detailed look at your expected retirement spending, the better able you will be to find ways to live more penuriously, both now and after you retire.

❑	❑	❑	**11. Downsize your home.** Down-

sizing your living quarters has advantages beyond the money you're able to pull out of the home (free of federal capital gains taxes in most instances) if you're a home owner. Your yearly utilities and property taxes will be reduced, and if you move into a newer home or a rental, upkeep expenses should be lower as well. (See chapter 8.)

❑	❑	❑	**12. Relocate to a lower-cost locale.**

You pay a big price to live in the big city. If you're anxious to lower your retirement expenses or you'd like to live where the livin' is easier, follow the well-trod path of those who are moving to lower-cost

SUCCESS STORY: FIFTY YEARS OLD AND NOTHING TO SHOW FOR IT

"When I turned fifty, I was a poster child for bad planning. Big spending, a divorce, a home foreclosure—you name it, and I did it. The last thing I wanted to do was take a look at my situation, because I knew it was hopeless. But when I got my Social Security benefits statement, my situation didn't look as bad as I thought. I finally mustered the gumption to take a look, and I'll never forget that day. I spent a Saturday on the Internet—reading, using a mutual fund company's retirement forecaster, and planning. For starters, I found that Social Security was going to provide almost half of what I needed when I retired. By using the calculators on the Internet, I found that if I saved about 15 percent of my income until I retired, I would be okay. It took me a couple of years to get up to that level, but I did, and stuck with it. I also bought a house after I cleaned up my credit record and should be able to pay it off about eight years after I retire. Incidentally, I'll be retiring in about three years and will have met the plan I established on that Saturday twelve years ago. My advice to those who find themselves in the same pickle I was in is not to avoid taking a hard look at what you need to do. Chances are, you'll discover that you can work toward a decent retirement."

and lower-taxed locales both in and outside the United States. Moving from a big city to a medium-size city could lower your living costs by 40 percent. Just moving to the suburbs can cut your living expenses to a much more retirement-friendly level. (See chapter 9.)

Delaying Retirement or Retiring Gradually: The Wave of the Future

One of the biggest trends in the twenty-first century is the preference for many, particularly baby boomers, to delay retirement or to retire gradually. Gradual retirement has a lot of appeal, for both lifestyle and financial reasons. Gradual retirement means working a reducing number of hours either in the same occupation or in a new vocation. A lot of workers simply can't imagine retiring cold turkey at sixty-five under any circumstances. Since this is a money book, I'd be remiss in not describing how much of a difference extra years of income can have on your retirement lifestyle. Delaying retirement and gradually reducing your work income one year means 10 percent extra annual income from your nest egg when you do retire; three years, 25 percent; and five years, 40 percent! Gradual retirement results in so much more retirement income for two reasons. First, your retirement savings have more time to grow before you begin tapping into them. Second, each year you continue working is one less year your money will be needed to fund your retirement. Also, by delaying the date you begin collecting Social Security retirement benefits, that income will increase as well. If, instead of retiring gradually, you work full-time and continue saving, your retirement-income increase will be even greater.

WORK SHEET
DELAYED RETIREMENT INCOME ESTIMATOR

You can use this work sheet to approximate the amount your retirement income will increase if you:

1. Delay retirement while continuing to make retirement contributions.

2. Retire gradually without making additional retirement-plan contributions.

The difference between the two approaches is, if you retire gradually without continuing to save, you will not enter any amounts in Step 3, additional savings.

Please keep in mind that these rules of thumb are estimates only and may vary depending on several factors, including your Social Security earnings history, your investment returns, and your life span. But this will provide you with a ballpark estimate of your expected retirement income at various ages between sixty-four and seventy, using age sixty-two as the base year.

The example cites a single person who plans to retire at age sixty-eight and whose income is $70,000, has $300,000 in retirement investments at age sixty-two, and expected annual retirement-plan contributions of $15,000 between age sixty-two and retirement.

Step 1: Estimate Your Social Security Benefits

	YOUR NUMBERS	EXAMPLE
Expected annual Social Security benefits at age 62	$_____	$14,500

Increase benefits by the following

percentages, assuming retirement at age:

64 - 18% (multiply by 1.18)

66 - 38% (multiply by 1.38)

68 - 63% (multiply by 1.63)

| 70 - 88% (multiply by 1.88) | ×_____ | × 1.63 |

Estimated Social Security benefits at

    planned retirement age $_____   <u>$23,635</u>

                                                          (Step 1 total)

Step 2: Estimate Your Retirement Nest Egg

Expected retirement, investments at

    age 62 $_____ $<u>300,000</u>

Annual income multiplier, assuming

    retirement at age:

        64 - multiply by .075

        66 - multiply by .09

        68 - multiply by .11

        70 - multiply by .13   ×_____   × <u>.11</u>

Estimated annual income from nest egg $_____   <u>$33,000</u>

                                                           (Step 2 total)

Step 3: Estimated Additional Income from Savings between Age 62 and Planned Retirement Age

Annual savings between age 62 and

    planned retirement age $_____ $<u>15,000</u>

Annual income multiplier, assuming

    retirement at age:

        64 - multiply by .06

        66 - multiply by .20

        68 - multiply by .38

        70 - multiply by .60   ×_____   × <u>.38</u>

Estimated annual income from additional

    savings $_____   <u>$5,700</u>

                                                           (Step 3 total)

Step 4: Estimated Annual Pension Income, If Any, at Planned Retirement Age

$_____ $0

(Step 4 total)

Step 5: Total

Total income in first year of planned
retirement age (Step 1+Step 2+Step 3
+Step 4) $_____ $62,335

In the above example, postponing retirement to age sixty-eight results in retirement income that is almost 90 percent higher than when retiring at age sixty-two! **w w w**

Timing is everything. What's your preference: early, late, or even normal? It's nice to have choices, but, of course, these choices have financial consequences. One of the most important choices is how much you want to spend when you're retired. Early retirees are usually content to live more modestly. Those who want a more lavish retirement are often willing to work a few extra years to achieve it. For the first time in history, baby boomers have the wherewithal to be able to choose when to retire. Relish the opportunity, but also make sure your plans are consistent with your means.

SUCCESS STORY: CAREER CHANGE PROVIDES POSTRETIREMENT OPPORTUNITIES

Baby boomers aren't the first generation to experience multiple careers. Here are the thoughts of someone from the preceding generation: "I first worked twenty years for a large technology company, but became one of many victims of the company's downsizing. At that point, I had had enough of the corporate rat race, so I went back to school to earn my teacher's certificate. While I really enjoyed teaching, after fifteen years it was time to leave, but I wasn't yet financially well-off enough to retire. I got a pension from the school system, but with only fifteen years in the system, it wasn't enough to live off. Still, I wanted out, so a couple of years before leaving I began to investigate how I could earn some money on my terms—at a reduced schedule. I soon found three promising areas, including substitute teaching, private tutoring, and, using my background in the tech sector, teaching part-time at a local community college. I'm sixty-eight and still work about twenty hours a week, although I take a couple of months off each year. This has worked out really well for me. I can retire now, but plan to keep on working for at least the next three years, simply because I like what I'm doing."

CHAPTER 8

Edifice Complex: What to Do with the Family Home

Your Home Is Your Best Investment, but for Most Boomers, It's Not an Investment

In recent years, baby boomers in most areas of the country have been basking in the wealth they've created simply by owning a home. Congratulations. But what are you going to do with all that equity you've built up—if anything? The only way that home equity can be considered an investment in the sense of providing resources for your retirement is if you intend to withdraw that equity by selling the house and either moving into a less expensive domicile or renting. But most people don't want to do that, and they should not be deluded into thinking that this big chunk of home equity is a substitute for saving for retirement the old-fashioned way, by putting money into retirement accounts and savings.

Caveat home owners. How much of your total net worth (assets minus liabilities) is comprised of the value of your house? Here's a

quick table to find out (you may need a calculator or, if you're so inclined, a slide rule to figure out the percentages).

Equity in your home (realistic estimate of
value minus mortgage[s]) $_____   _____%

Retirement and other savings/investments $_____   _____%

Total $_____   ___100%

When evaluating your net worth, careful attention should be paid to
how much of it is composed of the value of the family domicile(s). A
recent study indicates that the value of homes owned by working-age
people comprises about 50 percent of total net worth for those residing
in the heartland of the United States and almost 60 percent of net
worth for denizens of the east and west coasts. Many home owners
have enjoyed substantial gains in the values of their homes. The danger
of this, from a retirement-planning standpoint, is that while net worth
may seem adequate, if the value of the home represents a large percentage of total worth, you may be deluded into thinking that you are
better off financially than you are, unless you're prepared to downsize.

Example. Edward and Edie Edifice are within a decade of retirement and have what at first glance appears to be a darn good net
worth of $1 million. They have been running retirement income and
expense projections based on their $1 million net worth. But closer
inspection reveals that $650,000 of their net worth consists of equity
in their home, net of a sizable mortgage. Since they have no intention
of moving when they retire, the net value of the home should be ex-
cluded when analyzing retirement cash flow. The Edifices are so-
bered by these revised but more realistic projections.

Big-ticket items tell a lot. In speaking with individuals and families over the years, I've found that how they handle big-ticket items,

particularly the home, is a reliable indicator of how well they are preparing for retirement. I've talked with numerous singles and couples up and down the income ladder who, by middle age (*middle age: n.*, "anyone who is ten years older than you"), have accumulated a lot of retirement money, including a lot saved outside of their retirement plans, and have little or no debt. The vast majority of them have one thing in common: the value of their homes—or the amount of their rent—is way below what they could currently afford. There's no reason why anyone has to own a home commensurate with his or her income. Warren Buffett—not to mention closet millionaires in your community—doesn't own a mansion or drive a designer car. Despite a growing income, the notion of buying trophy homes doesn't even enter their minds. Rather, they're quite content living well beneath their means. You probably know some people who take the opposite tack—serial home owners. A week after they move into their latest home, they're contemplating moving into an even bigger palace with, of course, a bigger mortgage. The upshot is that by the time they start seriously thinking about retirement, they've probably built up some equity in their houses over the years, but that equity pales in comparison with the buildup in their mortgages. And because of their edifice complex, the notion of moving into something more affordable is anathema.

Whatever your housing situation, decisions you make between now and the time you retire could have a big effect on your retirement finances. The first thing to do is give some thought to what you might change, if anything, in your housing situation over the following years and decades.

Homebody's Wish List

As part of your retirement planning, you should give some thought to what you expect to do with your hacienda. Three primary considerations enter into housing decisions when you retire. (A fourth decision, where to retire, is covered in chapter 9.)

1. **Lifestyle.** Will you be content with your current home during retirement, or would you prefer a change in venue?

2. **Financial.** Will you want or need to increase your retirement resources by moving into less-expensive housing?

3. **Timing.** If a change in housing is in the offing, when do you want to make the change?

Probably	*Maybe*	*No or N/A*

Lifestyle considerations

❑   ❑   ❑ **Stay put.** There's no need to move. You love where you are and expect to stay there indefinitely.

❑   ❑   ❑ **Stay put, but renovate.** You don't want to move, but your old house could sure stand some improvements.

❑   ❑   ❑ **Move to easier-to-maintain housing.** The house is long in the tooth and keeping it up to snuff is likely to be a financial and physical burden. Thus, moving to a place that's easier to maintain is important.

Financial considerations

❑   ❑   ❑ **Downsize or rent to increase income upon retirement.** You want to sell the house and move to less-expensive housing to enjoy a more financially comfortable retirement.

Timing considerations

❑   ❑   ❑ **Move or renovate before retirement.** You expect to "make the move" or endure a home renovation project before you retire.

Probably	*Maybe*	*No or* *N/A*

❑   ❑   ❑   **Move or renovate when you retire.**
You'll wait until retirement to relocate or renovate.

❑   ❑   ❑   **Move or renovate after retirement.**
There's no rush. Any changes in housing can wait until after you
expect to retire.

Important planning matters. The following pages contain information and guidance on three important housing matters:

1. **Paying off the mortgage.** The sooner the mortgage is paid off,
   the better, and accelerating the payoff need not be too painful.
   See below.

2. **Downsizing.** Baby boomers are attracted to unlocking some of
   the equity they've built up in their homes by downsizing, which
   can definitely be beneficial financially. See page 191.

3. **Home improvements.** Homebodies who decide to stay in the
   family quarters often desire some renovations. From a financial
   standpoint, renovations can range from an excellent investment
   to a wasteful indulgence. See page 196.

Paying Off the Mortgage

I catch a lot of flak whenever I urge people to pay off their mortgages
early, but owning a mortgage-free home by the time you retire—or
shortly thereafter—dramatically improves your retirement prospects.
Paying off the mortgage could well reduce the amount of income you
need in retirement by 20 percent or more. Owning your own home
free and clear is not an impossible dream. In fact, 75 percent of all
retired home owners have paid off their mortgage, as have nearly half
of those age fifty-five to sixty-four.

Home, sweet (unmortgaged) home. A home will probably be the second-best investment you'll ever make (education is first, although marrying someone worth $10 million is even better). True, a home is a ceaseless drain on our hard-earned money, but home ownership still beats renting. Aside from the quality-of-life advantages of owning a home, two significant financial benefits of home ownership, particularly for baby boomers (beyond the obvious, but overrated, tax deductions for mortgage interest and property taxes), are:

1. A home gives you the opportunity to be mortgage-free by the time you retire or shortly thereafter, thereby improving your odds of enjoying a financially comfortable retirement.

2. A home is a potential source of additional income during retirement. Retirees who sell or downsize their homes can put up to hundreds of thousands of dollars of gains, most or all of which is federal income tax free, into their retirement kitty.

The financial savings of mortgage prepayment are easy to quantify. For example, making one extra payment a year on a $200,000 mortgage could save you more than $60,000.

Exceptions to Jonathan's mortgage prepayment entreaty. In reckless defiance of the criticism that's been heaped upon me, I still urge you to make extra payments against your mortgage, but if, and only if:

✦ **You've pretty much maximized any and all available retirement-plan contributions, including your retirement savings plans at work and an IRA.** While there are lots of financial benefits to reducing your mortgage sooner rather than later, tax-advantaged retirement savings plans offer better ones, so you should generally put as much as possible into retirement plans first.

✦ **You've paid off all other higher-interest loans, including credit card loans and car loans.** It makes no sense to make extra payments against your, say, 6 percent mortgage while you've got an 11 percent car loan and 18 percent credit card balances.

✦ **You've got a stash of nonretirement savings sufficient to pay at least six mortgage payments.** This will protect you in the event that you lose your job or some other calamity befalls you. Some people get so excited about making extra payments on their mortgage that they use all available money to pay down the loan. That's dangerous, because everyone needs some readily available rainy-day money.

Paying Off Your Mortgage Sooner, Rather Than Later

There are several ways to prepay a mortgage, and all of them work. They range from the informal to a formal refinancing of your mortgage to a shorter maturity.

Add a few bucks to the monthly payment. If you've got some money left over at the end of the month, add some of it to your standard mortgage payment. Even a few dollars every month can shorten the time it takes to pay it off. (See Table 8.1.) The beauty of this strategy is its flexibility. If you don't have any extra money, simply make the regular payment. If you have a small windfall, include a larger chunk of money with the next payment. Whether it's a few dollars or a few hundred dollars, you can't beat the good feeling of knowing that you'll pay off the mortgage before you become a great-grandparent.

Biweekly mortgages. These mortgages often fit nicely into the family budget, particularly if you're paid biweekly. By paying half of your monthly mortgage every other week, you make the equivalent of thirteen months' worth of mortgage payments (twenty-six biweekly payments) each year. That extra monthly payment will cut the time it

TABLE 8.1
A LITTLE BIT EXTRA CAN GO A LONG WAY

This table shows the effect of making regular extra payments on a $200,000, thirty-year, fixed 6½ percent mortgage with a regular monthly principal and interest payment of $1,265.

MONTHLY EXTRA PAYMENT AMOUNT	MORTGAGE WILL BE PAID OFF IN	TOTAL PRINCIPAL AND INTEREST PAYMENTS
$0	30 years	$455,000
100	24	399,000
200	21	365,000
300	18	341,000
400	16	324,000
500	15	311,000

takes to pay the darn thing off by several years. But be wary of high fees that many biweekly mortgage plans assess. You can accomplish roughly the same result by making one additional mortgage payment each year on your own, sans extra fees. **w w w**

Shorten the mortgage. If you're contemplating a mortgage refinancing, you could consider a shorter-maturity new mortgage. One troubling trend amongst your fellow baby boomers is taking cash out of the home equity to finance renovations or just plain frippery, and extending the loan maturity to keep the new mortgage payment roughly equivalent to the old payment. They're lengthening mortgages at a time when they should be shortening them. Beyond the obvious advantage of paying off the mortgage, those who have the wisdom to opt for a shorter-maturity loan will discover another advantage—a lower interest rate. It's not uncommon for fifteen-year mortgages to be available with interest rates that are 1/4 percent to 3/8 percent lower than equivalent thirty-year mortgages, and sometimes even lower. The disadvantage of shortening the maturity is that you absolutely, positively have to come up with the higher mortgage payment each month. The more informal mortgage prepayment strategies allow you to suspend your extra payments if, for whatever reason, they become temporarily unaffordable.

Doubling up the principal payment. This is a great prepayment strategy. First, doubling up doesn't require you to make two full mortgage payments each month. Rather, armed with a mortgage amortization table (they're easily found on the Internet), you simply make the current month's regular mortgage payment (principal and interest) and add the next month's principal payment. Then cross out both months on the mortgage amortization table and do the same thing each subsequent month. If you do this religiously, you'll pay off the mortgage in half the time. For a detailed look at how this works, go to the reader Web site. It works so well early in the mortgage because the principal payments are quite small. The extra monthly principal payment will grow modestly each month, but it still takes several years before they become burdensome. Presumably you'll be better able to make those larger payments as time goes on and your income increases. Whenever you do make extra payments against your mortgage, be sure to make it clear on your payment slip that the money is to be applied against your mortgage principal. Also, make sure the lender does in fact apply the extra to the mortgage principal. **w w w**

HOME EQUITY LOANS: A DOUBLE-EDGED SWORD

A home equity loan (HEL) is a wonderful and comforting source of money needed quickly. However, it's all too easy to impair your retirement as a result of abusing this seemingly painless form of credit. I spoke with a couple who could have been poster children for bad HEL habits. They had just retired and had paid off the mortgage a couple of years prior. But they also had a $150,000 home equity loan outstanding. The loan included five past and present cars and several vacations, and they had made only minimum payments on their ever-increasing balance. So this couple, who had worked so assiduously to pay down their mortgage, had substituted an HEL for it. They're going to have to take a not-so-small portion of their retirement income over the next decade to retire the HEL.

Here's how to manage your home equity loan to avoid that predicament. Home equity loan borrowers typically borrow for short-term purposes (vacations, home maintenance and repairs, payment of estimated income taxes, for example), intermediate-term purposes (automobiles), or longer-term purposes (making major home improvements or paying college tuition bills). Short-term loans should be paid off within a year, intermediate loans should be paid off over a few years at most, and longer-term loans should be paid off over a maximum of ten to fifteen years. In other words, match the repayment period to the period of time you benefit from whatever it is you borrowed the money for. Since a common use of HELs is to buy cars, it's crazy not to have paid off the loan on your current car before buying a new car. Yet it happens all the time. If you sense a bit of antipathy toward cars, I fully voice my opinions on these quintessential money wasters beginning on page 264.

Case Studies: Paying Down the Mortgage

Case study 1. Jill won't be retiring for twenty years, but she recently took out a thirty-year mortgage. She's interested in finding out how much extra she'd have to kick in each month to pay off the 6 percent, $250,000 mortgage ten years early. Much to her delight, Jill finds out that she only needs to add $250 to her $1,500 regular mortgage payment to reduce the payoff time by a decade.

Case study 2. Jack is about to retire, but he still has fourteen years until his mortgage is paid off and notes, "I don't want to be making mortgage payments when I'm eighty." His original mortgage was $150,000 at 6¼ percent. Jack says he can afford to pay an extra $400 a month toward his mortgage—the same amount he was paying on a car loan he just paid off. By so doing, he'll pay off the mortgage about five and a half years earlier. "If I do that," Jack says, "I'll still be young enough to spend the money I no longer have to apply to my mortgage on cruises, vacations, and other niceties."

Case study 3. Max and Maxine are in their mid-forties and just made a bunch of improvements to their digs. Rather than saddle themselves with a big home equity loan, they are planning to refinance their mortgage. It's a variable rate, and since interest rates are currently pretty low, going for a $300,000 fixed-rate mortgage makes a lot of sense right now. But they still have to decide whether to take out a thirty-year or fifteen-year mortgage. Maxine favors the shorter mortgage. "Our current mortgage has twenty years to go. We figured when we took it out that it would be paid off about the time we retire. If we take out a thirty, though, we won't pay it off until our mid-seventies." Max, on the other hand, worries that a fifteen-year mortgage would break the family bank. "The fifteen would cost a fortune." True, the shorter mortgage would hike the monthly payment, but many home owners are surprised to find that the payments aren't as high as they imagine. Max and Maxine can get a thirty-year, 6 percent mortgage on the $300,000 they need to borrow for a monthly payment of $1,800. Shorter mortgages usually have lower interest rates, and in the current market, the fifteen-year rate is 5.6 percent, which translates into a $2,470 payment. Max figured it would be a lot higher, so he's willing to take out the shorter mortgage.

Less-than-meets-the-eye department—tax savings from paying mortgage interest. Tax rates are a lot lower than they were not too long ago. The lower the tax rate, the lower the benefit of a tax deduction. Therefore, the mortgage-interest deduction simply doesn't save that much money. Please don't misinterpret me, though. Home ownership has numerous advantages and can be a big help on the road to achieving financial security. But taking out a big mortgage or adding to your mortgage to save taxes doesn't make a whole lot of sense. Here's an example: Someone in the 25 percent federal income-tax bracket who pays $10,000 in mortgage interest saves 25 percent of that, or $2,500 in federal income taxes. That's a big help at tax

---

MYTH DEBUNKER: "I CAN EARN MORE BY INVESTING THE MONEY RATHER THAN PAYING DOWN MY MORTGAGE"

You may be among the throngs of people, particularly those who are active investors, who argue that the rate they can earn on their investments is higher than the interest rate they are charged on their mortgage, and thus extra mortgage payments are a bad investment. This may be a valid argument, but only if all of your money is invested in stocks or real estate, which over long holding periods tend to earn higher returns. But since most investors diversify among stocks, bonds, and temporary investments, chances are that at least some of their money is invested in securities that pay less than the interest rate on the mortgage. For example, if you have a 6 percent mortgage, but regularly have some money invested in money market funds paying 4 percent or checking and savings accounts yielding even less, doesn't it make good financial sense to use some of that money to reduce the interest you pay on a 6 percent loan?

time, but remember that you had to pay $10,000 in interest to reap a $2,500 tax reduction. In sum, while the mortgage-interest deduction is nice to have, at this stage of your life you shouldn't add to your mortgage burden because you'll enjoy a bigger tax deduction. That dog won't hunt.

SUCCESS STORY: HEEDING THE IN-LAWS

"Although I didn't appreciate their advice at the time, it was probably the best advice we have ever received. At the time, like many of our fortysomething acquaintances, my wife and I were hell-bent on selling our home—which we had owned for only a few years—and buying a bigger one. My wife's parents, people of modest means, but who always seemed to have enough, said we were insane. Why, they asked, did we need a bigger and much more expensive home? That was a good question, so we decided to stay put. Here we are twenty years later with a free and clear home while many of our friends indeed have bigger homes, exceeded only by the size of their mortgages."

MYTH DEBUNKER: "BUT I NEED A MORTGAGE WHEN I'M RETIRED TO CUT MY INCOME TAX BILL"

Please don't delude yourself into thinking that a mortgage is a good thing in retirement because of the tax breaks. Compare the finances of two retirees, Jerry and Mary:

Jerry has a $1,000 monthly mortgage interest payment that saves him $250 in federal income taxes (a whopping

$3,000 a year). "The tax savings really come in handy at tax time." But he's still out of pocket $750 a month in interest, or $9,000 a year.

Mary paid off her mortgage by moving into a smaller house. She has the same income as Jerry, so her income tax bill is $3,000 higher than Jerry's. While Jerry probably thinks Mary's a chump for overpaying her taxes, she's a chump with a higher spending budget since her monthly expenses are $750 lower than those of Jerry, the tax genius. Actually, Mary is more than $750 per month better off because Jerry is also having to pay down mortgage principal and probably has higher property taxes than Mary.

Tax rates are now so low that the tax-savings impact of the mortgage-interest deduction isn't substantial.

FIND OUT IF YOU'RE STILL REQUIRED TO PAY FOR PRIVATE MORTGAGE INSURANCE

If you were required to carry private mortgage insurance when you took out your home mortgage (no one volunteers to have this coverage), check to see if you can drop it. Federal law requires lenders to stop charging for private mortgage insurance, or PMI, once you've built up enough equity in your home either through making sufficient payments to reduce principal or through price appreciation in your home. Ask your mortgage lender what the procedures are to eliminate PMI. You may be one of millions of home owners who are no longer required to pay those annoying PMI premiums.

Downsize Your Housing to Upsize Your Income

Downsizing—selling your current manse and buying a less-expensive home either before or after you retire—makes a lot of financial sense and could be a sensible lifestyle decision besides.

Downsizing is becoming more popular. Interest in downsizing is picking up steam in the United States, and those who think about these matters opine that the trend is likely to accelerate as the baby boom generation confronts retirement. There's more than anecdotal evidence to support this thesis. The average size of new homes has actually declined a bit in recent years to about 2,200 square feet.

Compared with prior generations, boomers are better traveled, more adventurous, and not as attached to their communities. There's less attraction to remaining in the family homestead when there are so many more exciting housing arrangements and areas in which to live. Indeed, many have had to bear with intransigent parents who insisted on staying too long in a too-large house that turned into a maintenance money pit.

Lifestyle advantages. Downsizing, particularly into a newer home, could reduce the time and inconvenience of maintaining your current home. Relocating to a place that has a less frenetic pace is attractive to some. Conversely, moving from the suburbs to the big city is appealing to others. Health considerations may also influence you to relocate to an area with a more salubrious climate. Proximity to family members is yet another reason to pick up stakes.

Financial advantages. The primary benefit of downsizing for most is financial. If money is no object, you might still want to consider a change in housing, but there's nothing to preclude your spending the same or more on the new home, particularly if you have an edifice complex. Here are the financial bennies:

1. **Reduced debt.** Eliminating or reducing a mortgage that might otherwise erode your retirement budget would greatly improve your retirement living standard.

2. **Tax breaks.** Uncle Sam rewards home sellers with a big break in capital gains taxes. You'll probably not owe any federal income taxes when you sell your home unless you have a big-league gain on the sale. **w w w**

3. **Increased income.** If your downsizing allows you to free up capital to invest, you'll enjoy more income throughout your retirement.

4. **Reduced housing expenses.** Downsizers usually also enjoy lower housing expenses—for example, property taxes and utilities.

5. **Reduced maintenance.** Most baby boomers have more pressing matters to attend to than fixing an old toilet, and they're probably not handy around the house to boot. If you downsize into more modern quarters, maintenance hassles and costs will be lower.

Downsizing can result in a financial home run, particularly if you're moving from a high-cost locale to a lower-cost area. Relocation is discussed in the next chapter.

Yet another downsizing advantage. The smaller the home, the less likely you'll have adult children moving back to the nest. While my better half isn't so enthusiastic, I'd like to move into a one-bedroom home when we retire.

ATTENTION RENTERS:
IT'S NEVER TOO LATE TO BUY A HOME

If you're a renter, even one who is just a few years from retirement, it's not too late to buy a home, particularly if you
intend to stay in your current locale indefinitely. While owning a home will probably be more expensive than renting,
even after the tax savings from mortgage-interest and
property-tax deductions are considered, home ownership
provides you with more stability since you would no longer
be subject to the landlord's whims. Home ownership also
affords you the opportunity to build equity in your home,
which could come in handy in late life should you need to
tap into the equity through, for example, a reverse mortgage. See page 293.

SUCCESS STORY:
LIFELONG RENTER TAKES THE PLUNGE

"I had always rented, but when my current landlord started
talking about selling the building, I began to wonder if renting
for the rest of my life was such a good idea. At the age of
fifty-six, I bought a condo. It turns out that owning didn't cost
a great deal more than renting, and I'll have more control over
my housing in the future."

Downsizing Decision Maker

While the decision may be many years off, this Decision Maker will
help you begin to think about whether downsizing, either before or
after retirement, makes sense for you.

❏   ❏   ❏ **1. Importance of lowering retirement expenses.** Moving into less-expensive housing will, of course, reduce your retirement expenses, perhaps considerably.

❏   ❏   ❏ **2. Importance of increasing retirement income.** Freeing up capital to invest for retirement will boost retirement income.

❏   ❏   ❏ **3. Desire to move to a lower-cost neighborhood or locale.** If you're interested in relocating anyway, a lower-cost home will improve your retirement finances, whether or not you need the extra money.

❏   ❏   ❏ **4. Desire to move into a newer and/ or lower-maintenance home.** If your home is now or is likely to become decrepit, downsizing or simply moving into a newer, lower-maintenance home could be the ticket.

❏   ❏   ❏ **5. Importance of having enough space to accommodate your children, grandchildren, or friends.** This is often the rationale for retirees to stay in a too-large house. But look at it this way: the money you save by downsizing will provide you with more than enough extra income to put up the children and grandchildren at the Ritz whenever they visit, and after a long day with the little hellions running hither and yon, at great risk to you and your antique stemware, all generations will be delighted when the offspring retire to the hotel.

Downsizing sooner, rather than later. Boomers are not only trendsetters in planning to downsize; many have already downsized, well in advance of retirement. Early downsizing can make a lot of sense. You can take advantage of a robust real estate market to get the most for your house, rather than waiting until retirement, when prices may be depressed. If you decide to sell before you retire, you can take more time locating the ideal new home because you're under no pressure to sell your current home. Moreover, lowering expenses during your working years will enable you to put even more money into your retirement cubbyhole. Finally, the tasks of selling the old house, buying a new one, and moving are a lot easier when you're younger.

SUCCESS STORY: EVISCERATING RETIREMENT EXPENSES

Here's the story of a couple who downsized and reduced their retirement budget by one-third! "When we retired, we hoped to cut our budget by $10,000 by moving into a smaller home, but we ended up saving $20,000 a year. Here's how it worked: We sold our old house for $525,000 and paid off the $150,000 mortgage, leaving us with $375,000. We moved to the Sun Belt, bought an almost new home for $300,000, and spent $25,000 in moving costs and for some new furniture and drapes. We added the remaining $50,000 to our savings. It's hard to believe, but here is how we ended up reducing our spending by $20,000: First, not having the mortgage saved $13,500. Our mortgage payments were actually $17,000, but taking out the tax savings from the interest deduction brought it down to $13,500. Then, we estimated annual savings from property taxes and repairs to be, conservatively, $4,500 a year. Finally, the extra $50,000 will give us $2,000 or so in additional income. So adding up $13,500 mortgage savings, $4,500 in lower carrying costs, plus $2,000 in extra income totals $20,000. We're still amazed at how much lower our expenses will be."

SUCCESS STORY: STAYING PUT WITH A PLAN

Downsizing isn't for everyone, but here are a couple who are wisely thinking way ahead about the disposition of their home. "My husband and I are still many years away from retirement. A lot of our contemporaries are making grand plans about selling their homes, moving to lower-cost areas of the country or even a foreign country. But we like our home and want to retire there. Some of our friends think we're bonkers, and one raised an interesting, albeit indelicate, question: 'Are you going to stay in that old house until they haul you out feet first?' That brought back memories of my mother, who insisted on staying in a big house that required a lot of upkeep. It was a constant concern for my siblings and me. She stayed there until a fall required her to move to an assisted-living facility. Then we were confronted with cleaning out the place and selling it. So my friend's remark really hit home. As a result, my husband and I came up with some contingency plans. We'll still stay in the house when we retire to be near family and friends. But we'll be more open-minded about how long we'll stay there. We'll travel a lot and may find another attractive region of the country. If so, a second home is not out of the question. But most important, we're going to be a lot more flexible in our attitude about where we'll live. I guess what I'm saying is that I don't want to be like my mother."

Making the Most of Your Home Renovations

Renovating your home is often preferable to selling it and moving into a similarly by priced wigwam. Moving also inevitably costs a lot more than you originally planned. The same can be said for home improvements, of course, but at least you're more in control of that project than you are in selling a home, buying another home, and moving.

Most home renovations require a substantial investment, and as with any major financial outlay, you need to pay attention to the return you can expect to receive on your investment. Some home renovations offer better returns than others, including:

✦ Remodel bathroom

✦ Remodel kitchen

✦ Add a deck

✦ Remodel attic or basement

✦ Replace siding

The home owner's return on investment is quite high for these renovations, but many others will also provide you with a decent payback when you eventually sell the house.

Here are some additional points to consider when contemplating home renovation:

✦ **Minor renovations yield a higher return.** When it comes to spending on home renovations, usually less is more. You'll likely recoup a higher percentage of the money you spend on minor renovations compared with major renovations.

✦ **Value of renovations varies by region.** There are some obvious regional differences in the value added to certain home improvements. You're likely to enjoy a higher return on your swimming-pool investment if your home is in Fort Myers, Florida, than in Fort Kent, Maine. But there are also more subtle regional differences in how the locals will value your home renovations. ᴡ ᴡ ᴡ

✦ **Consider how the next buyer will welcome your renovations.** This is important. Your taste may be a whole lot different from the taste of a potential home buyer. While kitchens and bathrooms are universally used, wine cellars, home theaters, ten-person saunas, planetariums, and boccie courts may not be to everyone's liking, as shocking as that may be to you if you're into any of the aforementioned. Some renovations are so bad that they actually impair the value of the home. A twenty-person hot tub, for example, is likely to cause a potential home buyer to wonder what kind of shenanigans went on in that house (not to mention wondering how much it will cost to remove it). By all means invest in an unusual, ego-gratifying home improvement of your liking, but view it as an investment in your own enjoyment, rather than an investment that will pay for itself when you eventually sell your manse. *Author's confession:* I recently converted our garage into a family fitness center. Not only do my wife and kids not use it, but soon after completing the project, I saw a list of the five worst home improvement projects, and it included turning a garage into a fitness center. So please do as I say, not as I do.

✦ **Never own the best home in the neighborhood.** Hopefully, you heeded this advice when you bought the joint in the first place. But some home owners, in their zeal to keep up with the Joneses down the street, end up renovating the money pit until it's the neighborhood Taj Mahal. Bad decision. It's okay to do stuff to your home to make it a better place, but it shouldn't be the best. In fact, when planning additions, consider the neighborhood norms. If most of the homes have three bathrooms and you have two, adding a third makes sense, but adding a fourth is pushing the envelope.

✦ **Avoid extensive renovations if moving is on the horizon.** Other than with minor renovations, such as modernizing an ancient bathroom or landscaping, you're unlikely to benefit handsomely from extensive renovations if you think you may be moving within the next five years or so.

✦ **Finance the renovations wisely.** Ideally, you will be able to pay off any financing costs before you retire or soon thereafter. If the latter, be sure to include the financing costs in your retirement budget in Appendix I.

CHAPTER 9

Deciding Where to Retire

B aby boomers, particularly those who are over fifty, should begin planning where they want to retire. Even if you're younger,
giving some thought to this matter will help you make a more
considered decision later on. Your generation will be redefining what
it means to be retired, and that includes considering a range of housing alternatives, as discussed in chapter 8, and exploring relocation
possibilities both within the United States and overseas, which are
discussed below. ❤ ❤ ❤

Where do you want to retire? Here is a mutually exclusive and col-
lectively exhaustive list of possible places to live after you retire, or for
that matter, before you retire. There are only four choices, but don't let
the seeming simplicity understate the importance of this decision.

Worth Considering	Never	
❏	❏	**1. Stay put.** Sometimes the best thing to do is nothing. You can stay put in the family homestead.
❏	❏	**2. Relocate in the same locale.** This alternative has particular appeal for boomers who

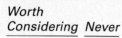

Worth
Considering Never

want to be near what's familiar, but who prefer a different housing arrangement.

❏ ❏ **3. Relocate to a more distant U.S. locale.** This is a major decision, which many boomers are considering, and needs careful evaluation.

❏ ❏ **4. Relocate to a foreign country.** If moving to a different region within the United States is a big decision, retiring to a foreign country is a mammoth one, but it will become increasingly popular as today's worldly baby boomers enter retirement.

1. Stay Put

The devil you know is often better than the devil you don't know. That's why staying put in your home or apartment when you retire has considerable appeal. After all, you don't have to rush into a relocation decision, and you may be perfectly content where you are. Also, a decision to relocate can always be made a few or many years into retirement. The only admonition is that the older you become, the more trying a move will be.

2. Relocate in the Same Locale

Staying in the same area is appealing to those who like where they live, but who prefer a change in housing. This move may be desirable to acquire:

✦ A smaller, more manageable home—or an apartment.

✦ A less expensive home to free up money for retirement.

✦ A rental instead of a place that you own.

✦ A home in the suburbs or exurbs instead of the city.

✦ A home in the city instead of the suburbs.

A move that keeps you in familiar environs doesn't generally require the same degree of investigation as a move to a different state. Nevertheless, the checklist below for those who are contemplating a more distant move may be useful for those considering a local move.

3. Relocate to a More Distant U.S. Locale

Many current retirees chose to move to a different region, and the pace of relocations will pick up dramatically as baby boomers retire. The combination of a yen to try new things and less attachment to a particular area will spur active consideration of relocation for some boomers. But this has never been an easy decision to make, even if you're already quite familiar with a particular locus of interest. Here's a checklist that will help you make a thorough evaluation of what will be one of your most important retirement decisions:

Checklist for Evaluating a New Locale

❑ **Cost of living.** Don't forget to factor in moving and other relocation costs. If you live in a high-cost area on the east or west coasts and want to move to the Sun Belt, you may find total living costs to be 30 percent to 40 percent lower. But moving from Manhattan, Kansas, to Manhattan, New York, for example, will hike your living costs, in the example, somewhere in the vicinity of 150 percent.

❑ **Housing.** Finding the right home or apartment is the most important task, of course. Spending a mere week finding a house in a new area might have worked when you were younger, but the older you get, the more a relocation takes out of you, so you don't want to make a mistake. You should subscribe to the local paper for a while. First identify the kind of housing you want—single-family, condo, etc.—and the price range. If you have friends in the vicinity, enlist their help, even though you'll probably eventually want to work with a Realtor. Be sure to set your target price at least $50,000 less than you can easily afford because, as you must know from past home purchases, you always spend more than you intended.

❑ **Weather.** You should spend some time visiting the area in "low season" when the weather is at its worst and the locals can't wait to get out of town. While you may also be planning to get out of town at the same time, realize that the time may come when it will be difficult to travel, so you'll have to stay put, perhaps when it's 120 degrees or minus 20 degrees outside.

❑ **Taxes.** States vary widely in the way they extract taxes from their residents, so it's important to learn about the following in your state of choice:

✦ State and local sales taxes

✦ Special tax provisions for retirees

✦ State income taxes

✦ Property taxes

Try to figure out how you'll be affected by the state's various taxes, because your lifestyle could influence your total tax burden. For example, if you're a homebody who wants a big house, but doesn't otherwise spend a lot, a state with low property taxes but higher sales taxes may be better for you than the reverse.

Also check on how the state treats any pension income that you will be receiving. While a state pension check may be tax-free if you continue to reside in your home state, it will likely be subject to state income taxes if you relocate.

In addition to income, property, and sales taxes, you should consider the state death-tax regulations. (A "death tax" is to a state what an "estate tax" is to the federal government. It's a tax that's due after you're dead, so credit the states for their clarity.) In recent years, many states have imposed more burdensome taxes, and wealthy people will gravitate to states whose tax rules are more favorable.

❏ **Health care.** While the United States generally has an excellent health care system, the quality of health care in particular communities varies. While you probably enjoy good health now, evaluate the health care in your desired new community based upon your need for more frequent access to the health care community as well as the area's ability to handle acute health problems. If you or your spouse have medical conditions that require specialized treatment, will the new location have the specialists and facilities to accommodate that need? In addition, will your retiree health benefits, if any, be transferable to the new location?

❏ **Transportation.** If you leave friends and family behind, you'll want to visit them and they'll want to visit you, so check out the local transportation system, including the airport, rail, and bus facilities. How easy is it to drive to and around the city? Ease of getting around by car or public transit is important to you as well as your visitors.

❏ **Employment opportunities.** If you're considering seeking gainful employ in your new destination, some research into employment opportunities for someone of your background and experience is important.

❏ **Volunteer opportunities.** Most communities welcome and can definitely benefit from the services of volunteers. If some volunteer activity particularly interests you, find out if the local community has a compatible volunteer program. After all, successful retirees don't retire. They recycle their energy, experience, and wisdom into other meaningful activities.

❑ **Cultural and educational activities.** If they're important to you, are the cultural and adult education opportunities in the area you're considering to your liking?

❑ **Leisure activities.** Ah, leisure. What floats your boat? Fishing, golf, hiking, skiing, ellipticals, movies, sporting events, watching the grass grow? Whatever your leisure activities are, you'll want to make sure there are an abundance of outlets for them.

IF YOU'RE THINKING OF RETIRING TO ANOTHER LOCALE, PUT A STAKE IN THE GROUND WITH A LAND PURCHASE

If you've got a hankering to relocate when you retire but aren't ready, psychologically and/or financially, to buy a home there, you might consider putting a stake in the ground by buying a building lot or other undeveloped land in that area. If you decide to relocate there, you have a nice hedge against rising home prices. If you decide not to, you won't be saddled with selling a home, but you will probably have a profitable asset to sell or hold on to until later in your retirement.

SUCCESS STORY: PLANNING IN ADVANCE FOR A RELOCATION

Retirees are on the move. One study of retiree mobility revealed that one-third of residents who lived in the largest cities—those with populations of 5 million or more—retired to cities between 1 million and 5 million. A slightly smaller percentage moved to cities with even smaller populations. Baby boomers are often planning such moves well in advance of retirement. "My partner and I knew that we didn't want to

> retire in the city. There's a vacation area that we have long
> liked—better climate, lower housing costs, and much lower
> cost of living. So several years ago, we bought a second
> home there where we plan to move when we retire. We'll sell
> the city place when we retire, which will provide a big boost
> to our retirement savings."

4. Relocate to a Foreign Country

The number of Americans retiring overseas is expected to rise as baby boomers, an adventurous lot, retire. A lot of retirees have already opted for living in foreign climes. An estimated 4 million Americans live abroad. While there is no data on how many are retired, according to the State Department, close to half a million Social Security checks are mailed abroad each month. But, unless you have family overseas or have spent a great deal of time in your chosen country, retiring abroad is a major decision that requires significant scrutiny and advance planning. Some of the important matters to consider follow.

Retiring Abroad Checklist

❑ **Quality of life.** It's hard to believe, but some people pick up stakes and move abroad after only one visit (when the weather was ideal). Some intrepid—or insane—souls go there sight unseen, based upon a brochure or a Web site. Better to visit the area several times, in all seasons, to get a feel for whether you'll be happy living there full-time.

❑ **Stability.** As delightful as the financial climate and weather might be, government and financial stability are crucial to positive overseas living. Crime and police corruption also need to be carefully assessed.

❑ **Language.** Are you conversant in the local language or are you prepared to learn the language? If not, will you be able to communicate with the locals, including emergency-room personnel, should the need arise?

❑ **Real estate.** If the average house in your Shangri-la costs less than a parking space in your hometown, there may be less than meets the eye. First, can you as a foreigner even own real estate, and if so, are there restrictions on what you can buy? Is construction quality up to snuff? Are building codes and development restrictions to your liking, lest a Marriott resort go up next door to your cottage? Are the utilities and services, including fire and emergency services, reliable?

As inexpensive as housing might be, moving to a foreign country is so fraught with uncertainties that you may be well-advised to rent a place for a year or so, which will not only give you time to find or begin building the ideal home, but will also let you know absolutely, positively that you want to spend your retirement years there.

❑ **The true cost of living.** Be sure to factor in additional costs of living overseas, including travel back to the United States. If you plan to maintain a stateside residence, factor that into your total costs lest you soon find such a lavish retirement is financially unsustainable.

❑ **Social Security.** You should be able to receive Social Security checks in your chosen country, although you'll probably want to have them deposited in a U.S. bank. Some countries have restrictions on receiving Social Security checks—the usual suspects—places you wouldn't care to live in anyway.

❑ **Taxes.** Don't wait until you arrive on the foreign scene to learn about the country's tax rules and how they relate to U.S. taxes, which are assessed on all U.S. citizens no matter where they live, although you will probably qualify for various deductions and credits against

U.S. taxes. Generally, federal taxes are payable on pensions sent abroad, and state taxes may be due on same. It will behoove you to speak with an accountant or lawyer who is familiar with the tax structure in your country of choice. While you're at it, find out what you'll need to do to revise your will and other estate-planning documents to conform to the country's regulations.

❑ **Financial matters.** Is the local banking system up to snuff, so that you're money isn't snuffed out by a banking failure? Ideally, your local banking relationship will be with a branch or affiliate of a large U.S. bank or multinational bank.

❑ **Property insurance.** Make sure you can obtain the necessary insurance coverage from reliable carriers for your property, including homeowner's and auto. Just as in the United States, these policies should include liability coverage.

❑ **Health insurance.** Big concern, since Medicare doesn't cover care outside the United States and its territories with the exception of certain areas of Canada and Mexico near the U.S. borders. If your employer will provide retiree health care benefits, check to see if the coverage extends to non-U.S. environs. Find out what it will take to secure health insurance coverage in your country of choice. Your best and least-expensive choice may be national health insurance, if it's available and you're entitled to receive it. But you also need to be okay with living in a country with national health insurance.

❑ **Health care.** This may be the most important item on your checklist. Americans are spoiled by their health care delivery system, and even many developed countries don't come anywhere close to the quality of health care we take for granted. Some expatriates delude themselves into thinking that if they get sick, they'll return to the United States for quality health care. But what happens if an emergency arises and you can't hop on a plane? So spend some time investigating the resources available to take care of your health in both normal and dire times. For the sake of your good health, an advance evaluation is essential.

HOW WILL FAMILY AND FRIENDS REACT TO AN OVERSEAS MOVE?

Relationships are important at all ages, but more so in retirement. Before relocating overseas, do some hard thinking about how the move will affect your relationships. Don't put a lot of stock in the excited reactions of your family and friends that they'll visit often. Perhaps they will, but maybe they won't. Will you end up spending a small fortune traveling to the States to maintain these relationships?

CHAPTER 10

Preparing for the Unexpected

L ife is full of unexpected and unpleasant financial surprises. They can range from minor annoyances, such as car repairs or an unanticipatedly large tax bill (are they ever unexpectedly small?), to a major disruption in your finances, such as a fire in the family home or the disability or death of a breadwinner. Table 10.1 summarizes these major life events.

One of the most essential things you can do to stay on course a great retirement is prepare for these unpleasantries, because you will certainly experience some of them if you haven't already. Four basic rules of thumb are the subject of this chapter:

1. Use savings and investments to pay for minor financial disruptions.

2. Use insurance for protection against most major financial disruptions.

3. Prepare a will and other estate-planning documents to protect your heirs.

TABLE 10.1
LIFE EVENTS THAT COULD NEGATIVELY
AFFECT YOUR FINANCIAL SECURITY

FAMILY

Family members with special financial needs

Aging parents

Separation and divorce

Death of a spouse or other close family member

Major losses from fire, flood, accident, or theft

Lawsuits

OCCUPATION

Decline in income

Unemployment

Forced early retirement

HEALTH

Disability

Old age

Chronic illness

Long-term care and rehabilitation

Terminal illness

---

4. Organize your records and documents through a letter of instructions to simplify your financial life now and help your loved ones later in the event of your death or incapacity.

Coping with Minor Financial Disruptions

One piece of financial advice your parents gave you when you started your first real job probably went something like this: "Now, the first thing you need to do is save about six months' worth of salary as an emergency fund. Keep the money safe in a savings account or checking account so that you'll be able to get at it quickly." If you were an obedient child (in stark contrast to your own children), you probably spent the next fourteen years or so setting money aside for your emergency fund. With all due respect to our parents, that advice wasn't so hot. Letting a lot of money, even emergency money, languish in accounts that pay low interest doesn't make a lot of sense. But today you can get access to your money in most investment accounts in a day or two or, in many instances, in a matter of hours. For a rundown of easy ways to access money on the q.t., see page 85.

Preparing for Major Financial Disruptions

If you think about the various types of major financial disruptions that can befall us (as uncomfortable as it is to contemplate such unwelcome events), they fall under two categories:

Major financial disruptions that cannot be insured against, in the traditional sense, at least, such as a job loss or divorce. The ability to survive these events financially basically depends on the amount of money you have available to cushion such financial blows.

Major financial disruptions that can be insured against, such as a fire, car accident, illness, disability, or death of a breadwinner. Insurance is, of course, an essential defense against most major financial disruptions, and important matters must be considered for the various categories of insurance that you should carry, or at least consider carrying.

Menu of Insurance Coverage

Insurance is one of those necessary evils in life and is probably one of the top three or four expenses in the family budget. You'd just as soon not have to pay for it, but there may come a time when you're awfully glad you did. While most people understand the importance of carrying adequate insurance, many still leave gaps in their coverage. Just one gap in insurance coverage can result in a loss that could wipe out years, if not decades, of hard-earned savings. Don't jeopardize all the hard work you've expended to get where you are financially today by leaving a hole in your insurance umbrella. Moreover, take care to understand each of your policy's limits. Your insurance agent should explain the coverage, although it doesn't hurt to read the policies yourself, admittedly not a stimulating activity. Remember, the big print giveth, and the small print taketh away.

Table 10.2 summarizes the various types of insurance coverage that you should typically have, although some may not be applicable, such as professional liability insurance. Two areas of coverage of particular import to baby boomers, life insurance and long-term-care insurance, are accorded more extensive treatment in the pages that follow. But please also take heed of the tips on other areas as well. Insurance is one financial matter that should not be given short shrift.

TABLE 10.2
HOW ARE YOU FIXED FOR INSURANCE?

OKAY	?	
❑	❑	Health
❑	❑	Disability
❑	❑	Home owner's or renter's
❑	❑	Auto
❑	❑	Personal liability
❑	❑	Professional liability (if applicable)
❑	❑	Life
❑	❑	Long-term-care

Health Insurance

Health insurance protects you from both the smaller out-of-pocket costs of health care and the large medical bills that major illness can bring.

Important matters to consider:

❑ If your employer offers a range of coverage, carefully evaluate the alternatives so that you select the policy that best fits your and your family's needs.

❑ If you are self-employed, check with local business associations or trade associations that offer health insurance to their members at group rates.

❑ Make sure that children who are in college or recently out of the nest have adequate health insurance coverage.

❑ If you plan to retire before Medicare kicks in, plan in advance to secure coverage during the interim. See page 299.

❑ Examine any medical bills you receive for accuracy. Even though you may not be paying the bill, it is incumbent upon all of us to make sure we're not being overcharged.

❑ As you near retirement, you should become familiar with health insurance needs of retirees (see page 298).

Disability Insurance

Disability insurance replaces part or most of your job income in the event of disability.

Important matters to consider:

❑ All working individuals should have enough disability insurance to replace 60 to 70 percent of their job income. Employer-provided disability policies may be unduly restrictive—examine the policy carefully. If the policies are restrictive, you may need to supplement them with other group or individual disability insurance.

❑ If you need to obtain your own disability coverage, first determine if it is available through any professional groups or associations that you can join. Although individually purchased disability insurance policies are the most comprehensive, they are also expensive.

❑ If your employer provides disability insurance coverage, consider reimbursing the employer for the premium that is paid on your behalf. By doing so, you will be able to receive disability benefits tax-free if you ever need to collect. If the employer has been paying the premium, the disability checks will be taxable. Talk to your company's HR department if you're interested in this.

Home owner's and Renter's Insurance

Home owner's insurance covers property—including the home, other structures, personal property, and general contents of the dwelling—against theft or destruction. Renter's insurance protects the personal possessions of the tenant. These policies also offer some liability protection in the event, for example, that someone has a problem navigating the stairs in your home.

Important matters to consider:

❑ In addition to the basic coverage, consider obtaining replacement-cost coverage for your personal possessions and, in the case of home owner's insurance, the home itself, if structural replacement cost is not automatically included in your policy. Construction costs are rising, so be sure your home owner's insurance coverage keeps pace, whether you have a mortgage or not.

❑ With regard to your personal possessions, replacement-cost coverage will generally pay to replace lost, stolen, or damaged items rather than giving you their depreciated value.

❑ Strict policy limits apply to valuable possessions. Any valuables should be appraised so that a floater policy can be added. Valuables stored in a safe-deposit box should be insured as well.

❑ If you're in an area that is prone to such calamities, obtain flood and/or earthquake insurance. Few people who suffer from these calamities have sufficient coverage, if they have any coverage at all. If you're at all in peril, and many regions of the country are, obtaining this coverage should help you sleep better at night and you might just avoid a financial calamity. Here's another suggestion if you reside in a hurricane-prone area: Read your home owner's insurance policy carefully to see how much coverage it offers for hurricanes. Many policies provide less coverage for hurricane damage than they do for losses from other causes, so you may need to improve the coverage. **www**

❑ If you're a renter, don't go without renter's insurance. Consider the impact on your financial situation of losing all of your personal possessions. It happens to people every day.

SAFE-DEPOSIT-BOX INSURANCE

If you store valuables such as jewelry in a safe-deposit box, the contents should be insured. Many people don't realize that the contents of safe-deposit boxes are not insured by the bank, and insurance under a regular home owner's policy is typically limited to $1,000 or less. A rider on your home owner's or renter's policy can add safe-deposit-box insurance at a rate that is usually far less than the cost of insuring valuables that are kept at home. An inventory of the box contents should be stored at home or in the office. At a minimum, your inventory may prevent a wasted trip to the safe-deposit box to retrieve some document or bauble that isn't there.

A home safe may be a viable alternative to a safe-deposit box. They don't cost any more than a few years' worth of safe-deposit-box rental fees, and losses are covered by your home owner's insurance if you have each valuable item listed in a floater policy.

Automobile Insurance

Automobile insurance protects automobile owners from the potentially large bills an accident could bring. Automobile insurance also protects the car owner from theft and provides some liability protection.

Important matters to consider:

❑ Buy sufficient coverage in essential areas such as bodily injury and personal liability, but reduce or eliminate coverage in other areas such as collision and comprehensive if you own an old clunker.

❑ Don't buy cars that cost a lot to insure and invite the attention of auto thieves. Really, your image won't suffer if you own a homely car.

❑ Don't waste money on car rental insurance if you don't need to. If you're going to rent a car, find out in advance if your automobile insurance policy will cover it (most do).

Personal Liability Insurance

Personal liability insurance, also called umbrella insurance, protects you from losing your assets or future earnings as the result of a liability suit arising out of your personal, but not job, activities. It provides additional protection on top of home owner's or renter's and automobile liability coverage and usually covers family members, including kids away at college (talk about frightening liability potential) and even pets.

Important matters to consider:

❏ You should have at least $1 million in umbrella liability insurance. If your estate is growing or you have a high income, you should probably have at least $2 million in coverage. It's quite affordable.

❏ Your umbrella liability insurance policy will need to be coordinated with the liability coverage provided on your auto and home owner's or renter's policies. Therefore, it's usually advisable to buy the umbrella policy from the same company.

❏ If you perform regular or heavy volunteer work, find out from the organization or your attorney if you are indemnified against personal liability.

Professional Liability Insurance

Professional liability insurance protects you from lawsuits arising out of job-related activities. Not all professions require liability insurance, but if you are in a business that could leave you open to a lawsuit, this coverage is essential.

Important matters to consider:

❏ If you're an employee, find out if your employer covers you for professional liability.

❏ Self-employed professionals or small-business owners should probably acquire professional or business liability insurance. If you need to acquire professional liability coverage, check with your professional association. If they don't offer the coverage, they can probably advise you on insurance companies that do.

HAVE YOU TAKEN A HOUSEHOLD INVENTORY?

Hardly a day goes by without a couple of serious house fires in the news, not to mention hurricanes, floods, and other calamities. Chances are the unfortunate home owners are going to suffer a second misfortune when they do battle with the insurance company over the worth of their lost furniture and personal property. Let's look at a worst-case scenario: your house or apartment burns down, blows away, or floats away. How accurately could you recall all of your possessions and how persuasively could you argue your case to a skeptical insurance company? A household inventory, which might only consist of a bunch of camera shots or a videotape of your sundry possessions, can go a long way toward assuring a fair and full insurance settlement should the worst happen. For an obvious reason, don't store your household inventory in your house. Abundant work sheets and Web sites are available to help you prepare and maintain your inventory. **w w w**

Life Insurance

Life insurance replaces part or most of your wage income in the event of your death and may also cover other expenses of your dependents during a readjustment period after death. Depending on where you are on the baby boomer age spectrum, two matters may be of particular interest to you. If you're a younger boomer with a young family, your life insurance needs may be as high as they will ever be. Older baby boomers may be wondering if and when their life insurance needs may decline. But first things first. You can use the following Decision Maker to summarize your life insurance needs.

Life Insurance Decision Maker

This Decision Maker will help you decide on the amount of life insurance you need and how long you'll need it.

CHECK IF YOUR SURVIVORS NEED COVERAGE TO:		NUMBER OF YEARS COVERAGE IS NEEDED			
		<10	10–20	21–30	>30
❑ Pay off the mortgage(s)	$_____	❑	❑	❑	❑
❑ Pay off other debts (credit cards, etc.)	$_____	❑	❑	❑	❑
❑ Pay for the kids' education (see Table 10.3)	$_____	❑	❑	❑	❑
❑ Provide a transition fund until your survivor(s) become financially self-sustaining	$_____	❑	❑	❑	❑
❑ Provide or augment a retirement fund for your spouse or partner	$_____	❑	❑	❑	❑
❑ Other needs (caution: don't unjustly enrich your survivors)	$_____	❑	❑	❑	❑
Total estimated life insurance needs	$_____				

TABLE 10.3
HOW MUCH LIFE INSURANCE DO YOU NEED
TO FUND COLLEGE TUITION?

If it's going to cost $200,000 or so to pay four years of tuition for your toddler, that doesn't mean you need $200,000 in life insurance. The necessary amount may be quite a bit less, depending on the age of the child or children. Here's a table that shows the approximate amount of insurance (the "present value" in mathematics parlance) necessary to establish an investment fund to meet college costs.

PRESENT VALUE OF COLLEGE COSTS

JUNIOR'S AGE*	PUBLIC COLLEGE	PRIVATE COLLEGE
0–5	$40,000	$100,000
6–10	45,000	110,000
11–15	50,000	120,000
16–18	55,000	130,000

* Here's a sobering thought: If you're a boomer with very young kids, you may be able to withdraw money from your IRAs and other retirement accounts to pay for college tuitions, since you'll be over age 59½ when tuition time comes. This is not recommended, however, since your retirement money should be used for—what else?—retirement.

CASE STUDY: FIGURING OUT LIFE INSURANCE NEEDS

Harry and Harriet Harried are really confused about the amount of life insurance they need, although they realize they need substantially more. They already have some small policies through their respective employers, but don't want to count on that insurance in the event they lose their jobs or become self-employed. Here's how the Harrieds analyzed their needs:

- Pay off the mortgage of $200,000 if either spouse dies. Mortgage will be paid off in about fifteen years.
- Education costs for two kids of $240,000 until the last one graduates in ten years.
- Transition funds, including additions to surviving spouse's retirement savings, of $100,000 until retirement fifteen years hence.

Since they need life insurance only over the next fifteen years, the Harrieds can meet these needs with term insurance. Here's what their insurance agent recommended:

1. Ten-year level term for $250,000 on each spouse to cover college costs.
2. Fifteen-year level term for $300,000 on each spouse to cover the mortgage and transition costs.

While the family's needs will decrease over time as college tuitions end and the mortgage is paid down, they wanted to maintain that level of coverage over the entire ten- and fifteen-year periods, because other events might arise that would require coverage beyond their current estimates—graduate school for the kids or a second home mortgage, for example.

Important matters to consider:

❑ Examine whether term and/or cash-value insurance will best meet your needs. The following section will help you resolve that dilemma.

❑ If you need to acquire more life insurance, keep in mind that the life insurance industry is competitive, particularly for plain old term and whole-life insurance. Comparison shopping by you or your agent could save you lots of money.

❑ Buy life insurance when you're healthy. If you wait until some major health problem arises, a life insurance policy will cost much more—if you can get it at all.

❑ Review your life insurance needs periodically, because changes in your financial or family circumstances may result in a change in coverage or a change in beneficiaries. There's nothing like having an ex-spouse listed as the beneficiary of your life insurance policies to cause your grieving widow a lot of unnecessary grief. Remember also that life insurance needs typically diminish as you age. For example, once you approach retirement and the children have left the nest, your life insurance needs may be nominal. Or they may not diminish if you have a spouse or other family member who would suffer financially without the coverage.

❑ If you're thinking about purchasing (or more likely being encouraged to purchase) life insurance to help pay estate taxes (second-to-die life insurance, for example), be sure to speak with an estate-planning attorney first to see if there are other ways to reduce your estate-tax bill without having to resort to expensive life insurance. ⬤ ⬤ ⬤

LIFE INSURANCE IS GETTING CHEAPER FOR BOOMERS

Life insurance rates, particularly term insurance, are declining, thanks to longer life expectancies and fierce price competition among the life insurance companies. It may be rewarding to survey the term insurance landscape if:

- **You need more life insurance coverage.** Don't assume that you're too old to obtain affordable term insurance. According to one survey, term insurance premiums have fallen about 50 percent in the past decade.

- **You already have a term insurance policy.** Because premium rates are coming down so fast, you may be able to reduce the premiums on an older term policy as long as your health is still okay. Of course, never drop an old policy in favor of a new one until the new policy has been signed, sealed, and delivered.

What kind of life insurance is best for you? Have you ever wanted the straight scoop on what kind of life insurance is best for you? Well, you've come to the right place. There are two basic kinds of life insurance: term, which is pure insurance coverage with no bells and whistles, and cash value, which comes in a variety of flavors, all of which provide insurance protection while at the same time building up cash over the years that can be accessed, if necessary. The most important consideration in determining whether term or cash value (which is also called permanent insurance) is preferable in your situation is how long the insurance is going to be needed. If the need is temporary and is not likely to extend into later life when such coverage could become prohibitively expensive, then term insurance may be sufficient. On the other hand, if the duration of the anticipated need for life insurance coverage is uncertain and is likely to continue indefinitely, cash value is the likely solution. But keep in mind that among the various kinds of cash-value insurance, the one that's being most vigorously promoted may not be the right one for you. So, do some independent investigation. Often, it's best to stick with the basics when selecting insurance, and the most basic form of cash-value insurance is whole-life insurance. You know what you're going to get with these policies—no rosy forecasts that may turn out to be a pipe dream.

Finally, as with most every other financial and investment product, the term versus cash-value dilemma should not be viewed as an either/or decision. Many people find a combination of both term and cash value to be the answer to the life insurance dilemma. **w w w**

Example 1. Robert and Roberta Roberts are reviewing their life insurance needs. They have two children under the age of five, and the only life insurance they now have is the minimal coverage provided by their respective employers. Roberta summarizes the situation this way: "Our major need is to provide for the children in the event one or both of us dies before they're out of college. Bob's and my parents are in good shape financially and won't need any support, and while we're not making a ton of money, the pension plans where we work are pretty good. But if one of us dies in the next fifteen or twenty years, we'd be up a creek with the mortgage and college expenses."

The Robertses' insurance needs are typical of families in similar situations: they need a lot of insurance for a discrete time. Term insurance is the likely solution—perhaps a twenty-year policy on each spouse. They should also consider adding additional and probably low-cost coverage through their respective employers.

Example 2. Larry and Laura Lawrence are self-employed professionals in their early forties. Since they are unlikely to have children, the couple had concluded that they don't really need life insurance. Larry notes, "We're both doing okay financially, so if one of us dies, the survivor should be able to get by okay." But after reviewing their overall situation, their financial planner came to a much different conclusion. The mortgage and the car payments currently consume almost half of their income. They have only recently been putting money aside for retirement. An additional complicating factor is that Larry is concerned that his parents, who are struggling financially, may need his financial assistance after they retire. The planner concluded that if one income disappeared, the remaining spouse would be unable to meet the current fixed obligations, much less put money aside for the future. Even more perplexing is that the need to replace the second income is likely to persist for at least twenty-five years, extending into the early retirement years—a situation not atypical of DINK (dual income/no kids) couples. Therefore, while term insurance could play a role in an insurance program, permanent insurance would be a key component since the Lawrences' insurance needs might well extend into a period where term insurance becomes extremely expensive. Permanent insurance also has the advantage of "forced savings," which would be particularly helpful for a couple more inclined to spend than to save.

Long-Term-Care Insurance

Deciding once and for all if you should buy long-term-care insurance. For many baby boomers, particularly those over fifty, this is probably their most nagging insurance question. A decade ago, I would have strongly discouraged obtaining LTC coverage. The only things worse than the limited coverage were the questionable sales tactics. I'll never forget a tearful call I received from a woman many years ago who said she had just been told by her insurance agent that if she didn't get a long-term-care policy, the statistics showed that she had a 95 percent chance of dying in poverty. Well, this single woman had a few million dollars of investments. I did a quick calculation and found that she had enough to stay in a nursing home for 141 years before going broke.

Fortunately, both the policy design and the sales pitches have much improved over the past several years. LTC coverage is well worth considering, yet it may still not be necessary or affordable. But I hope my following musings and suggestions on long-term-care insurance will help you make a decision one way or the other, so you can check this annoying task off your retirement to-do list.

Long-Term-Care Insurance Decision Maker

Here are some important questions that will help you assess your need for LTC coverage. The more "yes" responses, the more likely you might benefit from this coverage.

Yes	No	N/A	
❑	❑	❑	**1. Are you married or partnered?**

The biggest financial risk of incurring huge out-of-pocket expenses for long-term care is impoverishing the other spouse or partner. Single people don't face that risk, so, all other things being equal, singles have less need for LTC insurance.

| ❑ | ❑ | ❑ | **2. If you're single, are your total investments between $500,000 and $1 million?** |

Most objective observers of the LTC insurance scene believe that the ideal candidates for long-term-care coverage are those who can comfortably afford the premiums and can handle any future premium increases, which are becoming quite common. One common rough measure is net worth (excluding the home), or, more simply, the amount of investments you have. Those with less than $500,000 in investments might not be able to afford the coverage. Another more reliable measure is how much the insurance will cost you as a percentage of your expected retirement income. If the premiums are likely to consume more than 10 percent of your income, you probably can't afford it. Those singles with over $1 million in investments may want to consider self-insuring.

| ❑ | ❑ | ❑ | **3. If there are two of you, are your total investments between $500,000 and $1.5 million?** |

See the reasoning described above for singles. Those above the range may be able to consider self-insuring.

| ❑ | ❑ | ❑ | **4. Did your ancestors have chronic health problems or other conditions that required prolonged care in their dotage?** |

While far from a perfect predictor, the past

health patterns of parents and grandparents can be an indicator of what you have to look forward to.

Yes   *No*   *N/A*

❏   ❏   ❏   **5. Is passing on an inheritance to your children or other heirs an important financial goal?** While passing on an inheritance violates my mantra of trying to spend it all before you die, if this is important to you, an LTC policy could protect at least some of your assets for future generations.

Important matters to consider:

❏ Understand the policy limitations and features. Many purchasers don't really understand what they're getting—or not getting. Become an expert on long-term-care insurance before signing up for a policy. This insurance could be one of your biggest retirement expenses.

❏ Favor policies that provide comprehensive home health care coverage as well as nursing home coverage. Inflation protection is also an important feature for baby boomers who are considering this coverage.

❏ One alternative to long-term-care insurance that you may want to consider is investing the money you would pay in LTC premiums. According to recent statistics, only 37 percent of all sixty-five-year-olds will need long-term care in a nursing home or assisted-living facility. Most will stay less than two years.

❏ Faustian bargain: You can cut premium costs by limiting the policy to three years, but if you spend a lot longer than that in a nursing home, you may end up impoverishing yourself anyway. Eight percent of the population will spend more than five years in a "nursing facility."

❏ Chances are that you could accumulate a significant amount of money by the time you enter a nursing home (if you ever do) by self-insuring. If you're worried about a nursing home confinement impoverishing you and your spouse, consider investing some of your retirement savings in an annuity, which will at least assure you and/or a surviving spouse or partner a lifetime source of income that won't be forfeited to the nursing home (see page 143).

❑ You may lower premium costs by eliminating all the fancy, and expensive, bells and whistles, while keeping the inflation kicker. Lowering the daily reimbursement rate will also lower the premiums, as will increasing the waiting period until benefits kick in.

❑ If you can only afford to insure one party, note that women are more likely to spend extended periods in a nursing home.

❑ Many baby boomers will likely eventually consider continuing care communities (CCCs), which have been popular among their parents. CCCs provide three levels of care for their residents: independent living, assisted living, and nursing home. CCCs may obviate the need for an LTC policy.

When should you acquire an LTC policy? Opinions vary greatly as to the best age to acquire an LTC policy. Keep in mind that the annual premiums for LTC coverage are a lot higher if you wait to take out a policy until your sixties or later. Few objective experts on these matters recommend that coverage be purchased before age fifty or after age seventy, when premiums may become prohibitively expensive. While premiums are lower if the policy is purchased at a younger age, keep in mind that premiums are likely to be paid for decades before any benefits are collected, if ever (the average age that a senior enters a nursing home is eighty-three). However, one compelling argument for purchasing a policy sooner rather than later is that health issues may arise that render you uninsurable. Therefore, if your health is deteriorating, or you have a family history of early disability, or you engage in high-risk activities, you should probably acquire an LTC policy at a younger age.

LTC policy features worth considering. While "new and improved" insurance policies should often be viewed with skepticism, some enhancements, including the long-term-care genre, may be worth considering, particularly since every several years Congress further tightens eligibility requirements for Medicaid coverage of nursing home costs. Here are some examples of innovative long-term-care insurance policy features:

✦ **Combination policies.** Money that is not used for long-term care is paid out in annuity distributions.

✦ **Shared care.** Allows couples to tap into each other's policies in case either exhausts policy benefits.

✦ **Flexible payout.** Rather than receive the stated benefits, these policies will allow policyholders to change how they're reimbursed from month to month to better match their long-term-care costs.

W W W

LONG-TERM-CARE POLICYHOLDERS BEWARE: YOUR PREMIUMS MAY RISE

Most people who purchase an LTC policy believe that the premiums will remain fixed for life. But many policyholders have had to endure premium increases, in some instances of 50 percent or more in a single year. Those burdened with higher premiums can pay the higher cost, pay the original premium by accepting scaled-back coverage, or let the policy lapse. While it's impossible to predict whether and by how much premiums will be raised in the future (older policies have been most susceptible), it's important for LTC policy-

holders to understand and assess the possibility that premiums may be hiked in the future. If you're in the market for a
policy, ask the agent or the insurance company if they have
had to raise premiums on previously issued policies.

An alternative to long-term-care insurance. You've got to hand
it to the insurance industry's ingenuity in inventing new types of
insurance. While many of these policies are of dubious value, a
fairly new species of coverage may in some instances be a worthy
alternative to expensive long-term-care insurance, or purely for providing an income boost later in life. Longevity insurance, or "retirement income insurance," will pay you a lifetime income commencing
at a later age in exchange for a lump-sum payment. (The actuaries,
always eager to obfuscate, call them "advanced-life delayed annuities.") For example, here's what you get in exchange for a lump-sum
payment of $50,000 at age sixty with benefits starting at age eighty-
five. If a female policyholder survives until age eighty-five (that's a
big *if,* of course), the policy would pay $34,000 for life each year
thereafter. If a male policyholder survives until age eighty-five (that's
a bigger *if*), the policy would pay a lifetime $46,000 per annum. If
you're in good health and have ancestors who were entering middle
age in their eighties, these policies might be your cup of tea.

Beware of the fine print. There are all sorts of variations on this
theme, some of which offer a refund should you die before the age
when the payout commences. But these additional bells and whistles
come at a big price in the form of a much lower ultimate benefit. If
you're buying insurance as a substitute for LTC coverage, you want
pure coverage, unadulterated by features you don't need but pay
dearly for.

Saving on Insurance

Many people spend more than they should to secure adequate insurance coverage. Here are some of the many simple ways to reduce insurance costs and avoid costly mistakes:

✦ **Raise deductibles.** You can save as much as hundreds of dollars each year by raising the deductibles on your automobile and home owner's or renter's insurance policies.

✦ **Don't underinsure.** While you should certainly be encouraged to pare down unnecessary insurance costs, don't go without necessary coverage merely to save premium dollars. Eliminating needed coverage can be a costly mistake.

✦ **Earn discounts by purchasing all insurance coverage from one company.** Many carriers offer discounts to customers who purchase all their policies, such as automobile, home owner's, and umbrella liability insurance, from them.

✦ **Don't buy insurance through the mail without comparison shopping.** You may periodically receive direct-mail offers for life insurance from a credit card company, association, or famous TV personality. While most of these offers should be rejected, some, particularly those offered by professional associations, may be worth considering. Do some comparison shopping to determine if the mail order deal is a good one.

✦ **Reduce life insurance coverage when children leave home.** Life insurance needs often decrease when children are no longer financially dependent, if the parents live that long.

✦ **Avoid credit life insurance.** Credit life insurance (and credit accident and disability insurance) is almost always grossly overpriced and entirely unnecessary. If you need a policy to ensure that your loans can be paid off in the event of death or disability, you should buy death or disability insurance—not this overpriced waste.

✦ **Inquire about discounts.** Many insurers offer discounts for home owners who take protective measures against fire and burglary. The cost of installing these systems may be recouped fairly quickly through insurance premium savings. You may also qualify for special discounts on your automobile insurance policies without even realizing it. Check with your insurance agent or the company itself to find out about various discounts that may be available to you—such as those for driver-training courses, theft-deterrent systems, and automobile safety features.

✦ **Self-insure.** You may have sufficient capital to assume certain risks, either by raising deductibles or by canceling coverage altogether. The decision to self-insure is serious, however, and should only be made after careful analysis.

✦ **Avoid "dread disease" or other narrowly defined insurance coverage.** Stay away from cancer insurance, air travel insurance, and other types of insurance that protect against specific risks. These policies exploit fear and protect against risks that regular insurance already covers. A good medical policy, for instance, renders any disease-specific insurance unnecessary.

✦ **Pay insurance premiums annually rather than monthly or quarterly.** If it doesn't decimate the family budget, paying insurance premiums annually is usually cheaper than paying monthly or quarterly.

Planning Your Estate for the Here and Now as Well as the Hereafter

In the words of Woody Allen, "I don't want to achieve immortality through my work; I want to achieve immortality through not dying." While there's only anecdotal evidence to refute the notion that we're all immortal, it's still prudent to assume that our days are numbered. Let's just hope that it's a big number. There's no joy in contemplating our own mortality, but if you give forethought and advance planning to the settlement of your estate, you can be reasonably sure it will be distributed the way you want.

This section would not be necessary if all baby boomers had taken care of their estate planning, but the most generous estimate is that half of boomers lack wills and many others have outdated wills. Estate planning is depressing for the simple reason that you'll never live to see the fruits of your efforts. But that doesn't mean you should ignore it. Once you get it over and done with, you'll feel at least some comfort in knowing that your heirs aren't going to have to go through the considerable hassle of settling an estate that is bereft of a will and other estate-planning documents. At a minimum, you'll save your loved ones a lot of grief, and I'm not talking about the kind of grief that people suffer from the loss of a loved one. Instead, I'm talking about the grief that's caused by an improperly planned estate or, worse, no estate planning at all. Your money can go to three places—to charity, to the government, or to your heirs—and I don't know of anyone who prefers that his or her money go to the government. So unless you detest your heirs and you want to get back at them from the grave, here are some of the basic matters you need to think about and documents you need to have prepared. If you already have these documents, make sure they're up-to-date.

Every baby boomer should have three basic estate-planning documents:

✦ A will

✦ A durable power of attorney (or living trust)

✦ An advance directive

Don't try to prepare them yourself. Have an attorney do it. Unless your financial or family situation is unusually convoluted, it won't cost much. A lot of mistakes that we make in life can later be rectified, but if you mess up on your estate-planning documents, even a séance cannot help.

A fourth estate-planning document that I highly recommend, a letter of instructions, is discussed beginning on page 243. You don't need an attorney to prepare a letter of instructions.

NAME CONTINGENT BENEFICIARIES FOR YOUR IRAS AND OTHER RETIREMENT PLANS

Most people haven't named contingent beneficiaries for their retirement accounts. A contingent beneficiary will inherit the retirement-plan assets in the event that the primary beneficiary predeceases you. Otherwise, the benefits will be added to your estate and will then probably have to be withdrawn over a short time. Under current retirement-plan withdrawal rules, those who inherit IRAs or other retirement plans can stretch out the withdrawals over their life expectancies, resulting in potentially much lower income taxes on withdrawals and higher accumulations over the beneficiary's lifetime.

---

1. Will

Before your death, your will is a private document, the contents of which need not be known to anyone other than you and your attorney. Upon your death, however, the will becomes a publicly accessible legal document that is under the jurisdiction of the probate court system. Through the probate court, the state assures that your will is valid, that your assets are protected against loss or theft, that your bills and taxes are paid, and that all your remaining assets go directly to the beneficiaries you have designated in your will.

✦ **The heartbreak of intestacy.** If you die without a will, your heirs will have to go through the hassle of settling an "intestate" estate. In the event of intestacy, state law dictates how your assets are distributed, and the outcome can be frightening, particularly if you have children who may end up owning half of your estate.

✦ **Discuss the contents with heirs.** Despite the privacy afforded by a will, you should discuss its contents with your intended heirs. Doing so not only gives you the opportunity to explain or clarify certain will provisions to those directly involved, it also improves the chances that your will's provisions will be carried out as indicated, with a minimum of doubts and animosity.

✦ **Wills can always be changed.** A common misconception is that a will limits your flexibility; but a will can always be altered to reflect changes in your circumstances or desires. In fact, updating the will to reflect such changes is an important part of ongoing estate planning. Getting married or divorced, starting a family, losing loved ones, and becoming disabled— all are changes that will, more likely than not, require revisions in your will. Indeed, in many states, marriage, divorce, or a new baby invalidates any existing will. You can either write a new will that declares any previous wills invalid or append a codicil to an existing will. (Codicils are subject to the same legal stipulations as are wills.) Moving to a new state may invalidate a will drawn up under the laws of your previous state. Earlier wills should be saved for reference. If a current will is declared invalid, the latest-dated, legally valid will is considered your legal will.

✦ **How to treat the children.** The vast majority of parents sincerely want to treat each of their children the same when planning how their estates are to be distributed. But often, the children are not the same when it comes to their need for or ability to handle money. This is obviously a difficult matter to address, and many parents don't want to address it. But imagine how much harm might be done to, say, a spendthrift child who receives an inheritance and a year later has squandered it. Sometimes the most unfair thing to do is treat each child the same, both with respect to how they receive the money and when they receive it.

✦ **Choosing an executor who is up to the task.** When your will is created, you will have to appoint an executor (also referred to as a personal representative) to ensure that your estate is properly settled upon your death. Otherwise, the courts will appoint one. An executor ensures that your will is probated and that the wishes stipulated in it are properly carried out. The executor has a lot of responsibilities, all of which need to be settled in accordance with legal and tax requirements. Failure to do so may result in penalties. An executor should have financial knowledge, be a reliable record keeper, and be sensitive to the needs of your beneficiaries. Family members may or may not be up to the task. If you choose a family member to be your executor, you may set him or her up for criticism from other family members. One solution might be to appoint a family member as an executor but mention in your will that you expect the executor to hire necessary professionals (lawyers, accountants, and the like) to assist in settling your estate. If your estate is quite large or complex, you might consider appointing a bank trust department, estate-planning attorney, or other professional to serve as the executor. Assigning a professional to this position removes the burden from your family and lowers the possibility that any conflicts might arise. On the other hand, professionals may be rather impersonal for a family that has suffered a traumatic loss. A solution to this dilemma could be to appoint coexecutors (for example, a bank trust department and a family member) and thus get both the financial expertise and the personal touch.

✦ **Where to store your will.** Although it is advisable to make photocopies for your files and for family members, there should be only one original copy of a will at any time. Deciding where to keep the original is vexing. Options include a home safe, a business safe, a bank safe-deposit box, your lawyer's office, a trust company (if one has been named as an executor), or the clerk of your local probate court, who will hold it for safekeeping in a sealed envelope. Where you should store your will depends on state and local probate law. For example, many such laws automatically seal the safe-deposit box upon death, making the will inaccessible pending a court order and creating a messy complication. Wherever you decide to store your will, always be sure that family members or close friends know its location.

✦ **Things change.** Family circumstances shift, as does your financial status. People move to different states. Federal and state tax laws change. Therefore, you must periodically review and revise your will to ensure that its contents conform to current laws and regulations and that it still reflects your wishes. Dying with an out-of-date or invalid will can be almost as bad as dying without a will at all.

Planning for children and other family members with special needs. The number of individuals with a disability is variously estimated at 15 to 20 percent of the American population. Advances in health care are likely to increase the incidence of disabled family members, including younger-generation members who may well outlive the custodial parents or siblings. The challenges of providing for a disabled child or other dependent are difficult enough during the parent's or caretaker's lifetime, and the challenges become particularly troublesome if the parent or caretaker predeceases the disabled

---

PARENTS: HAVE YOU APPOINTED GUARDIANS FOR YOUR DEPENDENT CHILDREN?

Have you appointed a guardian for your dependent child in your will? Many parents fail to make this important arrangement. A guardian becomes responsible for a minor child's care and upbringing or a disabled adult's welfare if the parents die early. Failure to designate a guardian in your will can cause a lot of problems. With the increasing number of less-traditional family situations among baby boomer families, such as divorced parents and stepparents, the possible complications are even greater. Your attorney should advise you as to various possible steps, including dividing guardianship duties so that one person is responsible for the child's care and another for the finances.

---

family member. In these circumstances, it's vitally important to consult an estate-planning attorney, who may recommend a "special needs trust" to provide for a disabled family member.

2. Durable Power of Attorney

If you ever become incapacitated (through accident, illness, or just plain aging) and are unable to handle your own affairs, a court may appoint a guardian or conservator to manage your money. The court may not appoint the guardian whom you would have chosen. Even if the court ultimately does approve your choice of guardian, the approval will be subject to unnecessary red tape and confusion. The simplest way to protect yourself—and to ensure that your property will continue to be managed as you see fit—is to appoint a guardian for yourself through a durable power of attorney. No matter how it is arranged, your durable power of attorney may be canceled at any time, and it terminates immediately upon your death.

DO YOU NEED A LIVING TRUST?

Living trusts, an alternative to a durable power of attorney, can provide a variety of estate-planning advantages, such as avoiding probate and keeping your financial matters private. Living trusts—not to be confused with living wills—allow you to specify whom you want to take over your financial affairs if you become incapacitated. Residents of states where probate is particularly burdensome may prefer living trusts.

Living trusts are a hot product, and many attorneys and financial institutions have aggressively been promoting them, leading many people to believe that living trusts are the answer to every problem. This is not necessarily the case. For example, living trusts do not save income or estate taxes, although many people who have been sold them think they do. While some can benefit from living trust arrangements, others will find them to be a waste of time and money. How do you determine if a living trust makes sense for you? Speak with an attorney who is experienced in estate planning but who *doesn't* ballyhoo the supposed virtues of living trusts. In other words, consult with an attorney who can give you an objective evaluation of whether a living trust is right for you. ***w w w***

HEALTH PRIVACY RULES MAY REQUIRE A CHANGE IN POWER-OF-ATTORNEY OR LIVING-TRUST DOCUMENTS

The Health Insurance Portability and Accountability Act (HIPAA) was designed to protect medical privacy by, among other things, preventing doctors from speaking freely about a patient's medical condition without consent. But this well-intentioned law may create a problem if, as I hope, you've given power of attorney to someone to take care of your medical and financial needs if you're incapacitated. Under HIPAA rules, the person you have designated to act on your behalf may not be able to secure enough medical information to ascertain your incapacity.

The solution is to prepare a HIPAA authorization form that permits the person you have designated to act on your behalf to have access to your medical information. If you have a trust, the procedure to enable access to your medical records is more complicated, but is no less necessary. Check with your attorney in either case.

---

3. Advance Directive

Advances in medical technology mean, plain and simple, that people's lives can be sustained even when they are terminally ill and have no hope of leading an active, independent life. An advance directive gives instructions about your health care and what you want done and not done if you can't speak for yourself. Advance directives are not complicated, typically consisting of short, simple statements expressing your values and choices. The term *advance directive* includes health care directives, living wills, health care (medical) powers of attorney, and other personalized directives.

✦ **Health care directive** tells your, doctor and your family members what kind of care you would like if you are unable to make medical decisions. Unlike most living wills (described next), a health care directive is not limited to cases of terminal illness. If you cannot make or communicate decisions because of illness, a health care directive helps you keep control over health care decisions that are important to you.

✦ **Living will** usually only comes into effect if you are terminally ill, which generally means you have less than six months to live.

✦ **Health care (medical) power of attorney** lets you name someone (an "agent") to make medical decisions for you if you are unconscious or unable to make medical decisions for yourself for any reason. It may be incorporated within a health care directive or living will or it may be a separate document. Appointing an agent is particularly important. When a decision needs to be made, your agent can participate in discussions and weigh the pros and cons of treatments based on your wishes. Your agent can decide for you whenever you cannot decide for yourself, even if your decision-making is only temporarily affected.

An advance directive, including a health care (medical) power of attorney, has no legal effect unless you lack the capacity to make health care decisions or to give consent for care. By expressing your wishes in advance, you help family or friends, who might otherwise struggle to decide on their own what you would want done—a point that was amply illustrated by the Terry Schiavo case. Everyone, young or old, should consider preparing an advance directive; it can provide comfort to family members at a difficult time. Also (forgive me, but this is a financial book), an advance directive can save a lot of money. The cost of keeping someone alive by artificial means can drain a family's estate.

ESTATE PLANNING FOR UNMARRIED COUPLES

Estate planning for unmarried couples is complicated by the legal ambiguities that surround nontraditional couples. The legal status of cohabitants varies widely from state to state and even from city to city. In the absence of well-defined laws, unmarried couples are advised to use written agreements that specify their rights and obligations. Lawyers who are knowledgeable and experienced in matters pertaining to unmarried couples should be consulted, especially for unmarried couples who have custody of children, either biological or adopted, where laws tend to be especially murky.

Letter of Instructions

A letter of instructions is not the most pleasant item to prepare, but you will be doing your loved ones a big favor by preparing one, keeping it up-to-date, and letting them know where it's located.

A letter of instructions is an informal document that gives your survivors information concerning important financial and personal matters that must be attended to after your demise. As opposed to the other three essential estate-planning documents—your will, durable power of attorney, and health care proxy (living will)—which you should have an attorney prepare, you can prepare a letter of instructions yourself. Although it doesn't carry the legal weight of a will and is in no way a substitute for a will, a letter of instructions clarifies any special requests to be carried out upon death. It also provides essential financial information, thus relieving the family of needless worry and speculation. **w w w**

Information to include in a letter of instructions:

✦ The location of important papers, including the will, birth and marriage certificates, and military records.

✦ A summary of your investment accounts and insurance policies.

✦ The location of documents relating to your personal residence, including an inventory of household contents and warranties and receipts for expensive items. You may also want to include a list of mementos naming whom you would like to receive each.

✦ Details of the whereabouts of your safe-deposit box, its key, and a list of its contents.

✦ The locations of previous income-tax and gift-tax returns.

✦ An expression of your wishes about your funeral and burial preferences, including any advance arrangements that have been made.

✦ The names and addresses of people and institutions that should be notified.

Obviously, your survivors will greatly benefit if you prepare a letter of instructions. But you will also benefit since a well-prepared letter is a great way to organize your personal records—something all of us should do.

Keep it up-to-date. After you prepare your letter of instructions, please keep in mind that things change in your life, which inevitably requires you to change the letter of instructions later on. While an out-of-date letter is nowhere near as perilous as an out-of-date will, you should still strive to keep it up-to-date by reviewing it at least annually or making any obvious changes when they arise.

Tell the world where your letter of instructions is located. Finally, put a copy of your letter of instructions in an easy-to-find location and make sure your loved ones know where they can find it. Incidentally, my wife and I have taped our letters of instructions to the refrigerator door, amongst our kids' paraphernalia. Our friends think this is rather maudlin, but at least it's well-known where the darn things are located. Why don't you do the same?

CHAPTER 11

Healthy, Wealthy, and Wise

There's more to preparing for a great retirement than the customary triad of saving regularly, investing those savings wisely, and getting your debt under control. This chapter is devoted to your good health and various family matters, including helping your parents and, if perchance you have violated a fundamental tenet of sound financial planning by taking responsibility for things that eat, dealing with spouses or partners and children, without sacrificing your financial future. Here are my brief thoughts on these matters:

1. **Health.** Taking care of your health during your remaining working years can make a big difference in how well and how long you'll be able to live the good life in retirement. Money and health are not mutually exclusive, and you can stack the odds for a long and healthy retirement by improving your health habits.

2. **Family.** Senator Clinton once observed, "It takes a village to raise a child," to which I add, from an expense standpoint, it costs about the equivalent of two houses in said village to raise a child. There's nothing like the specter of a skein of college tuition bills to engender images of having to delay retiring by a few decades.

But, as with preceding generations, boomer families can surmount that hurdle without impairing their retirement goals.

3. **Parents.** While only a small percentage of parents require financial help from their children, as your parents age, they may increasingly need some assistance with their own financial and investment management. Providing some helpful guidance during their retirement years is not only the right thing to do, but also might enhance your own retirement well-being, as discussed beginning on page 259.

4. **Cars.** Cars are included in this "family" chapter because in our jaundiced society, we love our cars almost as much as family members, probably treat them better, and may spend more money on them than on the rest of the family. I'm having difficulty trying to hide my disdain for cars, as you'll understand beginning on page 264.

5. **Your career.** Don't overlook your most profitable investment— your career. Striving for excellence and advancement in your job will be one of the most important contributors to your financial security.

What Good Is Wealth without Good Health?

Baby Boomers Can Look Forward to a Healthier Retirement

According to "65+ in the United States: 2005," a U.S. Census Bureau report on the aging population, today's baby boomers are markedly different from previous generations in their health prospects. The report notes that older Americans are more prosperous and healthier than their forebears, and those differences will widen when the first boomers reach retirement age.

One of the report's key findings is that seniors are showing substantially less disability, which points to an improved quality of life for retired boomers. Researchers use the term *health expectancy* to describe how long a population can expect to live free of disability. Health expectancy is expected to increase substantially in the future. In 1982, more than 26 percent of those over age sixty-five had a disability that resulted in a substantial limitation in a major life activity. By 1999, less than 20 percent of the over-sixty-fives had a disability, and this downward trend is expected to continue.

The report concludes that all of the positive trends in health are expected to accelerate. "The future older population is likely to be better educated than the current older population, especially when baby boomers start reaching age sixty-five. Their increased levels of education may accompany better health, higher incomes, and more wealth, and consequently higher standards of living in retirement."

The director of the Census Bureau also noted that as younger workers become scarcer, employers will have to find ways to convince their older workers to stay on the job longer.

It's Never Too Late to Improve Your Health Prospects

You can do several things not only to greatly reduce the probability of premature death, but also to make your remaining working years and your retirement years a lot healthier. It would be a shame to do all the right things financially to ensure that you're going to have a great retirement only to have your money eroded or spent on preventable infirmities simply because you didn't take sufficient care of your health. Even if you've had lousy health habits in the past, changing those bad habits now can reduce future problems and lengthen your remaining life.

✦ **Diet.** We all know the foods that make up a well-balanced diet, but that doesn't mean that we eat them. Fresh fruits, vegetables, whole grains, fish, and lean meats in moderation will help you maintain good health for a longer time. Consult your doctor about a food regimen that's best for you.

✦ **Exercise and stress reduction.** Moderate to vigorous exercise of at least thirty minutes several days a week will work wonders in reducing stress, improving your overall outlook (and look), and preventing or postponing later-life health problems. Be sure to include strength and flexibility in your exercise regimen.

✦ **Checkups.** Screening tests as part of regular doctor visits will help identify diseases or other health problems early, making them easier to treat. Unless you're not too enthused about finding out such matters in advance, keep up-to-date on the state-of-the-art in diagnostic tools. **w w w**

The Mind Needs Work, Too

✦ **Developing a social portfolio.** Develop and nurture meaningful relationships with family and friends. Having such people in your life is conducive to a longer, healthier life. Further, these relationships will add to your enjoyment of life and help you better manage stress.

✦ **Keeping mentally sharp.** A lot of what you do to keep yourself physically fit will also promote mental fitness. Neuropsychologists urge those of us who have a few decades under our ever-widening belts to participate in cognitively challenging activities—in other words, exercising parts of your brain that haven't been used much. Ideally, pursue new activities that are difficult. Learn a new language or a musical instrument (I want to learn how to play the steel drum), or try crosswords, Scrabble, painting, or the like. When you get good at it, move on to something else. Forty years of research has shown that undertaking (excuse the poor word choice) cognitively challenging activities as an adult has been shown to delay the onset of dementia and to slow its progression.

✦ **Keeping busy.** There's no question that baby boomers are staying busy, which is important to your mental health. Leading a full life doesn't end with retirement. For more ideas on planning an active retirement, see chapter 12.

HOW FAMILY HEALTH INFLUENCES YOUR FINANCIAL PLANNING

Family health is an important albeit often overlooked factor in financial planning. For example, the financial planning for a sixty-year-old whose health is poor (or whose spouse's or partner's health is poor) must be viewed in a considerably different light from that of others who enjoy good health. The health status of other family members (e.g., children or parents) who are currently or may become financially dependent should also be considered. Several areas of financial planning may be affected by family health matters, including insurance coverage, investing, and retirement and estate-planning strategies.

The health history of your immediate family may also be important in your financial planning. The longevity and disease patterns of older-generation family members may be helpful in making important financial decisions—for example, the way in which retirement benefits are received (lump sum versus annuity) and the efficacy of purchasing long-term-care insurance.

Tips for Family Financial Felicity

Here are some suggestions for minimizing marital money strife and raising financially savvy children.

Involve your spouse or partner in all important financial decisions. In close relationships, one spouse or partner usually oversees the investments and other family financial matters. But planning for retirement, particularly the big decisions, requires closer collaboration.

Even if you've had some difficulty seeing eye to eye on financial issues before, weighty retirement decisions must be made jointly. These discussions should commence many years before you intend to retire. It wouldn't hurt to set aside a "financial planning day" on the same date each year to discuss where you stand financially and your strategies for the future.

REVERSE KEEPING UP WITH THE JONESES

A study on consumer debt found that people in general base their savings and spending decisions not only on their own resources, but also on the spending patterns of their peers. In general, if consumers feel peer pressure toward conspicuous consumption, a higher level of consumption may result. My advice is to resist the temptation to keep up with the Joneses. True, you need to encourage your friends and neighbors to spend lavishly, because the health of our economy depends on heavy consumer spending. But the economy won't collapse if you restrain your spending. I like to refer to this approach— encouraging everyone else to spend while you limit your own spending—as "reverse keeping up with the Joneses."

Talk about money matters with the younger generation. Money shouldn't be a taboo subject in the family. Here's an easy way to help your children—even the adult children—learn about money. Simply discuss family finances and investments in their presence. You might even want to give them some stock to further stimulate an interest in investing. Several years ago, I surveyed over a thousand mutual fund managers. One of the questions I asked was how they learned about investing. Most of the managers attributed their early knowledge to hearing their parents and grandparents discuss the family's investments. Incidentally, the vast majority of the money managers

surveyed came from middle-income families. So involve the youngsters in your life in family money discussions.

Allowances can be a valuable teaching tool. The weekly allowance can be a powerful tool in teaching children about the importance of developing sound spending and saving habits. As well, it can
teach them to distinguish between "needs" and "wants"—something
that many adults are not particularly adept at. One way to impart
lasting money lessons (at least we hope they'll be lasting) is to divide
the weekly allowance into three equal parts:

1. **Spend as you wish.** The child can spend one-third of the allowance on anything he or she wishes. This helps your daughter or
   son understand that total income is always much greater than the
   amount that may be spent. The remaining money must be put
   aside for later. Also, the amount that can be spent immediately
   must last a whole week (an eternity for most kids). If the child
   chooses to spend it all within ten minutes of receiving the allowance, so be it. She'll have to wait another week unless she chooses
   to tap into her short-term savings.

2. **Short-term savings.** The second part of the allowance is put
   into a short-term savings fund that is kept handy. The purpose
   of this fund is to gradually save up for something "big" that the
   child wants and couldn't otherwise afford with the weekly allowance. Once the child catches on, you'll probably see the
   short-term savings account mounting up in anticipation of some
   large purchase. This helps the child learn about the importance
   of setting money aside for future use, just as adults must do to
   pay for large expenditures—either expected or unexpected—
   without wreaking havoc on the family finances. It also helps
   Junior realize that you have to be patient and wait awhile to
   accumulate sufficient money to afford the good (i.e., expensive)
   things in life. Hopefully, your child won't become a wisenheimer

like my youngest, who insists that she has no money to contribute toward a nontrivial purchase because she's "saving for retirement."

3. **Long-term savings.** The final third of the weekly allowance should be earmarked for long-term savings. Therefore, it should be invested in some type of account that lets the youngster see that money set aside for a long time will grow in value. Parents and grandparents of young children might consider a "parental savings bank" that provides a higher rate of interest than banks so the kids can bear more rapid witness to the miracle of compounding to grow their dollars. An investment account that could be invested in stocks and mutual funds might be opened for older children to help them really begin to learn about investing. Stocks and mutual funds will also help youngsters learn about risk because, once they start following their investments in the newspaper, they will learn a crucial lesson that every successful long-term investor must learn: all worthwhile long-term investments will periodically decline in value, but over the long term, gains should handily outweigh losses. Savings accounts and U.S. savings bonds simply don't impart that lesson, since they never lose value (and, as a result, barely keep up with inflation).

MYTH DEBUNKER: "YOU SAVE MONEY WHEN YOU BUY SOMETHING ON SALE"

A lot of people think that one way to save money is to buy something on sale. But it's impossible, as the following example illustrates. A coat has a retail price of $120, but Wally Wastrel buys it on sale for $100. Wally thinks he saved $20 on the purchase. But he saved nothing. Instead, he spent $100. You can go broke saving money by buying stuff that's on sale.

Don't overindulge your youngsters. Sadly, many children reach adulthood with such appalling financial habits that their only hope is to receive a fat inheritance. Parents used to have no problem teaching their children about financial limits because most didn't have a whole lot of money to spend on them in the first place. But we've become a more affluent society, so many of us have more money and "things" than our parents did. Even if we don't have more than our parents, there's an insidious financial malaise permeating our society that causes many parents to indulge their children financially beyond their ability to comfortably do so. If you don't believe me, take a look at the expensive cars parked in the local high school's student parking lot. Whether you can afford to or not, bestowing many and expensive material goods on a child will stack the odds in favor of that child's becoming a financially irresponsible adult. You set limits on other aspects of a child's life. Set financial limits as well. Sometimes, the best financial advice you can give to a rapacious child is: "We can't afford it." Here's the incentive: imagine how much better your retirement will be if you don't have to provide financial support to your financially inept adult children.

Give an IRA to a child. Giving an IRA to a child or other younger-generation family member is an excellent way to show the importance of saving for retirement even though it's way off in the future. The rules for establishing IRAs, even for minors, are pretty easy. Most mutual funds and stock brokerage companies will permit custodial IRAs for minors. **w w w**

Set a good example for the youngsters in your life. It's not easy raising children. Never has been. But it seems to be harder now than it was for earlier generations. One of my former professors once observed, "Just keeping our kids from suffering grievous injury is a sign of parental success." While there are far more important child-rearing responsibilities, the one I'd like to proffer is to strive to set a good *financial* example for the children in your life. This includes being prudent in the way you spend, save, and invest money.

SUCCESS STORY: GETTING RELIGION AT FORTY-FIVE

When they married twenty years ago, the wife knew that marrying a minister involved, as she politely describes it, "certain financial challenges." She goes on to say, "Having two kids in the first three years of marriage didn't do a lot for the family finances." But now that both kids will soon be in college and having mastered the art of being a minister's wife, she thinks it's time to start earning some money so they can afford something nice every once in a while and also begin to save for the future. "While we'll eventually be receiving a pension from the church, it'll barely be enough to get by on. Also, we'll lose the free housing we now get." Despite her initial concern about having been out of the workforce for two *decades,* she soon found a job as a fund-raising assistant at a nonprofit organization. "It doesn't pay a lot right now, but it could lead to more income in the future. And even with the small salary, I'm able to contribute to the 403(b) plan and we can both contribute to IRAs for the first time. Best of all, there's enough left over to actually be able to afford a summer vacation with the kids. Compared to where we were a few years ago, we're downright affluent!"

Paying for College and Staying on Track for Retirement: An Impossible Dream?

As if preparing for retirement isn't challenge enough, many baby boomers are also confronted with the additional burden of paying college tuitions for their progeny, and, for those mature boomers who birthed babies in their twenties, helping pay for their college-age grandchildren. Yikes. While their popularity has diminished somewhat, 529 plans, also called qualified tuition plans, are still the vehicle of choice for investing college savings because their tax advantages surpass those of any alternatives. One exception is if your young scholar is very near college age, in which case setting up a 529 plan may not be worth the hassle. The waning interest in 529s is the result of some unsavory publicity surrounding high fees and self-serving sales tactics among some of the financial planners who sell these plans. But the offending states and firms are cleaning up their acts and lowering their expenses to boot. **w w w**

Should you set up a 529 plan in the first place? Don't put any money into a 529 plan, or any other college savings account, until you have contributed sufficiently to all available retirement savings plans, including IRAs. Of course, it's almost impossible for anyone to contribute to the maximum, given the high limits available in most plans, but even so, contribute as much as you can to these plans each year because, as I mentioned earlier, it's a "use it or lose it" proposition. Every year you forgo making the largest retirement-plan contributions you can afford is a year you can't make up in the future.

College is a frightfully expensive proposition. But families manage the challenge. Sure, Betty Baccalaureate may be saddled with some student loans, but, hey, that may provide Betty with an added incentive to find a job. On the other hand, some people are coming up short when retirement comes around. Saving for retirement is simply too important to stop to fund college savings plans. If money is tight in the old homestead, but your parents are flush, perhaps they could do the heavy lifting by funding a plan themselves for their grandchildren.

Moving a custodial account into a 529 plan. If you or your parents have set up custodial accounts for the young Einsteins, consider transferring that money into a 529 plan, which offers more tax advantages.

You first have to sell all of the custodial account investments because the 529s will only accept cash. This could trigger a tax on the sale of the custodial account investments, but it's not likely to be much. You should probably check with the 529 plan administrator and/or your tax person to make sure everything is done properly. Incidentally, similar transfers from Coverdell Education Savings Accounts into 529 plans can also be arranged. **w w w**

Choosing the right plan. Every state offers at least one plan, and your own state's plan may—or may not—be the best choice. If you deign to put money into a 529 plan, here are some tips for selecting the right one:

- ✦ If your own state plan offers tax breaks (about half do), opt for this plan unless the expenses are high or the performance is lackluster.

- ✦ Whether your home state offers tax incentives or not, compare expenses and performance of your own state plan against the plans of other states.

- ✦ If you're comfortable making your own decision, select a 529 plan on your own; if not, ask an investment adviser for help.

Managing the account. Unless you're really into actively managing all of your investment accounts, opt for the "age-based" 529 plan alternative. The age-based option will automatically rejigger the investment mix as the young scholar gets ever-nearer college age. In short, the younger the child, the higher the percentage of money in the plan that will be invested in stock. As the child nears college age, the percentage devoted to stock will gradually be reduced, which makes a lot of sense because the last thing you want is to lose a lot of money from a stock market tumble just before those damned tuition bills have to be paid.

TIPS FOR BOOMERS WHO ALREADY INVEST IN 529 PLANS

- **Consider more than one state plan.** If you're socking away quite a bit of money, it may pay to have a second manager for the money. Just as you probably don't invest all of your money with a single mutual fund company, by selecting a second state plan, you have the benefit of another group of managers looking out for your college money.
- **Move the money to another 529 plan if the one you're in is a stinker.** While most of the state plans are reasonably good performers, you may sour on your plan. If so, the regulations allow you to, in effect, roll over the money to a new state plan without tax penalty, so long as you do so no more frequently than once a year.

College scholarships: success is the reward for the diligent. Students and their parents must not only meet the challenge of gaining admission to college, but most must also grapple with daunting financial-aid applications to help pay the ever-increasing costs of a college education. (Costs at many colleges are now rising at *twice* the rate of inflation.) One way to help meet those costs is to exhaustively review all possible sources of scholarships. Private scholarships (i.e., those offered by nonacademic organizations) for academic, athletic, and leadership achievement are common. Parents and students should also consider any military, company, union, trade, civic, religious, or ethnic affiliations they have that could lead to other sources of funds. Particularly diligent families have been able to cobble together several small scholarships, $500 here and $1,000 there, to reduce the cost of college. Every little bit helps, and many scholarships are not granted for lack of qualified candidates, or, more likely, for lack of any applicants since no one knew of the scholarship. Your child doesn't have to excel at something to win a scholarship. Thousands are available for young people who have just about any interest or ambition.

When you begin to search for scholarships, take a two-pronged approach:

1. **Look first for scholarships in your community.** Civic groups, businesses, and churches often have small scholarships for townies.

2. **Research scholarships nationwide.** There are seemingly several trillion scholarships available nationwide, but the Internet can help you manage the search.

A caveat. A plethora of scholarship search companies have popped up that purport to search for scholarships for a small or not-so-small fee. While these services may be legit, some aren't, and scholarship experts say that these services offer no more service than you could obtain by doing a little digging on a free Web site. **w w w**

Helping Your Parents as They Age

Thanks to delayed child rearing and lengthening life expectancies, baby boomers will become particularly aware of the meaning of *sandwich generation*—adults with both dependent children and dependent parents. All of our parents say, "We don't want to be a burden on you." Well, chances are, they will be. While most of us won't have to provide financial support, as your parents age, they are likely to become more and more dependent on their children, close relatives, or acquaintances to help them manage the inevitable challenges of senior citizens.

Financial Challenges of Aging Parents

Here are four particularly important matters to attend to as your parents age:

✦ **Housing.** I wish they would pass a law in this country that would require anyone who reaches age sixty-five to discuss with their family members various later-life housing options. And by *housing options,* I mean, of course, the possibility of having to go into an assisted-living facility or, perish the thought, a nursing home. Because if it's not discussed before the decision has to be made, you can pretty much be assured what the response of your mother or father will be: "Shoot me rather than put me in a nursing home." This is unfair. It sends the child on a permanent guilt trip when, if these matters had been discussed earlier, the possibility of having to go into a nursing home could have been discussed more rationally.

✦ **Insurance.** Make sure your parents keep and maintain the right kind and amount of insurance. A lot of seniors are either victimized by unscrupulous insurance agents or they go out on their own and buy narrowly defined coverage (cancer insurance, for example) that's a waste of money.

✦ **Health care.** A lot of seniors are reluctant to ask for the health care that they deserve and are entitled to. Sometimes a younger-generation family member will have to intervene to make sure that the senior is receiving appropriate health care.

✦ **Day-to-day money concerns.** Finally, be alert for money problems. A sudden change in spending habits, late filing of tax returns, late payment of bills, may indicate that a senior is simply unable to maintain his or her day-to-day finances. It doesn't necessarily mean that a parent is having trouble making ends meet, but the assistance of a child or other family members is probably necessary. Also, seniors are all too often the victims of scam artists. They are easy marks and are often too embarrassed to complain to anyone. If you're a child, relative, or close friend of a senior, encourage him or her to check with you before making any major expenditure. Whether it's an investment, a driveway paving job, or whatever, encourage the parent or other family member to get your independent opinion. Perhaps you should suggest the "$500 rule," which has well served the extended Pond family. If the parents are going to spend more than $500 on anything, they first check with one of the kids. This has helped our family avoid several problems.

If your parents live quite a distance away, most cities have agencies to meet the basic needs of the elderly, from home health care to companionship and escort services. **w w w**

REQUEST DUPLICATE INVESTMENT STATEMENTS FOR THE SENIORS IN YOUR LIFE

If you've got a parent or other older-generation family member who isn't paying much attention to his or her investments, you should ask the relative to request duplicate copies of the investment statements to be sent to you, even if they use an adviser, so you can monitor what's going on.

Can You Count on an Inheritance?

The statistics are mouthwatering. Over the next twenty years, baby boomers will inherit trillions of dollars. But before you step up your spending and curtail your retirement-plan contributions, you need to consider how much wampum, if any, you can reasonably anticipate. This whole discussion may seem mawkish, because it is. After all, by definition, the passage of an inheritance requires the passage of a family member from this world. So a sad event results in a happy event in the form of a financial windfall.

A tremendous amount of wealth will be passed down over the next couple of decades, but as in most matters financial in a capitalistic society, the distribution will be uneven. Those who already have a lot of money will probably receive the majority of the wealth, while those in most need of a boost will receive little or nothing. But most of us are in between, and taking a possible inheritance into consideration is an exercise in uncertainty. A lot of us in the immense middle may be surprised or chagrined.

The prudent course. Perhaps the prudent thing to do in your planning is assume you'll receive no inheritance unless your parents are loaded, penurious, or, ideally—from the standpoint of inheritance maximization—both loaded and penurious. Even then, the inheritance you receive could be a fraction of what you (or your parents) currently think you'll inherit.

My Inheritance Expectancy Estimator

❏ Whopping ($1,000,000+)

❏ Commodious ($250,000 to $1,000,000)

❏ Middling ($75,000 to $250,000)

❏ Scanty ($25,000 to $75,000)

❏ Naught ($10,000 to $25,000)

❏ Not even enough to pay for the funeral (evidence of exquisite planning) (<$10,000)

Your inheritance expectancies can move down the above list. Uninsured nursing home or home-care costs or just plain medical expenses can quickly dissipate even a fairly comfortable estate.

What will you do with an inheritance? Don't be surprised if you feel dissonant about an inheritance. After all, a loved one has died and you would like to be a responsible steward of your parents' or other relative's sacrifice and generosity. What would they want you to do with the money? The best way to minimize these inevitable feelings is to discuss this important matter while your parents or other benefactors are still alive.

ARE YOUR PARENTS INVESTING THEIR AGE?

Here's a common dilemma that many retirees, perhaps including your parents, aren't even aware that they should be considering. Affluent retirees might not realize it, but they may well be investing not only for themselves, but also for their children, grandchildren, nieces, or nephews—including you. If so, the way such a person should invest may be quite different from the somewhat more conservative guidelines that are often recommended to retirees. Consider, for example, a couple that has two adult children, four grandchildren, and a sizable investment portfolio in addition to their pensions and Social Security. Whom are they investing their money for? The appropriate answer in this and many other situations may be: for three generations. Therefore, they shouldn't be investing all of their money as if it were all going to be used by the eldest family members. One approach your parents want to take if they're in this fortunate situation is to divide their total investments into two portfolios. The first would be invested to meet the parents' anticipated needs, while the second would be the portfolio earmarked for younger generations. While this may be a delicate matter to bring up with your parents, it's nonetheless important for the entire family that they give some consideration to who will ultimately be receiving their money and what the best way is to invest that money for the intended recipients.

Controlling a Car Addiction

I fully realize that, in our culture, cars assume almost godlike qualities. A fancy car supposedly bestows upon its driver respect in the community. I've never been high on cars. I've yet to understand why Americans have such a love affair with their mobile phallic symbols. They're expensive to purchase and maintain, and while you're pouring money into car payments and repairs, the darn thing is depreciating in value, which violates a basic tenet of sound financing: "Never borrow to buy a depreciating asset."

My cars embarrass my children. They prefer to be dropped off a block away from school so that their classmates won't see the car. My neighbors apparently aren't pleased with our cars, either. Shortly after we moved into our house, I found a piece of paper on my windshield one morning that said, "Your car violates this neighborhood's standards of good taste." Too bad you feel that way, neighbors. It's because I didn't waste money on cars that I can afford to live in your neighborhood.

> **Question:** What's the quickest way to lose $2,000?
>   A. Bet $2,000 on a horse that finishes out of the money.
>   B. Drive a new car off the dealer's lot.
>
> **Answer:** B. You've lost $2,000 in seconds. (It takes longer—over a minute—for your nag to finish out of the money.)

The rich are different. It's perfectly natural to want to own an expensive set of wheels. "If only I had Warren Buffett's money, then I could own the car of my dreams." So what does someone who has Warren Buffett's money (i.e., Warren Buffett) drive? A 2001 Lincoln, according to *Forbes* magazine.* Software multibillionaires Bill Gates and Paul Allen prefer Porsches. Gates has a 1999 and 1988,

---

* Update: According to the latest news reports, Mr. Buffett bought a *new* Cadillac to show his support for General Motors. He paid cash.

Allen a 1988. Another tech billionaire, Steve Ballmer, isn't quite so flamboyant with his 1998 Lincoln. Retailing titans aren't any more exciting in their car choices. Jim Walton of Wal-Mart fame seems to favor late-model cars, specifically a 2002 Dodge, while Ingvar Kamprad, the founder of Ikea, owns a 1993 Volvo. So the next time you look askance at some loser driving a not-so-nifty car, it might be a billionaire who doesn't feel compelled to display his or her wealth.

While it's hard to persuade people to break long-held habits, hope springs eternal, so I'm going to present two analyses that compare the costs of car ownership, starting with a comparison of what it costs to operate. That will be followed by a strategy for getting out from under car loans (or car leases, which are worse) once and for all. Then, mercifully for some of you, I'll drop the subject. **w w w**

BAD NEWS FOR LATE-MODEL CAR LOVERS

The National Highway Traffic Safety Administration came out with a report that will refute an oft-cited reason that late-model car lovers use to justify their expensive addiction, to wit: cars last longer. How many times have you heard someone say something to the effect of: "I trade cars every x years"—where x is a number equal to four or less—"because after x years cars become undependable." Here's a summary of the government study:

- In 1977, half the cars on the road survived until they were ten and a half years old with an expected useful life of 107,000 miles.
- By 1990, half the cars put into service stayed on the road for twelve and a half years with an expected useful life of 127,000 miles.

- Using 2001 data, the government agency found that 50 percent of cars lasted thirteen years, and drivers could expect a useful life of 152,000 miles.

The Costs of Owning a Car

In addition to the cost of the beast itself, how long you keep the car and whether you finance it strongly influences the total cost of ownership. Table 11.1 compares the cost of car ownership for a typical car under three scenarios for a car driven 12,000 miles per annum. *Viva la différence!* While a few thousand dollars a year may not seem like a lot, it will add up to a lot over the decades, particularly during your retirement years.

TABLE 11.1
COMPARISON OF ANNUAL CAR-OWNERSHIP COSTS

	TRADE EVERY 4 YEARS	TRADE EVERY 10 YEARS	BUY 4-YEAR-OLD CAR AND TRADE AFTER 4 YEARS
Pay cash	$8,640	$6,600	$4,320
Finance over 4 years	$9,600	$7,080	$4,800

Dr. Jonathan's Car Loan Addiction Elixir

One part of your retirement planning should be to get into the habit of paying cash for your cars if you have heretofore been borrowing incessantly for them. This will lower your car-ownership costs both during your remaining working years and throughout your retirement.

Indeed, paying cash for cars can work wonders on your retirement nest egg. If you want to get into that wonderful habit, please see "Dr. Jonathan's Car Loan Addiction Elixir" on the *You Can Do It!* Web site. **w w w**

Your Best Investment Is Your Career

With all my prattling on about money matters, please don't lose sight of your best source of future financial security: your career. Keeping up-to-date in your field, striving to advance, and, if necessary, changing careers will provide you with the wherewithal to achieve your financial dreams on your own terms. Strong career skills will also enhance your chances of being able to retire gradually, if that is your intention (see page 172).

What's unique about baby boomers' attitudes toward work and career. A sizable portion of baby boomers expect to make career changes or start their own businesses before finally retiring. According to a recent AARP poll, over three-quarters intend to work beyond normal retirement age, which would reverse a decades-old trend toward earlier retirement. But baby boomers will likely cut their own swath when it comes to deciding when and under what terms they will retire. Here's a look at what's unique about the baby boom generation compared to younger and older generations:

✦ Boomers are assertive and have always competed intensely among themselves and other generations for career advancement.

✦ The work ethic is alive and well. Unlike any other generation, boomers define themselves through their careers.

✦ Personal relationships at work are important, as is the feeling of being part of a team.

✦ Because of downsizings and streamlinings, boomers have often experienced career disruptions and job changes. As a result, they often bring varied and valued experiences to the workplace.

It's no wonder, therefore, that you are called the TGIM generation—"Thank God It's Monday." No wonder employers are beginning to fear the time—and it's not too far off—when boomers will be leaving the workplace.

Honing your skills. Your career can provide a return greater than any financial investment you will ever make, including increased lifetime income and protection from unemployment, not to mention the psychic income that comes from a satisfying work life. In the words of Confucius, "If you enjoy what you do, you'll never work another day in your life."

Career success requires careful planning, consistent performance, and keeping up with knowledge advances in your chosen field. Investing in your career includes:

✦ Possessing the skills necessary for peak performance.

✦ Developing ideas to help you and your employer work more effectively and efficiently.

✦ Keeping up-to-date with the developments in your area of expertise.

✦ Cultivating networks within and outside your workplace to enhance your marketability.

✦ Approaching your work with a level of enthusiasm and flexibility that will set you apart from your coworkers.

✦ Taking risks, whether it's accepting a new and difficult challenge at work or changing careers. Important job and career moves are always anxiety-provoking, however.

✦ Having both long-term goals to keep your career aspirations in sight and short-term goals to sustain your enthusiasm and cope with the inevitable setbacks.

CHAPTER 12

For Richer or for Poorer, but Never for Lunch: What Are You Gonna Do When You Retire?

Money aside, retirement can be a time of abundant enjoyment or considerable misery. Psychologists who look at such matters say that adequate planning well in advance of retirement can make a big difference in how well you adjust to your new status. You can retire with tons of money, but what good is it if you don't know what you're going to do to make you happy? Have you thought about what you will do the day after you retire? You may know people who retired without having a clue as to how they were going to manage their time. It was almost as if they'd given up at the get-go, passing their time before the grim reaper paid a visit. How sad. **w w w**

Thinking about retirement? Only one out of ten retirees devote any serious time to planning what they're going to do when they retire. Just as during your working years, retirement is a balancing act—keeping yourself busy while maintaining enough flexibility to do new and interesting things when they arise. Most important, baby boomers will seek activities that are both satisfying and meaningful. For baby boomers, retirement will be less a transition into old age and more of a continuation of middle-age life. I plead guilty to a lack of adequate planning, but I've still got some time. I do often dream of retirement, but only in the context of every night being a Friday night and every day a Saturday. I still need to do a lot of planning. How about you?

PAIGE'S SAGE ADVICE FOR THOSE WHO ABHOR THE IDEA OF GETTING OLDER

Here's a wonderful observation from Leroy Robert "Satchel" Paige (Negro League and Hall of Fame pitcher): "Age is a question of mind over matter. If you don't mind, it doesn't matter."

This will not be your grandparents' retirement. Your primary frame of reference as to retiree lifestyle may be your parents or grandparents. Don't rely on what they did or are now doing during retirement as an example of what you'll be doing. Baby boomers will forge a new definition of retirement. The notion of a life of leisure is being replaced by a search for meaning and fulfillment. Golf, bridge, and early-bird dinners are being replaced by exotic travel, active volunteerism, and gourmet cooking.

What a difference a few generations make. A couple of generations ago, planning for a long retirement wasn't a big issue. In 1940, American life expectancy was sixty-four, so those who made it to retirement suffered from poor health or exhaustion from a lifetime of what was typically hard, physical labor. Today, only one in four pre-retirees and retirees think that retirement is a time to take it easy and enjoy leisure activities. But just keeping busy won't be enough for baby boomers. They will also insist on having a meaningful retirement, which may encompass part-time work. While the majority want to do so for psychic reasons, the financial benefits of gradually retiring through part-time work can be substantial, as explained on page 172.

Don't delay. If you're a boomer of relatively tender years, you may think that getting your financial act together supersedes any thoughts of what you'll actually do after you retire. If you've paid attention to the media reports, you've probably concluded that you'll be so impoverished during retirement that your primary activity will be dumpster diving. Hopefully, you have come to understand that any connection between the predictions of those media doomsayers and reality is purely coincidental. You should start thinking about these things in your fifties, at the latest. Give some activities a dry run during your working years. Just as you are well advised to spend considerable time vacationing in an area where you might want to retire (see chapter 9), you should also try out activities of interest. For example, if you want to learn to play golf, why wait until you retire? Get lessons now so you can experience both the occasional exhilaration of a good drive or putt as well as the constant frustration of failing to string a few good shots together on the same hole. Early planning is essential. It's not enough to put these decisions off until you actually retire. The experts on these matters say that those who count on developing new interests and social relationships after they retire often don't.

Active boomer years = an active retirement. The skills, knowledge, and self-discipline you have acquired during your working years will help you perform a variety of activities during retirement, even if some of them are brand-new and have nothing to do with your job aptitude. The best activities for retirees are those that challenge your mind, such as taking up art, learning a new language, or playing a musical instrument for the first time.

Thinking about a second career or starting a business? Some boomers want to begin a second career or start a business after they "retire." Again, don't wait around dreaming about it during your remaining working years. Learn all you can about your desired vocation and test the waters before your retire, if possible. Then, you will minimize the possibility of disappointment just after you retire if your plans don't pan out. If you want to start your own business, perhaps by turning a hobby or other passion into something remunerative, be realistic about the time and money that will be required. A postretirement business (remember, most new businesses fail) can soon become a money canyon at a time in your life when you can least afford a financial disaster.

Volunteer activities. Volunteerism is going to be particularly popular with retired boomers. Heaven knows our society benefits mightily from volunteers! Volunteering for some cause you believe in can provide immense satisfaction. Knowing that you are doing good things that are needed and appreciated can give your retired life far more meaning. You can choose work that makes you comfortable or work that is as challenging as anything you've ever undertaken. Plus, you can augment or replace the friendships you gained at work with those you'll make as part of your volunteer activities—with people who share your interests. But as with other planned retirement adventures, it pays to plan in advance.

> ## SUCCESS STORY: OCTOGENARIAN REVELS IN KIDDY MATH
>
> This is a success story of a retiree who stumbled upon a fulfilling volunteer opportunity. "I was enjoying an active retirement, but never as active as it became when I was in my midseventies. I was picking up my granddaughter from her grammar school one day and mentioned to the teacher that I was pretty good in math and would gladly spend some time with any students who needed extra math help. To say the teacher was delighted is an understatement. For almost ten years I have been working at that school and a second in the inner city, with small groups of kids, and it's the most gratifying work—it really isn't work—I've ever done!"

Managing the Transition to Retirement

The transition from work to retirement has never been a cakewalk, and it's likely to be even more difficult for boomers, particularly those who identify heavily with their careers. Your work is a source of intellectual stimulation, gives you purpose and self-esteem, and provides structure to your time. Here are a couple of tips to ease the transition:

◆ **Seek the advice of retirees.** Speak with acquaintances and relatives who are already retired about their experiences—both positive and negative—making the transition. Unhappy retirees fall into two camps: those who haven't really found anything that's stimulating, and those who are so busy that they don't have any flexibility in their schedules.

◆ **Involve your spouse or partner.** This really needs to be a collaborative effort, beginning many years before retirement. Important decisions need to be made about when you're going

TABLE 12.1
YOUR RETIREMENT GOALS

Baby boomers expect to do great things when they retire, just as they did during their working years. Goals were important during your childhood, they remain important throughout your working years, and they are just as important when you retire. What do you want to accomplish when you're retired? Use this space to begin recording the great and more mundane goals you will have once you're retired.

1. _____
2. _____
3. _____
4. _____
5. _____
6. _____
7. _____
8. _____
9. _____
10. _____

to retire (see chapter 7) and where you're going to retire (see chapter 9). What are your travel plans? How much time do you expect to spend together? Recognize that the private time you both enjoyed when one or both of you were working will be infringed. It's wise to assume that some degree of marital conflict and dissatisfaction will arise after you retire and will subside as you both adjust to your new status and relationship.

Special advisory for boomer workaholics. If you are heavily tied to your work (be honest, now), retirement will be a major challenge.

You need to be especially diligent in planning what you're going to do after you retire.

Developing a Social Portfolio

When you retire, you'll have an investment portfolio, but what about a social portfolio? A social portfolio consists of a diversity of activities and relationships that will have you looking forward to every day. Be sure some of your endeavors stretch your mind. New hobbies, taking up a new language, anything that keeps your mind active, will slow down your mental aging.

World-renowned psychiatrist and aging specialist Gene D. Cohen, author of *The Mature Mind,* encourages baby boomers who are planning for retirement to develop a social portfolio that's similar to the financial portfolio that tends to predominate in retirement thinking. The financial portfolio involves three major concepts that influence its growth and development: (1) assets to draw upon, with emphasis on diversification; (2) insurance as a backup should disability or other loss occur; (3) the importance of starting early and building over time.

The social portfolio is designed with the same three concepts in mind.

1. **Diversification.** Your assets are the diversified interests and relationships that you can develop and draw upon.

2. **Insurance backup.** This is addressed by focusing on individual versus group activities and high energy/mobility versus low energy/mobility activities. It is important to prepare for later life by balancing individual with group activities and high mobility/energy activities (that require significant physical exertion) with low mobility/energy activities.

    If and when your health declines, not all the interests you have developed should require high energy or high mobility.

Similarly, if you lose a spouse, partner, or friend, you should have interests that do not require the involvement of another.

3. **Starting early.** The earlier you start (even before retirement) developing your social portfolio, the better able you will be to thrive during retirement. However, it is never too late to start or revise your social portfolio.

TABLE 12.2
"WHAT ARE YOU GONNA DO?" ACTIVITY PLANNER

Use this work sheet to plan your retirement activities. It's never too early to start planning. This will be ongoing, so don't feel compelled to fill up your week. Take a few minutes to write down the things you expect to be actively involved in. Be as specific as you can as to how you'll implement your various activities, particularly if you're fairly near retirement. If you have any difficulty coming up with a plan, Table 12.3 has an example from someone whom I hope is near and dear to you.

ACTIVITY   **HOURS PER WEEK**

SOLO ACTIVITIES

_____   _____

_____   _____

_____   _____

_____   _____

GROUP ACTIVITIES

_____   _____

_____   _____

_____   _____

_____   _____

Total planned hours per week   _____

TABLE 12.3
SAMPLE OF JONATHAN'S RETIREMENT ACTIVITY PLANS

ACTIVITY	HOURS PER WEEK
Golf (joint activity with wife)	12
Aerobics and strength training	6
Volunteering in adult literacy program	6
Resisting the temptation to tell our daughters how to live their lives	4
Studying the investment markets	8
Learning to play the steel drum	10
Marriage counseling because of steel drum obsession	1
Applied enology*	8
Total planned hours per week (so far)	55

* Wine consumption

TABLE 12.4
TRAVEL WISH LIST

Retired baby boomers are expected to be big travelers, and if you have a modicum of wanderlust, use the space below to describe your dream destinations. Don't hold back.

DESTINATIONS I'D LIKE TO VISIT	TRIP HIGHLIGHTS
_____	_____
_____	_____
_____	_____
_____	_____
_____	_____

The goals of the social portfolio are to enhance individual mastery and interpersonal growth, while balancing grief with enduring relationships. The social portfolio is a way of helping people develop new strengths and satisfactions throughout retirement, even in the face of loss.

CHAPTER 13

Retire Rich and Die Destitute: What's Different about Your Investing and Financial Planning When You Retire?

I f your financial life is pretty much on track when you retire, contrary to popular opinion there isn't a whole lot you need to do differently. But some of the areas where changes might be called for are important, and that's the subject of this chapter.

Unfortunately, the financial services industry hasn't paid much attention to the financial needs of retirees. But that is changing as the industry begins to realize how much wealth will move from the ranks of the working class to the leisure class as you and the other 77 million baby boomers retire. In fact, the big mutual fund companies, brokerage firms, and banks are scared to death of losing your business. That's a good thing, because at last retirees will get the kind of attention and good deals they've always deserved. Baby boomers lead the way yet again!

"Retired" planning. The need to plan, monitor, and revise your personal finances doesn't end at retirement, even if you retire with not one scintilla of financial concern.

✦ **Investing.** Investing wisely goes without saying. This requires a balancing act between investing for income for such annoying things as paying your bills, and investing for growth to keep up with inflation over the decades, because those pesky bills are only going to increase in the future.

✦ **Withdrawing from your nest egg.** Deciding how much can sensibly be withdrawn from investments at retirement strikes fear in almost everyone planning for retirement. The amount withdrawn in the first few years of retirement sets the course for the rest of a retiree's life.

✦ **Considering a reverse mortgage.** Reverse mortgages may come in handy later on in retirement for those who have a bundle of their money tied up in home equity, but that's a decision that's usually best made later, rather than sooner.

✦ **Taxing matters.** Retirees are often surprised and chagrined about the magnitude of their income taxes. But retirees can use some straightforward strategies to reduce income taxes.

✦ **Health insurance.** If you think navigating the health insurance system is complicated enough already, are you in for a surprise when you retire.

✦ **Life insurance.** Retirement is a good time to revisit any life insurance you may hold, because your needs often change once you retire.

✦ **Estate planning.** The estate-planning documents that were prepared during your working years—you have prepared them, haven't you?—should stand you in good stead, but in some circumstances they may need to be revisited.

You'll find a retiree checklist at the end of this chapter to remind you of important matters to attend to when you retire at last.

Risks Aplenty for Retirees

Despite the good news about the financial health of the baby boomer generation, most have some trepidation about the whole idea of retiring. Perhaps that's why so many boomers don't even know when they'll retire; all they know is that they want to work indefinitely. Some measure of apprehension is to be expected. After all, once you're retired, you're pretty much stuck with whatever your financial circumstances might be. There's something frightening about that prospect. Just think of the threats to one's postretirement financial security. Forewarned is forearmed, so at the risk of scaring the daylights out of you, Table 13.1 presents a rather comprehensive list of the myriad risks in retirement and how to protect against them.

Investing When You're Retired

It's natural to think that you'll need to make a lot of changes in your investments once you retire. After all, you're leaving what is called, in investment parlance, your "accumulation" phase and are entering your "withdrawal" phase. Not so fast. You'll find from your retirement income and expense projections that you're probably going to continue adding to your retirement investments until you're eighty or so, to keep up with rising living costs in later life. Life expectancies are so long these days that it's no longer sufficient to just keep your principal intact. You need to add back some of your investment gains so that you can withdraw ever greater amounts in the future as your cost of living rises. Therefore, one of the most important decisions made at retirement is the percentage of your retirement money that you can prudently withdraw in your first year of retirement. This is discussed on page 290.

TABLE 13.1
POSTRETIREMENT RISKS

Retirees, like working-age people, face a lot of financial risks. But unlike the younger generations, retirees don't enjoy the luxury of having years, if not decades, to make up for financial setbacks. So it's important to review the various risks that retirees may need to confront as well as ways to protect against these risks. The following is a list of possible risks as well as a brief description of ways to cover each.

RISK	COVERING THE RISK
Longevity: outliving retirement resources	Social Security, pensions, annuities; adjusting spending so that money will last longer
Death of a spouse	Life insurance; annuity benefits for surviving spouse; proper estate planning
Inflation	Social Security; investment allocation; investing for growth
Interest rate risk*	Income annuities; owning bonds of varying maturities
Stock market risk	Diversification within and outside stocks
Business risk (i.e., business failure)	Pension Benefit Guaranty insurance, state insurance funds; avoiding too much employer stock in company savings plans
Employment risk	Ability to retire gradually; honing career skills

(continued)

TABLE 13.1 (CONTINUED)

RISK	COVERING THE RISK
Public policy risk (higher taxes, reductions in entitlements)	Roth IRAs, municipal bonds
Unexpected health care needs and costs	Medicare, Medigap, Medicare Drug Plan, HMOs
Loss of ability to live independently	Long-term-care insurance, continuing-care communities, Medicaid
Changes in housing needs	Adequate resources, continuing-care communities
Change in marital status	Laws provide for splits in event of divorce; pre- and postnuptial agreements
Unforeseen needs of family members	Adequate retirement planning to provide for these needs
Lack of available facilities or caregivers	Advance research to discover locales with adequate facilities
Incapacity	Durable powers of attorney; access to caregivers

* The possibility that the price of a bond or bond fund will decline because of a rise in interest rates.

The days of "living off interest and dividends" are past. Way back, it used to be possible to live quite well in retirement solely from dividends and interest. Back then interest rates were higher in relation to inflation, as were dividend payouts. Moreover, inflation was benign and retirees weren't living as long as they are now. Short of having an enormous retirement nest egg, you simply can't earn enough interest and dividends to pay your bills. Attempting to do so may lead a retiree to prefer risky high-yield bonds and stocks that offer big dividends but limited appreciation potential such as real estate investment trusts, utilities, and preferred stocks. Such a strategy could work for a few years but risks leaving you short later on.

Retiree investing no-no's. If you think you don't have a lot of time to make up for investment bloopers during your working years, imagine how you'd feel if your money didn't go anywhere when you're retired or, worse, you suffered big losses. Here's a reminder list of four common investment snafus that plague retired investors:

⬇ **No-no number 1—investing too conservatively.** The fear of losing money impels many retirees to invest too conservatively, emphasizing low-yield, short-term securities such as CDs and money market funds. But investing this way has its own risks. Low yields will just as surely erode long-term cash flow as the failure of a zirconium limited partnership. Investing too conservatively always risks the loss of purchasing power, because the return on these "safe" investments can rarely keep abreast of inflation.

⬇ **No-no number 2—chasing high-interest investments.** This is common, especially when interest rates are declining or are quite low. Rita Retiree was doing well with her 7 percent CDs, but when they came up for renewal and the bank was only offering 4 percent because of a decline in overall interest rates, she started looking for something that paid 7 percent, not realizing this investment maxim: the higher the interest, the higher the risk. Faced with declining investment income, many retired investors unknowingly take on increased risk to gain more income. Invading principal is anathema to many retirees. But if a retiree's nest egg is well diversified among stocks, bonds, and temporary investments, invading principal is not a concern so long as the overall value of the nest egg continues to grow in the early years of retirement. Of course, unfriendly investment markets may cause the nest egg to decline periodically. But so long as the longer-term trend is upward, no problema.

⬇ **No-no number 3—succumbing to spurious investment ideas.** The airwaves are infested with people touting their latest investment products or ideas. They're awfully slick to boot. Retirees should be particularly wary of any investment product that they don't fully understand. My long-standing guideline is: if it can't be satisfactorily explained to you in one sentence, don't buy it. Even if someone from a respected company recommends an investment on a respectable TV or radio station, proceed with caution. These touts often have a hidden agenda that is not in your best interests.

⬇ **No-no number 4—holding on to investments for sentimental reasons.** Some retirees refuse to sell consistently awful investments out of feelings of loyalty or emotional attachment. Often it's something that was inherited, or it might be a sizable holding in a former employer's stock. But there is only one reason to own an investment: it has an attractive long-term return. The retiree should consider the financial impact of holding investments with no discernible potential. If a retiree is holding on to a large block of stock for sentimental reasons, couldn't he or she be just as sentimental holding only one share?

So how should you invest? There's usually not much to change in the way you invest when you retire. That may seem a bit odd, and it is often violated by persons nearing retirement age. Retirees often think they need to reduce the riskiness of their investments. After all, they're no longer adding to their investments to make up for *losses*. Also, retirees think, quite appropriately, that they're going to need income from their investments to help meet living expenses. But investing during retirement requires balancing the dual goals of income and investment growth. After all, a typical retiree will need income to last for thirty years or more. So the most important consideration is how long you're going to need your money to last. That's called your investment horizon. Think about it. Your investment horizon on your first day of retirement is only one day less than it was the last day you worked. So in most instances, if you are already well diversified before retirement, major shifts in your investments should not be necessary. Chapter 3 contains all manner of information on investment diversification, for working baby boomers and, when the time comes, retired baby boomers.

A case study that illustrates fine-tuning diversification and holdings can be found on the special reader Web site. **w w w**

CONSIDER A CHARITABLE GIFT ANNUITY TO PROVIDE REGULAR RETIREMENT INCOME

Income is important for retirees, of course, and one way to earn a lifetime income for those of us who are charitably inclined is to consider a charitable gift annuity. As good as simply writing out a check to a worthy charity feels, other ways of giving to charity provide even more benefits to the donor than a tax deduction. In one common arrangement, known as a charitable gift annuity, you'll receive a partial charitable income-tax deduction, and the gift may reduce estate taxes. Also, if you donate appreciated securities—stocks that don't pay dividends, perhaps—you won't have to pay capital gains taxes on them. Finally, and best of all, you receive a lifetime income. The income rate is the annual percentage paid out based on the value of the cash or securities originally put into the charitable gift annuity. For example, Philipa Philanthropist, age sixty, contributed $100,000 to her local symphony's charitable gift annuity. She will receive an income of 5.7 percent of her $100,000 impartation, or $5,700, each year for the rest of her life. Here is an example of the approximate percentages of income that these gifts provide for a single donor (rates are subject to change), based on the age when the donation is made. Gift annuities can also be made over joint lives, which usually results in a slightly reduced income rate.

AGE OF DONOR	LIFETIME INCOME RATE
55	5.5%
60	5.7
65	6.0
70	6.5

Not bad, particularly for money languishing in savings accounts or in stocks that pay little or no dividends. Charitable gift annuities typically require a donation of at least $10,000, but they are an excellent way for the charitably inclined to boost their income. You can also arrange with your favorite charity to make the contribution now (and receive a charitable deduction), but defer collecting the income until a later date, presumably when you retire. By doing so, you'll boost your income considerably over the amounts indicated above. (See page 110.)

The ideal investment for retirement. As noted above, the ideal retirement investment provides both rising income, to help you pay your always rising living expenses, and growth of investment capital, so you'll have sufficient money to keep up with inflation over a retirement that is likely to span decades. The only two mainstream investments that provide both growth and rising income are income-producing real estate, which can provide rising rental income and appreciation in property value, and stocks of companies that have a tradition of regularly raising their dividends (or mutual funds that invest in such companies). This is not to say that bonds have no role in a retiree's portfolio, but arguably equal or greater emphasis should be placed on growth investments. While the notion of being a land-lord may be anathema, if you harbor even a scintilla of interest in real estate investing, you'll find some ideas beginning on page 362. Investing in companies that regularly raise their dividends is certainly an easier way to enjoy both growth of capital and rising income, and Table 13.2 shows the dividend records of some well-known companies.

SUCCESS STORY: INCREASING RETIREMENT INCOME BY DOING NOTHING

"We retired almost ten years ago, and my husband and I decided that we were going to be too busy in retirement to worry about our money. That may not be the best strategy, but that was what we did. We put half in U.S. Treasuries and half in blue-chip stocks that paid dividends. A decade ago, the interest income, combined with Social Security, was just enough to support us. It's interesting to see where we stand right now. We reinvested the Treasuries as they matured, but at a lower rate of interest. On the other hand, the dividends on our stocks have actually increased by almost 50 percent, which has helped close the gap. But the best news is that our stocks have more than doubled in value, so we've been able to make up for our income shortfall by selling a bit of the stocks. Overall, our plan has worked quite well."

TABLE 13.2
COMPANIES THAT PAY RISING DIVIDENDS

For retirees who would like to enjoy *rising* income, here is a sampling of companies that have consistently raised their dividends (no promises for the future, though).

	GE	COCA-COLA	MERCK	PROCTER & GAMBLE	JOHNSON & JOHNSON
1996	.32	.50	.71	.40	.37
1997	.36	.56	.85	.45	.43
1998	.42	.60	.95	.51	.49
1999	.49	.64	1.10	.57	.55
2000	.57	.68	1.21	.64	.62
2001	.64	.72	1.37	.70	.70
2002	.72	.80	1.41	.76	.80
2003	.76	.88	1.45	.82	.92
2004	.80	1.00	1.49	.93	1.10
2005	.88	1.09	1.52	1.03	1.23
1996–2005 increase in dividends	175%	118%	114%	158%	232%

Timing the purchase of income annuities. If you are planning on investing some of your retirement money in income annuities, doing so at retirement might not be the best course of action. See page 149 for more ideas on timing the purchase of income annuities.

How Long Will Your Money Last?

Front and center on the retiree worry list is the hellish decision about how much can prudently be withdrawn from the nest egg without having to worry about losing ground to inflation or, worse, running out of money. This financial decision is difficult to undo, short of having to sharply curtail your living expenses in late life. Once you establish a pattern over the first couple of years of retirement, you'll pretty much have to live with it, so you'll want to pay close attention to your intended withdrawal rate.

Table 13.3 can help you estimate how long your money will last based on the percentage of your money you will withdraw and the estimated percentage annual investment return. The table factors in 3% annual increases in money withdrawn to account for rising living costs.

When you get around to running your own retirement-withdrawal projections, keep in mind that there are a plethora of ways to determine prudent withdrawal rates, and many come up with first-year withdrawal rates considerably lower than these. What's most important is to run your own projections using an approach you (and/or your adviser) are comfortable with.

Whatever methodology you use, the investment returns you earn make a huge difference in the amount of income you can spend throughout your retirement, as illustrated on page 98. Check out the *You Can Do It!* Web site for resources and case studies dealing with the important matter of deciding how much you can prudently withdraw from your retirement nest egg. ⚙ ⚙ ⚙

Which Investments Should Be Drawn Down?

Retirees who are concerned about maintaining a sensible withdrawal rate—that's about 98.6 percent of them—might find the following approach of interest. It's based on a typical retirement portfolio consisting of:

✦ **Temporary investments** in a sufficient amount to fund a year or two of retirement spending. This allows you to keep some money very safe, although the retiree may want to draw against bonds or stocks to meet current spending needs, as described below.

✦ **Bonds and bond funds** of varying (laddered) maturities, primarily for income.

✦ **Stocks and stock funds** diversified across the major investment categories, primarily for growth.

Source of withdrawal depending on market conditions. Since the income earned from dividends and interest is probably insufficient to meet spending needs, a retiree is forced to sell some investments to

TABLE 13.3
HOW MANY YEARS YOUR MONEY WILL LAST

WITHDRAWAL	RATE OF RETURN											
	1%	2%	3%	4%	5%	6%	7%	8%	9%	10%	11%	12%
12%	7	8	8	8	8	9	9	10	10	11	12	13
11	8	8	9	9	9	10	10	11	12	13	14	15
10	9	9	10	10	10	11	12	13	14	15	17	19
9	10	10	11	11	12	13	14	15	16	18	21	26
8	11	11	12	13	14	15	16	18	20	24	30	*
7	12	13	14	15	16	18	20	22	27	36	*	*
6	14	15	16	18	19	22	25	31	44	*	*	√
5	17	18	20	22	24	29	36	*	*	*	√	√
4	20	22	25	28	33	42	*	*	*	√	√	√
3	25	28	33	39	*	*	*	*	√	√	√	√
2	35	40	50	*	*	*	*	√	√	√	√	√
1	*	*	*	*	*	*	√	√	√	√	√	√

Note: This table assumes that you'll increase the amount you withdraw after the first year by 3 percent per year to account for inflation.

* — Money will never be exhausted

√ — Original investment will never be reduced

Source: Deena Katz, Evensky and Katz, Coral Gables, FL

fill the gap. Which ones, though? Rather than simply randomly selling off a stock, bond, or mutual fund; or selling stocks and bonds pro rata; or ridding yourself of a lousy-performing stock, bond, or mutual fund, here are the decision rules:

1. **If the stock market has risen, liquidate stocks.** This forces you to "sell high," after the stock market has risen, which is exactly what successful investors have done forever.

2. **If the stock market is down, liquidate bonds.** While the temptation to sell stocks after they've declined can be extreme, retirees should give the stocks time to regain value. Otherwise, they're reducing investments with growth potential at the worst time.

3. **In years when investment returns are low or negative, try to reduce the amount withdrawn.** This is tough to do and may not be possible. But if a retiree fears running out of money because of poor investment performance, a temporary midcourse spending reduction can reduce the possibility.

See page 296 for some guidelines on deciding whether to withdraw money from your retirement accounts or from nonretirement accounts.

When Might a Reverse Mortgage Make Sense?

Many baby boomers, particularly those who reside in or near urban areas on the east and west coasts, have accumulated substantial equity in their homes. It's natural, particularly for those whose home equity exceeds their retirement savings, to be attracted to using that home equity to provide retirement income. Chapter 8 provides abundant (and, in the not-so-humble opinion of your author, thought-provoking) ideas on what to do with the family villa, but it purposely left out a discussion of reverse mortgages because those who are not yet retired should almost never consider them as part of their retirement projections. Too many things can happen in retirement to justify a reverse mortgage during the initial years of retirement. But a reverse mortgage may come in handy later on.

Options for receiving payments. The reverse mortgage industry is still evolving. Currently, there are five common ways to tap into home equity with a reverse mortgage.

1. **Tenure.** Equal monthly payments as long as at least one borrower lives and continues to occupy the property as a principal residence. This is usually the most prudent alternative. If you need a reverse mortgage to help pay bills and those bills will continue for the rest of your life, you should opt for lifetime payments.

2. **Term.** Equal monthly payments for a fixed period of months. Attractive because the monthly payments are higher than with a lifetime benefit, but dangerous unless your needs for the extra money are absolutely, positively temporary (for example, if you fully intend to sell the house at the end of the term).

3. **Line of credit.** Unscheduled payments or in installments, at times and amounts of the borrower's choosing until the line of credit is exhausted. Sounds great. It's like a home equity credit line that you never have to make payments on. But only the most financially disciplined retirees should take the risk of a credit line, because if the credit line is exhausted, the only feasible way to get access to additional home equity, if any, is to sell the house and pay off the reverse mortgage obligation— perhaps at an age when a move would be highly disruptive.

4. **Modified tenure.** Combination of line of credit with monthly payment for as long as the borrower remains in the home. This

option results in a lower monthly payment than a straight lifetime-payment reverse mortgage, but could be preferable in unusual situations where monthly income requirements can be met with a lower payment and the line of credit can be used for financial emergencies.

5. **Modified.** Combination of line of credit with monthly payments for a fixed period of months selected by the borrower. This combination is only appropriate when the borrower knows that the need for additional monthly income is temporary.

When reverse mortgages make sense. In your author's opinion, reverse mortgages are best considered a "late-life trump card" for veteran retirees, say in their eighties, who are intent on staying in their home for the duration, but could use a boost in income. Certainly they can work well in other situations, but the permanence of a reverse mortgage should not be taken lightly. Too many things can happen during a long retirement, and the equity in your home is like an insurance policy. Tapping into a reverse mortgage is like cashing in a life insurance policy. Furthermore, would-be reverse mortgagors are chagrined at the rather paltry payouts from a reverse mortgage, as illustrated in Table 13.4. After all, the mortgage company holds the reins and wants to profit from the deal even if you live into the twenty-second century.

Three additional points. First, if a reverse mortgage is in your future, timing the transaction can help, because the lower interest rates are at the time you take it out, the higher the payment(s) you will receive. Second, as with any other financial product, be sure to shop around for the best reverse mortgage deal. Finally, be particularly wary of anyone who encourages you (or your parents) to take out a reverse mortgage to purchase an investment product, such as an annuity. Those who pull this charade should be pilloried.

TABLE 13.4
REVERSE MORTGAGES—LESS THAN MEETS THE EYE?

Income or lump-sum payments based on a $200,000 home owned free and clear (payouts will change depending on interest rates):

AGE*	MONTHLY INCOME	LUMP-SUM PAYMENT
65	$600	$ 99,000
75	810	120,000
85	1,240	142,000

*Age of younger home occupant

Income Taxes

The last thing you want to do when you're retired is pay more income taxes than you have to. In the words of noted jurist Learned Hand, "There is nothing sinister (or illegal) about rearranging your affairs to make your taxes as low as possible." But a lot of retirees don't heed that advice. That's unfortunate, because minimizing income taxes is quite easy, and you don't have to be a tax guru to make tax-smart decisions.

Timing is everything. Here's a straightforward strategy that could save you many thousands of dollars in unnecessary income taxes during the important early years of retirement. In fact, this strategy is so simple, it can be explained in a mere ten words.

✦ **Withdraw already-taxed money first.**

✦ **Withdraw retirement account money last.**

Example. Tad and Tara Taxsavvy just retired and are trying to figure out the best way to withdraw the $40,000 that they estimate they'll need for living expenses over their first year of retirement. They have $650,000 in retirement accounts and $350,000 in brokerage accounts and CDs. They first asked their lifelong friends Ollie and Olivia Overpayer for advice, since the Overpayers had retired several years earlier. Ollie said, "This is a no-brainer. You should take all of your retirement money out of your retirement accounts. That's what they're for—retirement." But Tad and Tara put pencil to paper and came up with this analysis:

	SOURCE OF RETIREMENT MONEY	
	IRA ACCOUNT	MATURING CDS
Amount of withdrawal	$53,000	$40,000
Subtract income taxes		
(25% on retirement accounts)	–13,000	0
Amount available for		
living expenses	$40,000	$40,000

Here's how Tara explains it: "Ollie's right. This is indeed a no-brainer decision, but he's got it backward. Since withdrawals from retirement plans are taxed, in our tax bracket we'd have to withdraw $53,000 from our IRA accounts and then pay out a whopping $13,000 in income taxes, leaving us with the $40,000 we need. On the other hand, since our CDs aren't in a retirement account, we can take $40,000 from them and not owe any taxes. Even if we withdrew money from our brokerage account investments, we'd only have to pay a small capital gains tax on the stocks in the account. So we're going to fund our first few years of retirement out of our already taxed money, leaving the IRAs alone so that they can continue to grow tax-free until we have to begin making minimum distributions at age 70½."

Roth IRA conversions. Many people whose incomes were over the limit for a Roth IRA conversion during their working years may qualify once they're retired and their income declines. A Roth conversion may be attractive for both tax planning and estate planning. The downside of a Roth IRA conversion is that you have to pay federal income taxes on the conversion amount. But the upside is that all of the money you convert to a Roth, plus future gains in the account, can eventually be withdrawn free of federal income taxes. So when you're in your sixties or even your seventies, it's still not necessarily too late to do a Roth conversion, so long as you're confident you won't need to withdraw the money for at least a decade. Then, you'll be able to enjoy tax-free income later in life. See page 74 for more information on Roth IRA conversions.

Retiree Health Insurance

Adequate health insurance is doubly important for retirees. Actually, it's four times as important, because retiree health care costs are quadruple what they are for those in the workforce. Here's what's needed:

✦ **Medicare.** Medicare, which is available to virtually everyone who's age sixty-five or over, is the foundation of a retiree health care plan, but it doesn't cover anywhere near every medical cost. A word to the wise: if you plan to live or travel outside the United States when you are retired, with only a few exceptions Medicare will not cover health care costs incurred in foreign duchies.

✦ **Medicare drug coverage.** The Medicare Drug-Benefit plan can help reduce pharmaceutical costs, particularly for those with titanic drug bills.

✦ **Medicare gap.** Medigap policies, as they're called, fill in many of the gaps that Medicare doesn't cover. The ten standard Medigap policies each offer certain basic benefits.

The following sections will help you make sound decisions regarding two thorny retiree health insurance decisions—maintaining coverage if you retire before age sixty-five and choosing a Medicare Drug-Benefit plan.

Health Insurance Checklist for Early Retirees

If you retire before Medicare kicks in, obtaining health insurance during the interim is crucial. If your employer will cover you until you're Medicare-eligible, that's marvelous. Skip this checklist. But if not, this checklist will help you organize the search for the right coverage at the right price.

❑ Find out how much health insurance will cost between the time you retire and age sixty-five, when you become eligible for Medicare. Note that baby boomers will qualify for Medicare before they qualify for full Social Security retirement benefits.

❑ If you have health problems, health insurance coverage may be more expensive, if it is available at all.

❑ If cost is a problem, but you can afford to self-insure a portion of your coverage or raise the deductible and copayments to lower the premium, investigate the options. This may be particularly effective if you enjoy good health.

Plan on investing some time to find the best coverage at a reasonable price. Here are some suggestions, in order of priority:

❑ Continue coverage through your employer. Most employers are required under COBRA regulations to allow you to continue coverage for up to eighteen months, so long as you pay for the coverage, plus an administrative cost of no more than 2 percent. This is often your best choice, particularly if you have already left the company and need coverage quickly. If you'll reach Medicare age before the eighteen months are up, all the better.

❑ Absent coverage from your employer, check with any professional associations that you either belong to or could join if they offer group coverage to their members.

❑ Contact your insurance agent or other agents in your vicinity about obtaining health insurance.

❑ If you're thinking about setting yourself up in business, you may be able to join an association that offers group coverage. For example, by joining the local chamber of commerce you may qualify for health insurance.

❑ Check with local, state, and federal agencies about programs that provide coverage.

❑ Short-term health insurance policies are commonly available. A year's worth of coverage is commonly offered, although the policy limits and exclusions aren't the best, especially if you have a preexisting condition.

Whatever the outcome of your search, make sure any coverage you're thinking about using offers the scope you need.

Soon-to-be-Retiree Homework Assignment: Evaluating Medicare Drug-Benefit Plan Options

The Medicare Drug-Benefit plan initially caused considerable confusion and angst among Medicare beneficiaries, who were saddled with a complex array of choices. By the time you retire, the decision making will be a lot easier. As you approach age sixty-five, however, it will behoove you to do a little advance homework to make sure you choose the plan that best meets your current and future pharmaceutical needs. Here are some tips:

✦ **Compare the various plan offerings.** Don't rely solely on a plan that someone may be trying to sell you. Check with www.medicare.gov to compare current plan offerings.

✦ **Consider the drugs you currently use.** Plans vary both in the array of drugs they cover and the copayment for each drug. The plan may also impose quantity limits. So it's crucial to evaluate available plans against drugs you're currently taking.

✦ **Consider the big unknown: future drug needs.** Many Medicare recipients, particularly those with minimal drug needs and who enjoy good health, are forgoing participation in a Drug-Benefit plan. But this may be shortsighted, as one of the most important features of the plans is that they offer "catastrophic coverage" should later health complications skyrocket your drug costs. You don't want to be one of those unfortunates who are regularly featured in the media whose drug costs are fourteen times their annual income. **w w w**

Life Insurance

Your life insurance needs may change when you retire. Life insurance needs often decrease, but if you've got a lot of dough, you may actually need more life insurance to pay estate taxes (see page 302). Another possible exception to that sweeping statement is if you need to replace any life insurance you had through your employer to support family members who remain dependent on you after you retire. The following Decision Maker delineates some possible exceptions to the commonly held belief that retirees no longer need life insurance. If you are married or partnered, these questions should be answered in the context of each party's life insurance needs.

Retiree Life Insurance Decision Maker

Yes	No	N/A
❑	❑	❑

1. Will a surviving spouse or partner suffer a large decline in income? A small decline is probably okay, because one can live on less income than two. If there is a major decline, life insurance may be necessary, although it can be expensive for retirees.

Yes   No   N/A

❑   ❑   ❑ **2. Is your estate likely to incur estate taxes?** This is unlikely for most retirees. If your attorney (not your insurance agent) thinks that estate taxes loom, an "irrevocable life insurance trust" may provide a tax-advantaged way to pay eventual estate taxes, but life insurance gets expensive when it's taken out by sexagenarians. A better way to avoid said taxes is to whittle the estate down to size through lavish spending and, perhaps, making annual gifts to younger-generation family members who could probably benefit from the beneficence.

❑   ❑   ❑ **3. Is passing on an inheritance important?** Some retirees are anxious to pass on an inheritance to their children or other younger-generation family members. Sometimes this is essential if any heirs are disabled or are having real difficulties succeeding financially.

❑   ❑   ❑ **4. Will your survivors need any extra money to pay for "final expenses"?** These expenses might include your funeral, funeral pyre, costs of catering at a soiree following the funeral, a Mercedes, and bereavement costs, including a three-week South Pacific cruise for thirty-five family members.

If you need to acquire additional life insurance at retirement, particularly if you'll need the coverage indefinitely, rather than over just a few years, you'll almost certainly need cash-value insurance rather than term insurance. While term insurance was inexpensive in your younger years, it can become prohibitively expensive in your later years. Consider sticking with old-fashioned whole-life insurance rather than the newfangled cash-value life policies. (See page 224.)

Employer-provided insurance. Soon-to-be-retirees may have the option of continuing the life insurance coverage provided by their employers. For example, a group life insurance policy may be convertible to an individual policy without having to pass a medical exam. Continuing this coverage may be particularly appropriate for those with health problems.

Estate Planning in Retirement

Retirement is often a good time to ask your attorney to review your will and other estate-planning documents, particularly if it has been a while since anyone has looked at them. Retirement entails financial change, and changes in your estate planning may be necessary to protect your assets for yourself and your heirs.

Major life events. *Major life events* is a euphemism for those often or always unavoidable occurrences that usually require that you revisit your financial planning, such as chronic illness, terminal illness, or the death of a spouse or other family member. Not all major life events are so depressing, though. For example, the arrival of grandchildren (imagine that) may require a revision of your will.

Revisit your appointees. Retirees should also exercise more diligence in appointing those who will take over for them (executors and other fiduciaries) in the event of disability, terminal illness, or death. Your letter of instructions also becomes more important (see page 243). I'm trying to be circumspect here, but the truth is that once you enter the retirement years, you are more likely to need these various estate-planning documents. If you doubt that, peruse the obituary page.

Imminent-Retiree Checklist

Save this checklist until a year or so before you retire. It will serve as a memory jogger of important matters for nascent retirees.

Yes   **No**   **N/A**

❑   ❑   1. Are you keeping close tabs on your income and spending? This is important in the first few years of retirement to ensure that your available resources are sufficient to cover your actual spending.

❑   ❑   2. Are you planning to acquire adequate health insurance coverage, including Medicare supplemental coverage?

❑   ❑   ❑   3. If you are retiring before age sixty-five, will you be able to acquire adequate health insurance until Medicare takes effect?

❑   ❑   4. Are your investments well positioned to meet your retirement income needs as well as provide future growth of principal?

❑   ❑   ❑   5. If you qualify and can afford the up-front taxes, are you considering converting some or all of your traditional IRAs into a Roth IRA?

❑   ❑   ❑   6. Are withdrawals from your investment accounts being made with an eye toward minimizing income taxes? (See page 106.)

❑   ❑   ❑   7. Have you reviewed your life insurance coverage to determine if it can be decreased or needs to be increased?

❑   ❑   8. Are your estate-planning documents, typically including a will, power of attorney, and advance directive, up-to-date?

❑   ❑   9. Do you have an up-to-date and readily accessible letter of instructions that reflects your new status as a retiree?

CHAPTER 14

Countdown to a Great Retirement

Wherever you are on the boomer age spectrum—from your early forties to your early sixties—***You Can Do It!*** will help you prepare for a great retirement throughout your working years. As questions arise in your financial life, check out your guide for answers and strategies. ***You Can Do It!*** will be your reliable source of helpful guidance—an indispensable "second opinion" to counter the plethora of biased, self-serving, and just plain dopey financial ideas that are so prevalent today. This is truly a guide for all your boomer years.

The special reader Web site will always be up-to-date with the latest investment ideas and all-star mutual fund recommendations as well as the best ways to take advantage of future changes in the income-tax rules (which are only going to get better for both workers and retirees). Please visit the site often.

Baby Boomers on the Hot Seat?

Most of us are enjoying a pretty good life, but retirement looms. As I mentioned at the outset, however, judging from the news headlines, we're headed for the poorhouse. You could become discouraged by all of the studies and reports that seem to draw the same conclusion: baby boomers are going to pay a heavy price for their profligacy. But the reality is quite the contrary. Across almost all income levels, baby boomers are better prepared for retirement than any previous generation. In fact, boomers are far better prepared than their parents were at the same age.

A report by the Congressional Budget Office (CBO) concludes that the situation is far from dire:

> *Some studies have compared boomers' finances with those of preceding generations; others compare them with the official poverty level. Those studies conclude that, on the whole, boomers will almost certainly be better off in retirement than their parents and will be much less likely to live in poverty.*

Baby boomers have benefited greatly from productivity growth, rising real (inflation-adjusted) wages, and the increasing participation of women in the labor force. Although the benefits of prosperity have been distributed unevenly, boomers generally have higher per-capita income than their parents did at the same age, are preparing for retirement at largely the same pace as their parents, but have accumulated more wealth.

Don't be discouraged by the relentless media reports that portray you and your fellow baby boomers as apathetic profligates who are on a one-way trip to retirement penury. It's not so, but it has led too many people to avoid looking at their own situations or, worse, to give up any hope of ever achieving financial security.

The Big Four

I trust you have found many ideas on these pages that you can put to work to help you achieve your retirement dreams. Some are so obvious that I haven't insulted your intelligence by devoting much space exhorting you to, for example, save more and borrow less. But there are some less-than-axiomatic topics that can have a major impact on just how well ensconced you will be for retirement. Here are my top four:

1. **Diversification is essential.** Most investors understand the importance of diversification, but few pay more than scant attention to it (nor do many of their advisers). Diversification prevents the big investment losses that can erase years, if not decades, of hard-earned retirement savings.

2. **Select the best investments.** Devoting a few hours each year to making sure each of your retirement and brokerage accounts contains the best possible investments that you can own will add significantly to your retirement coinage. Baby boomers don't like to be average, so why settle for average investment results?

3. **Make the most of your home.** The typical baby boomer is sitting on, or more accurately living in, an asset that has greatly appreciated in value and will likely continue to appreciate smartly. It may be or become your biggest asset—one that has grand potential as a retirement resource. Those who can pay off their mortgages by the time they retire or soon thereafter will enjoy a much reduced budget. Others may want to consider downsizing, an alternative that is likely to be very popular with boomers desirous of both a more manageable living arrangement and a more abundant retirement lifestyle.

4. **Decide when and where you want to retire.** Baby boomers will enjoy as many opportunities in retirement as they did

during their working years, including the luxury of deciding when and where to retire. Each of these decisions has important financial implications, so they should be considered well in advance of retirement. The typical boomer isn't enamored of the idea of retiring early or even at age sixty-five. Delaying retirement will increase retirement income, often significantly, as will relocating to a lower-cost area of the country—or overseas.

Don't forget to visit regularly the *You Can Do It!* special reader Web site for checklists that will help you identify particularly important things to keep in mind as you continue to plan for retirement, no matter if you're a young or veteran boomer.

w w w

WILL WASHINGTON MESS UP YOUR RETIREMENT PLANS?

I was born and grew up in the Washington suburbs at the height of the nuclear scare, the old "duck and cover" days at Bethesda Elementary School. The specter of the enemy dropping an atomic bomb on Washington was a big concern. But my father reassured me that a nuclear bomb would never obliterate Washington. "Why?" I asked. "Because it would end all the confusion," he replied. There's more wisdom in that remark than that needed to allay the fears of a little boy. Our political system, for better and for worse, is designed to move slowly.

The current political scene in Washington is a piece of work, isn't it? To listen to the rhetoric, Social Security is going bankrupt and Medicare is far worse off than Social Security. There's talk about hiking taxes, and some doomsayers are even suggesting that tax breaks for retirement savers should be curtailed. You can lose sleep over these dire predictions or, worse, alter your financial life based on what some people think might happen in Washington. For example, some people aren't contributing to Roth IRAs because they think Congress will vote to tax Roth distributions. It's still fashionable to say, "I'm not planning on receiving any Social Security because they're going to do away with it." These people should get real. My exhortation is to assume that government regulations affecting our financial lives will continue pretty much on the same path as they always have.

So don't fear that Washington is going to mess up your planning. With respect to pocketbook issues in particular, our Washington solons aren't going to impair your retirement. If anything, they're going to make it better for the 77 million boomer voters who are becoming concerned about such things. **w w w**

BE HAPPY WITH WHAT YOU'VE GOT

As important as it is, there is far too much preoccupation with money these days. Baby boomers are accused of leading the pack in obsessing over money. Instead, boomers should be thinking of ways to do better with what they have. Too many people think they'd be happier with a fancier car, an imported kitchen, or a larger house. But if you can be happy with what you've got, you'll find it a lot easier to achieve financial security. That doesn't mean you should be so content that you don't aspire to do better in your career, earn more money, and increase your investment returns. After all, "rich is better." But life is a series of choices, and as long as you think you're deprived of things, you're going to want to acquire more things. More things won't make you happier, but more things could put a dent in your financial future. Think back to when you were growing up. Your parents were pretty happy with what they had, and they probably had a lot less than you do now. So be happy with what you've got.

TABLE 14.1
MY RETIREMENT-PLANNING TO-DO LIST

The preceding chapters have discussed a wide-ranging array of money matters, and if you're like the vast majority of boomers, you have checked off a lot of "Need to Do" boxes in the above checklists. It's easy to feel overwhelmed. But you don't need to do everything right away. Certainly, some matters, such as diversifying your investments, obtaining needed insurance, or preparing a will, have more urgency than others. The following to-do list will help you identify the most important financial and investment areas that need your attention. Then, one by one, over the next year or so, you can put yourself squarely on the road to a great retirement.

Done

1. _____ ❏
2. _____ ❏
3. _____ ❏
4. _____ ❏
5. _____ ❏
6. _____ ❏
7. _____ ❏
8. _____ ❏
9. _____ ❏
10. _____ ❏
11. _____ ❏
12. _____ ❏

Go forth and (let your money) multiply. You and your fellow baby boomers have so much to look forward to. You are becoming the standard-bearers for a new future, both in the workplace and, within just a few years as boomers begin to retire, in completely redefining what it means to be retired. I hope the ideas in this guide, along with my updates on the special reader Web site described on page xix, will help you achieve all of your retirement dreams, while enjoying a more prosperous and fulfilling life during the rest of your working years. Good luck. You *can* do it!

Budgeting for People Who Hate Budgets

I hope that you will consider preparing a budget. If you're more likely to complete these budget work sheets if they're available on the Internet, I strive to please. You can find them on the *You Can Do It!* special reader Web site. **w w w**

At this stage in your life, budgets can help you in two important areas:

1. **You can monitor your current spending patterns to identify areas in which to reduce expenses.** If you're already saving 25 percent of your income, you probably don't need to budget, but if you could stand to boost your savings a mite, a budget will help you find out where you might be able to cut back. Speaking of saving 25 percent, according to an extensive research study into the health and money habits of centenarians and their offspring, centenarians, their children, and their grandchildren all had savings rates of about 25 percent, in recognition of their need for lifelong income.

   While 25 percent may be a pipe dream, budgets *can* help

you increase your savings. There's a good chance that whatever your occupation, you're subject to some sort of budget. Why people don't budget their own spending has always confounded me, but I'm also a realist.

2. **You can begin to estimate how much you'll spend when you're retired.** This is something you should periodically be doing, even if you're still twenty years from retirement. Of course, if retirement is just a few years off, you should sharpen the pencil and take a pretty hard look at your expected retirement budget.

The work sheets that follow will ease the chore of preparing either or both budgets. I grant that doing so is about as exciting as taking a household inventory, but you'll be glad you did. If you'd prefer to get a quick-and-dirty look at how much your retirement expenses are likely to be, see page 14.

SUCCESS STORY: THE FUDGE FACTOR

"This may sound simple, but the best thing we ever did when we were planning for retirement was build in a 'fudge factor' of extra expenses that we could not anticipate. My wife figured this out. She was a budget officer for the military, so she was well versed in making sure budgets were beefed up for the inevitable overruns. She insisted that we add 20 percent to our budget, which included everything we knew we'd spend in our first year of retirement. Sure enough, at the beginning of the second year, when I was about to suggest ways to spend the extra money that we had left over from our first retirement year, the air-conditioning system went, I needed major dental work, and our son got into a bit of a financial bind. None of these had been anticipated, but as my wife said, 'They can't be precisely anticipated, but they are inevitable.'"

BUDGET WORK SHEET 1
ANNUAL BUDGET PLANNER

This work sheet allows you to summarize your current income and expenses to identify areas to reduce your spending. It can also identify areas where you can spend more if you think you're not spending enough—an almost unheard-of occurrence among baby boomers, but, hey, this is the land of opportunity, after all. Here's an explanation of the expense categories:

- **Fixed expenses.** Expenses that you have little control over without making some major changes in your finances, including mortgage or rent, utilities, and medical insurance.
- **Semidiscretionary expenses.** Budget items that cannot be totally eliminated but can be controlled to some extent, such as food, clothing, and transportation.
- **Discretionary expenses.** Optional expenses that can be eliminated altogether if necessary, including entertainment and gifts.

INCOME	CURRENT LEVEL	PLANNED INCREASE (DECREASE)	BUDGETED LEVEL
Gross salary	$ _____	$ _____	$_____
Interest	_____	_____	_____
Dividends	_____	_____	_____
Bonuses/ profit sharing	_____	_____	_____
Alimony/child support received	_____	_____	_____
Distributions from partnerships	_____	_____	_____
Income from outside businesses	_____	_____	_____

Trust
   distributions   _____   _____   _____

Pension   _____   _____   _____

Social Security   _____   _____   _____

Gifts   _____   _____   _____

Proceeds from sale
   of investments   _____   _____   _____

Other:

• _____   _____   _____   _____

• _____   _____   _____   _____

• _____   _____   _____   _____

I. Total income $ _____ $ _____ $_____

FIXED EXPENSES

Income taxes,
   Social Security
   taxes $ _____ $ _____ $_____

Rent/mortgage   _____   _____   _____

Home heating   _____   _____   _____

Electricity   _____   _____   _____

Natural gas   _____   _____   _____

Water   _____   _____   _____

Garbage
   collection   _____   _____   _____

Telephone   _____   _____   _____

Loan payments   _____   _____   _____

Tuition payments   _____   _____   _____

Property taxes   _____   _____   _____

Auto insurance   _____   _____   _____

Medical/dental
   insurance   _____   _____   _____

Savings and retire-
   ment contributions   _____   _____   _____

Other:_____   _____   _____   _____

**2. Total fixed
   expenses** $ _____ $_____ $_____

SEMIDISCRETIONARY AND DISCRETIONARY EXPENSES

Food, alcohol,
   tobacco $ _____ $_____ $_____

Household
   maintenance   _____   _____   _____

Furnishings,
   equipment   _____   _____   _____

Clothing   _____   _____   _____

Transportation   _____   _____   _____

Medicine,
   medical/dental care _____   _____   _____

Personal care,
   grooming   _____   _____   _____

Education   _____   _____   _____

Recreation   _____   _____   _____

Contributions,
   donations   _____   _____   _____

Gifts   _____   _____   _____

Laundry,
   dry cleaning   _____   _____   _____

**3. Total semidiscretionary and discretionary
   expenses** $ _____ $_____ $_____

**4. Big-ticket items,
   from Line 8 of
   Work Sheet 3** $ _____ $_____ $_____

**5. Excess (shortfall) of income over expenses
   (Line 1 minus lines**

   2, 3, and 4) $ ════════ $ ════════ $════════

BUDGET WORK SHEET 2
RETIREMENT LIVING EXPENSE BUDGET PLANNER

This work sheet can be used to help you estimate how much it's going to cost you to live at the time you retire. First, put your current living expenses in the left column. Second, estimate what your living expenses would be (in today's dollars) if you retired tomorrow and enter those amounts in the next column. Most expense items are likely to stay the same, but some may decline and some may increase.

	CURRENT LEVEL	**ESTIMATED LEVEL AT RETIREMENT (IN TODAY'S DOLLARS)**
Expenses that may decline or be eliminated when you retire:		
Savings, including retirement-plan contributions	$ _____	$ _____
Mortgage	_____	_____
Loan and credit card payments	_____	_____
Clothing	_____	_____
Transportation	_____	_____
Professional and business expenses	_____	_____
Child care	_____	_____
Alimony and child support payments	_____	_____
Tuition and education	_____	_____
Life insurance	_____	_____
FICA tax withholding	_____	_____

Expenses that may rise when you retire:

Medicine and medical/dental

   care   _____   _____

Health and longterm-care

   insurance   _____   _____

Recreation and travel   _____   _____

Hobbies   _____   _____

Expenses that are likely to stay the same when you're retired:

Rent   _____   _____

Utilities   _____   _____

Food   _____   _____

Personal care, grooming   _____   _____

Property taxes   _____   _____

Property and liability insurance _____   _____

Household furniture and

   equipment   _____   _____

Home maintenance   _____   _____

Contributions and gifts   _____   _____

Income taxes   _____   _____

Other: _____   _____   _____

Other: _____   _____   _____

Big-ticket items, from line 8 on Work Sheet 3:
   _____   _____

Total living expenses

   before taxes   _____   _____

Add income taxes   _____   _____

Total living expenses   \$ _____   \$ _____

BUDGET WORK SHEET 3
BUDGETING FOR BIG-TICKET ITEMS

The budget busters listed on Work Sheet 4 are bad enough, but big-ticket items that come along less frequently than every year can be budget killers. Prudent budgeters will anticipate these and build them into their monthly or annual budgets.

	ESTIMATED TOTAL EXPENSES OVER NEXT TEN YEARS	ESTIMATED TOTAL EXPENSES OVER FIRST TEN YEARS OF RETIREMENT
1. Home improvements	$ _____	$ _____
2. Major home maintenance	_____	_____
3. Cars	_____	_____
4. Relocation expenses	_____	_____
5. Extensive travel	_____	_____
6. Other:		
_____	_____	_____
_____	_____	_____
_____	_____	_____
7. Total big-ticket-item expenses	$ _____ /10	$ _____ /10
Divide above total by ten		
8. Estimated annual big-ticket expenses	$ _____	$ _____

Transfer the total to the appropriate line on
Budget Work Sheet 1: Annual Budget Planner

Transfer the total to the appropriate line on
Budget Work Sheet 2: Retirement Living Expense Budget Planner

BUDGET WORK SHEET 4
BUDGETING FOR BUDGET BUSTERS

Large bills that come every year, but less frequently than monthly, whether expected or an unpleasant surprise, can easily ruin your budget, not to mention your checking account. The trick is to set aside enough funds each month to meet these bills when they come due. Many people do this—honest. You can use this work sheet to summarize your expected irregular expenses in the left column. Once you do that, divide the number by twelve to give you the average impact of these expenses on the household budget.

While you're at it, you can use the right column to estimate the amount of the various expense items that you'll still be incurring when you're retired. For example, you'll probably still have to pay property taxes, but let's hope the kids' college tuition payments are gone, long gone. Incidentally, don't try to forecast what your inflation-adjusted expenses will be when you're retired. Use current expense levels instead. On the other hand, if you expect to move to a lower-cost locale, come up with an estimate of what the expenses might be. For example, if your property taxes are $5,000 but you expect to retire to a place where the cost of living is 20 percent less, it probably makes sense to lower your property tax estimate by 20 percent to $4,000.

	ESTIMATED CURRENT ANNUAL AMOUNT	ESTIMATED ANNUAL AMOUNT IF RETIRED
1. Property taxes	$_____	$_____
2. Health insurance	_____	_____
3. Home owner's/ renter's insurance	_____	_____
4. Life insurance	_____	_____
5. Other insurance	_____	_____
6. Home maintenance	_____	_____

7 Furniture	_____	_____
8. Seasonal fuel/ electricity	_____	_____
9. Vacation	_____	_____
10. Holidays/gifts	_____	_____
11. Tuition/school expenses	_____	_____
12. Club membership dues	_____	_____
13. Charitable contributions	_____	_____
14. Estimated income taxes	_____	_____
15. Retirement-plan contributions	_____	_____
16. Other:		
_____	_____	_____
_____	_____	_____
_____	_____	_____
Total annual expenses	$ _____	$ _____

Budgeting without the Budget

Did you diligently prepare the above budget work sheets? Probably not. Budgeting can be a useful exercise, but most people have neither the time nor the inclination to prepare a household budget. The purpose of a budget is to motivate you to live beneath your means, that is, to spend less than you earn. Of course, even a well-prepared budget is of no use unless you are prepared to live within its strictures. But another way to spend less than you earn, without going through the drudgery of budgeting, is through an investment or savings account.

✦ **Workplace retirement savings plans.** If your employer offers a retirement savings plan, such as a 401(k) or a 403(b), then by all means start there. If the employer offers a match, all the better, but even if not, contributions to these plans are, in effect, tax-deductible.

✦ **Regular contributions to an IRA account.** After contributions to workplace plans, transferring money into an IRA account (and, if you have income from self-employment, a self-employed retirement plan) is the next priority. The investment company will be happy to hit up your checking account every week or month and put the money into your IRA account. That's a lot easier than trying to come up with a few thousand dollars to fund an IRA contribution all at once.

✦ **Plain old savings.** With your instructions, any bank, credit union, or investment company will happily withdraw some money from your checking account or, if allowable, your paycheck and place it in an investment or savings account. Automatic investing is a great way to both begin and stick with a regular savings program.

I refer to automatic investing (with apologies to General Electric) as "better living through electronics," since the money you're setting aside for the future is electronically transferred from your paycheck or bank account. The money is thereby removed from any financial temptations that might arise. The result is relatively painless budgeting. Since you never get your hands on the money, it shouldn't be missed, particularly if you start small and gradually increase the amount that's transferred. If you put away a meaningful percentage of your gross (not net) income—in the realm of 15 to 20 percent (even more is better)—you may not need to prepare a household budget. But you still should prepare an estimated retirement budget.

Organizing Your Financial and Personal Records

I lied. This appendix isn't entirely about budgets. Amidst the challenges of an active, if not hectic, life, baby boomers tend to overlook the importance of organizing crucial family information, both financial and nonfinancial. Yet, virtually any person (rich, poor, young, old, single, or married) has information that will benefit those they will leave behind—information typically only stored in their heads that can forever be lost at death or incapacity. Organizing family information not only benefits those who have to care for an incapacitated person and those who survive, but it also provides benefits to you in the present by facilitating easy access to crucial records and information. In short, an effective personal record-keeping system saves both time and angst now and in the future. Below is a checklist of important matters to include when organizing your financial and personal life. The *You Can Do It!* Web site includes a variety of resources to help you organize your records and other important information. **w w w**

FAMILY INFORMATION ORGANIZER CHECKLIST

	OK	TO BE DONE	N/A
FAMILY INFORMATION			
- Personal background	❏	❏	
- Details of military service	❏	❏	❏
- Information on children and grandchildren	❏	❏	❏
- Summary of professional advisers	❏	❏	
- Location of important documents	❏	❏	
MEDICAL INFORMATION			
- Summary of medical professionals	❏	❏	
- Family medical history	❏	❏	
PERSONAL POSSESSIONS			
- Inventory of household possessions	❏	❏	
- Inventory of valuables	❏	❏	❏

	OK	TO BE DONE	N/A
- Motor vehicles	❏	❏	❏
- Summary of warranties	❏	❏	❏
- Summary of individuals who assist with home maintenance	❏	❏	❏

EMPLOYMENT AND BUSINESS

	OK	TO BE DONE	N/A
- Employment information	❏	❏	❏
- Company retirement plans	❏	❏	❏
- Other company benefits	❏	❏	❏
- Family business information	❏	❏	❏

FINANCIAL

	OK	TO BE DONE	N/A
- Insurance coverage and policies	❏	❏	
- Banking information	❏	❏	
- Investment holdings	❏	❏	
- Home and other real estate	❏	❏	❏
- Family budget	❏	❏	
- Financial obligations	❏	❏	❏

ESTATE

	OK	TO BE DONE	N/A
- Final wishes	❏	❏	❏
- Funeral and other final arrangements	❏	❏	❏
- Estate documents	❏	❏	
- Special bequests	❏	❏	❏
- Information on care of pets	❏	❏	❏
- Other thoughts and messages for surviving family members	❏	❏	❏

PAY YOUR BILLS ONLINE

Less than one-third of U.S. consumers pay their bills online. I guess many boomers still prefer the monthly drudgery of sorting through bills, filling out checks, and mailing them. Most banks offer free online bill paying, and they will either transfer your payment electronically or generate and mail a paper check. To further reduce your paperwork, you can arrange to receive bills electronically. Unless you've got a lot of spare time, do yourself a favor and begin to pay your bills online. It's also a big help when you get around to budgeting and doing your taxes because a by-product of online bill payment is that your expenses are summarized and can be categorized.

Investing 101

I f you are an inexperienced investor or just feel you need a refresher course, this appendix will help you with the basics and to better understand the suggestions and ideas contained in the three investing chapters, 3, 4, and 5, as well as Appendix III. Investing isn't orthopedic surgery. If you can arm yourself with some basic investing knowledge, you will be able to make better investment decisions and/ or ask better questions of your investment adviser. Investing simply isn't as complicated as most people think. Once you know the basics, it's really not that difficult. If you decide to use someone to advise you on investing, you should still read this section, because the more you understand about investing, the better you will be able to work with your adviser.

What Do You Want Your Money to Do for You?

The first step is to determine what goals you have for your money. Accumulating enough money to retire comfortably is certainly a goal for all working-age people, especially baby boomers. Everyone should be concerned with retirement, even those who are a couple of decades away from it. But your goal may be something more immediate, such as buying a car or taking a vacation, saving for a house or saving for college for the kids. Once you're retired, your financial goals will focus on having enough income to live comfortably and to be able to keep up with inflation.

Take a moment now to summarize your financial goals. I've taken the liberty of including your first goal.

MY FINANCIAL GOALS

To be able to afford to retire in the style to which I have become accustomed.

_____

_____

_____

_____

When Do You Want to Achieve Your Goals?

Now that you've determined your financial goals, you next need to decide how soon you want to reach each of them. If you need money for a goal within three years—to buy a car, for example—consider that a short-term goal. A long-term goal is eight or more years. Consider anything in between as a medium-term goal. Because, as we'll see later, the time when you need your money to meet your goals will be important in making your investment choices.

Typically, we have all three types of goals—short-term, medium-term, and long-term. At different stages of our lives our goals differ, so our strategies for investing will often need to change as we move through life. One of the most important factors in deciding where to invest your money is how soon you are going to need it. For short-term goals, safety is the most important factor; you don't want the value of money you'll soon be spending to drop just before you need it.

For long-term goals, growth is important; your money needs to in-crease in value enough to stay ahead of inflation. Deciding how much of each you need—how much safety and how much growth—is one of the most important parts of deciding how to invest.

A third factor is important to many people: income. Just as you earn a paycheck, your investments can earn money for you that can be spent on day-to-day expenses or reinvested. When you retire, income becomes a more important goal (to pay living expenses), but growth is also important to help you keep up with inflation throughout your re-tirement. Deciding where to put your money means thinking about those three things: safety, growth, and income. When you expect to need a certain part of your savings in just two or three years, you need to keep that money safe. You don't want the value of those savings to go up and down a lot. On the other hand, when your investment goals are long-term, say over eight years away, then you want to focus on some combination. Perhaps you'd want some growth to help build your savings and some income to help balance out the ups and downs of investing for growth.

Three Investor Profiles

To discuss further how growth, income, and safety fit into your in-vesting strategy, consider the three typical hypothetical situations below.

Profile 1: Frank

Age: Forty-three

Status: Single

Income: $40,000

Financial goals: New car; contributing to company retirement plan

Profile 2: Janet

Age: Fifty

Status: Single; one child, age sixteen

Income: $57,000

Financial goals: College tuition for her son; saving for retirement; replacing worn-out car

Profile 3: Earl and Jennifer

Ages: About five years from retirement

Status: Married, empty nesters

Income: $110,000

Financial goal: Retirement

Each of these people has a different set of needs for money, is at a different stage of life, and requires a different approach to investing.

FRANK: Let's start with Frank. Frank's biggest concern is income to buy a new car. Like a lot of people his age, he is primarily focusing on short-term goals.

But what about his investment future? He may want to buy a house in a few years. If so, that would be a medium-term goal. At his age, Frank may not be thinking much about retirement, but he should be. He has a long time for his money to grow for retirement if he starts saving now. Even if it's just a modest amount now, savings can make a big difference in how much he has when he retires.

JANET: Now let's look at Janet. Right now she is primarily thinking about sending her son to college. She also knows that she needs to save for her retirement. At her age, she needs to think of growth for her retirement goals since it's still a long time off. College is another situation. She will probably need a combination of growth and income for her medium-term goal of getting the child through college. She also has some short-term goals, goals that need to be paid for within three years. Her son will be entering college in a couple of years, and she needs to replace her car soon. She'll need to set aside some money for the car and the first couple of years of college in a safe place.

Since Janet is a single parent, you may think she should be pretty conservative with her money. She certainly does need safety for her short-term goals, but for her long-term goals, she'll need to focus on growth so that she won't lose ground to inflation.

EARL AND JENNIFER: Finally, let's look at Earl and Jennifer. They are five years from retirement and are worried about safety—protecting their nest egg. They know they are going to need to live off their investments when they retire, so they don't want to take any risks with them. For Earl and Jennifer, retirement seems like a short-term goal. But think about it. What happens if they live into their nineties—that's another thirty years! For Earl and Jennifer, retirement fits into short-term, medium-term, *and* long-term goals. So even when you are close to retirement, you still need to consider it a long-term goal as well as a short-term goal, because you are likely to need that money to last for a long time. Retirees need to invest for both income (to pay their living expenses) and growth (so that they can keep up with ever-rising living costs later in life).

Now that you understand a bit more about your investment time horizon, please go back to the goals you listed earlier and indicate next to each whether it is a short-term, medium-term, or long-term goal. Remember that in some instances (for example, when you have a child about to enter college or if you're about to retire), a particular goal may cover more than one period.

Risk Is Not a Four-Letter Word

No one wants to risk losing money, especially losing money on investments. But there are two kinds of risk: the kind you can see and the kind you can't. The kind you can't see is the risk that comes from inflation and what it means to the buying power of your dollars. Here's an example: With 3½ percent inflation per year, your cost of living doubles every twenty years. It could go higher than that, although we all hope it will be lower. Alas, we can't predict these things, so it's best to err a bit on the high side when it comes to inflation estimates. With 3½ percent annual inflation, for every $20 you spend today, you'll need $40 in twenty years, and double that again after the next twenty years. In forty years, for the $20 you need today, you'll need $80 to purchase the same items.

So let's consider someone at age forty-five whose living expenses are $50,000 today. Assuming he retires in twenty years when he is sixty-five, he'll need to spend $100,000 for the same expenses if inflation averages 3½ percent per year. In another twenty years, when he's eighty-five and still going strong, he will need $200,000 to enjoy the same purchasing power that he had forty years earlier. While your living expenses will almost certainly decline when you retire, the important thing to remember is that whatever your spending level is, it will increase each year throughout your retirement due to inflation.

These numbers are pretty scary, I admit. But they show how much risk is involved in just letting your money sit and not letting it grow enough to outpace inflation. Some people fear investing because they can see the stock market go up and down and interest rates go up and down. That's the kind of risk you can see. So they think they should put their money somewhere where it will be safe, but that pays low interest. If you don't take into account what you can't see from inflation, you will really be missing the boat. Table II.1 compares inflation risk with investment risk.

Now, you may conclude that there is a risk in everything. And there is, but you can minimize the risk that you can see—the visible risk from investments. Inflation is an invisible risk—you can't see it and you have no control over it and everyone has to deal with it. You actually have more control over visible risk—the kind you have when you invest in stocks and bonds—because you can control how much

TABLE II.1
INFLATION RISK VS. INVESTMENT RISK

INVISIBLE RISK OF INFLATION	VISIBLE RISK FROM INVESTMENTS
Means your money loses purchasing power over time	Means the value of your investments could go up or down
Is caused by increases over time in the cost of living	Is caused by different factors that depend on the type of investment
Is less of a potential problem in the short term	Is historically less of a problem over the long term
Can be managed by investing to try to get a rate of return that is higher than or keeps pace with inflation	Can be managed by deciding how much and what kind of investment risk to take, and how much to diversify
Is associated mostly with temporary investments that can lose purchasing power over time	Is associated mostly with stocks and bonds

and what kind of risk you take. There are several ways to reduce your amount of visible risk.

The Three Main Types of Investments

As we have seen, one of the most important factors in deciding where to put your money is how soon you'll need it. Do you need your money to grow over the long term? Do you need it to produce income? Do you want it to stay safe because you'll need it fairly soon?

The three main types of investments are each geared mostly toward one of the three key things you need from your money: growth, income, and safety. I say mostly because an investment behaves very differently over the short term—say two to three years—than it does over the long term, say eight years or more. The same investments can behave very differently over different periods. The three basic kinds of investments are temporary investments, bonds, and stocks.

1. Temporary investments. Let's lead off with temporary investments, also called short-term investments, since they are the most familiar. The main temporary investments are short-term bank certificates of deposit (CDs), bank savings accounts, money market funds, and U.S. Treasury bills. Temporary investments maintain a stable value, pay interest, and can easily be changed into cash, which is particularly helpful if you need money fast. Of the three types, temporary investments almost always pay the lowest rate of return. So why invest in them at all? Well, people buy them primarily for safety. You do get some income from them, but what's most important is their stability. When you go into a temporary investment, you can be sure how much money you'll get out of it. You are not taking much visible risk of losing money. The principal values (prices) of these types of investments don't go up and down the way those of other investments do.

So when would a temporary investment be a good choice? If you are going to buy something in the next year or two, it's good to know the money will be there when you need it. Also, when you eventually retire, you might want to invest some of your retirement money in temporary investments to meet your living expenses over the following year or so. On the other hand, if you're not going to need the money within a few years, you may not want to keep it in a temporary investment, because of the much greater invisible risk of the principal losing ground to inflation.

2. Bonds. Bonds are like IOUs. When you lend somebody money, you get an IOU from the borrower. (Of course, if you lend money to your child and get an IOU, good luck trying to get the money back.) With a bond, you lend money to a corporation or a government agency in return for regular payments of interest on the loan you made as well as the repayment of principal when the loan matures. The interest provides income. That's the most important reason people buy bonds. That income—called yield—can help them pay their bills or can be reinvested. The income can also help even out the ups and downs that both bond and stock prices go through in daily trading in the bond and stock markets.

Bonds usually pay more interest than temporary investments, but like stocks, their prices can change. When interest rates decline, bond prices rise. But when interest rates rise, bond prices will likely decline. (The way interest-rate changes affect bond prices is difficult for investors to visualize. Think of a seesaw, with interest rates on one seat and bond prices on the other. If interest rates rise, that side of the seesaw rises, and the bond price side descends, or declines, and vice versa. That means that if you have money in bonds, the overall value of that investment could go down even though you are receiving interest income.) Bond interest rates stay fixed until the bond matures—that's why they are often called fixed-income investments. But their prices go up and down depending on what interest rates in general do. The longer the bond's maturity—that is, the longer until the loan will be repaid in full—the more the price can go up and down.

3. Stocks. When you own a share of stock, you own a share of a company. How much of the company you own depends on the number of shares you have. Stocks are sometimes called equities because they are like the equity in your house. You own a part of something—in this case, the company. With your house, the bank has the rest of your equity. With stock, the other stockholders share the equity in the company. People invest in stocks primarily for growth.

As a group, stocks go up and down in value more than any other type of investment over the short term. But over time, stocks have been one of the few types of investments that have beaten inflation. There's no guarantee that what has happened in the past will continue in the future, of course, but the average yearly return on stocks has been a little over 10 percent. Historically, stocks have been more profitable than bonds and temporary investments.

People are often afraid of stocks because they hear about bear markets or stock market crashes. And that should be a concern to anyone who will need the money within just a few years. But over the long run, there is more risk of losing money to inflation if you don't invest in stocks. Yes, the visible risk of stocks periodically losing value is higher in the short term than the risk with other investments, but with proper diversification, you can protect yourself from those risks *and* from loss from inflation (see page 337). That's why most investors need a generous dollop of stocks in their investment holdings. Baby boomers should almost always have a majority of their money in stocks.

Mutual Funds

Many people think mutual funds are a fourth kind of investment in addition to temporary investments, bonds, and stocks. They actually are not. Mutual funds are a way to put money into the three types of investments that were discussed above. Mutual funds are a way for individuals to help protect themselves against the risks of investing in just one company or with one borrower. They allow you to pool your money with that of other investors. Then the fund manager buys one of the three types of investments to concentrate on and picks many different stocks, or many different bonds, or many different temporary investments. Some mutual funds invest in both stocks and bonds.

Each fund has its own way of trying to make money, called its investment objective. Based on those guidelines, a professional manager decides which stocks and/or bonds to buy. Stock mutual funds and bond mutual funds are pretty much self-explanatory. *Balanced* mutual funds invest in both stocks and bonds. A money market fund buys temporary investments.

One other investment term that is important to understand is *total return*. Total return includes not only income earned from an investment through interest paid by bonds and temporary investments or dividends paid by some stocks, but also any increase or decrease in the price of the investment. For example, if you get 6 percent interest on a bond, but the price of the bond drops 10 percent, your total return is minus 4 percent—bummer. On the other hand, if you get 6 percent interest on a bond and its price rises by 8 percent, your total return is plus 14 percent. Total return, rather than simply the interest or the dividend that an investment pays, is the best way to compare different types of investments and to evaluate how your investments have performed.

Managing Investment Risk through Diversification

Now that you understand the various kinds of investments, it's time to look at managing the risk that each poses. The best way to manage risk is to put time on your side. While younger-generation family members may think you're as old as Methuselah, we know that your money is going to have to last you a long time. Investing for long periods means that you have a long time to ride out the ups and downs experienced by the stock market. As I noted earlier, stocks go up and down in the short term, but the trend over time has been up.

Second, avoid putting all your eggs in any one basket. This is known as diversification. If you don't understand diversification, bear with me for a couple of minutes and you'll get the drift. There are three components of diversification.

Diversification Part I: Investing in all three types of investments—temporary investments, bonds, and stocks. First, you can control your investment risk by investing in all three types of investments: stocks, bonds, and temporary investments. The fancy term for this is *asset allocation* or *investment allocation,* which means nothing more than how you divvy up your savings among the three types of investments.

Combining the three major types of investments can help minimize risks, because if one type is doing badly, another may be doing quite well. That way, you don't have to do everything right, you just have to do more right than wrong. If everything is in one basket, you have only one chance to get it right. While investment allocation does not guarantee against a loss, it can help you minimize both the visible risk—that investments and stocks and bonds will periodically decline in value—and the invisible risk of inflation. But there's more to successful investment diversification than simply putting money into each of the three types of investments, which is explained next.

Diversification Part II: Spreading your money among the various categories of temporary investments, bonds, and stocks. As you may be aware, there are a variety of different categories of temporary investments, bonds, and stocks. For example, bonds may be issued by corporations, states and municipalities, and last but certainly not least, the U.S. government, which is world-renowned for its borrowing zeal. Just as the three types of investments periodically go through good and bad times, so do the various categories within each investment type vary in their relative performance. By further spreading your money out among these categories, you can further diversify your investments. Before moving on to Part III, here are descriptions of the most important categories of temporary investments, bonds, and stocks, along with some suggestions for investing in each.

Temporary Investments

✦ **Certificates of deposit (CDs).** A debt security offered by banks or savings-and-loan associations. Generally, a CD is issued for a specific dollar amount, for a specific period, at a preset, fixed interest rate. Government insured.

✦ **Savings accounts.** A deposit account at a bank or savings and loan that pays interest and can generally be withdrawn at any time. *Money market accounts* are a variation of savings accounts that may have more stringent rules regarding withdrawals. Government insured.

✦ **Money market funds.** A type of mutual fund that invests in short-term (less than a year) debt securities of agencies of the U.S. government, banks, and corporations. Not government insured, but generally safe.

✦ **U.S. Treasury bills.** A debt obligation issued by the U.S. government, having a maturity of one year or less.

Top tip for investing in temporary investments. The key to investing successfully in temporary investments is, simply, to shop around for the best interest rate. Since these securities are all safe relative to each other, the trick is to find the highest return. At any time, one or a couple of categories may be paying higher interest than the others. (See page 120.)

Bonds

✦ **U.S. Government bonds.** Backed by the full faith and credit of the U.S. government, these offer total protection from bond default, although the value of government bonds will fluctuate with interest rates, as do all bonds and bond funds. Of the types of U.S. government bonds, U.S. Treasury bonds (actually, most issues are called notes rather than bonds) are the best known. A second category of U.S. government bonds are mortgage-backed securities, such as those issued by the Government National Mortgage Association (GNMA or, phonetically, "Ginnie Mae"). There are also agency bonds issued by various government agencies.

✦ **Foreign bonds.** While not commonly used by U.S. investors, foreign bonds offer an additional means of diversifying a bond portfolio. The only feasible way to do so is through an international or global bond mutual fund. These funds typically invest primarily in bonds issued by foreign governments.

✦ **Municipal bonds.** The primary attraction of municipal bonds is that the interest they pay is generally not subject to federal income tax. Since municipal bond fund prices do not appear in the daily papers and the bonds are inconvenient for the individual investor to buy and manage, municipal bond mutual funds are a useful way to invest in them. Interest earned from bonds issued in the investor's own state, including those of "single-state municipal bond funds," is generally free of both federal and state income taxes.

✦ **Corporate bonds.** As the name so amply suggests, these are bonds issued by corporations. Depending on the financial strength of the issuing corporation, there are two categories of corporate bonds and mutual funds that invest in these bonds. *Investment-grade corporate bonds* comprise higher-quality corporate bonds and provide interest income with limited risk; *high-yield corporate bonds* are issued by weaker companies. These bonds (called junk bonds in less polite company) pay higher interest, but the risk of default—of possibly losing your original investment—is also higher.

Bonds come in different maturities. Bonds and bond mutual funds are also divided up according to the length of maturity of the individual bonds or the bonds that the fund manager puts into the portfolio. There are three maturity levels:

1. **Short-term bonds and bond funds** (also called limited-term bonds and funds) comprise bonds with an average maturity of between one and four years.

2. **Intermediate-term bonds and bond funds** include bonds sporting maturities of between four and ten years.

3. **Long-term bonds and bond funds** comprise bonds with a maturity typically of greater than ten years.

Top tip for investing in bonds. One of the most widely accepted strategies for investing in bonds is called laddering maturities. Rather than putting all of your money into single-maturity bonds or bond funds—be it short, intermediate, or long—invest in mutual funds or individual bonds with a variety of maturities. This reduces somewhat the risk of losing a lot of principal because of a change in interest rates. For example, if you have all of your bond money in long-term bonds and interest rates rise, you could stand to lose quite a bit of principal value. That's because the longer the maturity of a bond or bond fund, the more the principal value changes (both downward and upward) in reaction to a change in interest rates. On the other hand, if you had laddered your maturities by owning some short- and/or intermediate-term bonds or bond funds as well, you wouldn't have been hit as badly as a result of a rise in interest rates. Incidentally, with the exception of U.S. Treasuries, investing in individual bonds can be a minefield for investors since bonds are traded in very large denominations and the prices of most bonds aren't published, so it's hard to determine if you're paying a fair price. Therefore, most investors should stick with bond funds, including bond index funds and exchange-traded funds.

Speaking of bond funds, if the whole idea of investing in bonds has your head spinning, you might consider a *multisector bond fund.* These funds can invest in just about any kind of U.S. or foreign bond, although municipal bonds are usually off-limits. Multisector bond funds have amply rewarded investors in recent years, so they're certainly worth a look.

Stocks

Stocks are commonly classified according to the value of the stock, called its capitalization. Capitalization is simply the number of shares issued by the corporation multiplied by the current market value of the stock. For example, a stock that has 100 million shares outstanding and is currently trading at $50 per share would have a market capitalization or "cap" of $5 billion. Whether a stock is classified as large, midsize, or small varies depending on who's doing the talking. One such categorization is:

Large-cap: Market capitalization over $10 billion

Midcap: Market capitalization between $2 billion and $10 billion

Small-cap: Market capitalization below $2 billion

But how U.S. stocks are categorized is less important than what they can offer an investor who's interested in diversifying and making money.

✦ **Large-cap.** Stocks of the largest companies are classified as large-cap. Because of their size, they are not expected to grow as rapidly as smaller companies. Successful midcaps and small-caps tend to outperform them over time. Still, investors looking for dividends and preservation of capital with some growth potential choose large-cap stocks. They pay relatively more in dividends than small- and midcap stocks. Finally, investors who want their money to remain relatively safe over the long term are often attracted to large-cap stocks.

✦ **Midcap.** Midcap stocks are typically stocks of medium-size companies. They offer growth potential and also some of the stability of a larger company. Many well-known companies that have been in business for decades are midcaps. Many midcap stocks have had steady growth and a good track record. They tend to grow well over the long term. Midcap stocks, like small-caps, emphasize growth rather than dividends.

✦ **Small-cap.** The stock of small companies that have the potential to grow rapidly is classified as small-cap. Many of these companies are relatively new. How they will do in the market is often difficult to predict. Because of their small size, growth spurts can affect their prices and earnings dramatically. On the other hand, they tend to be volatile and may dramatically decline. Because they look to grow rapidly, small-cap stocks are likely to forgo paying dividends so that profits can be reinvested for future growth of the company. Small-cap stocks are popular among investors who are looking for growth, who do not need current dividends, and who can tolerate price volatility. If successful, these investments can generate significant gains over time. Because small-cap stocks tend to be riskier than larger-company stocks, the most prudent way to invest in this important stock sector is through a diversified small-cap mutual fund whose manager has expertise in this specialized investment arena.

✦ **International.** International stocks are stocks of foreign companies. Some trade on U.S. stock exchanges as American depository receipts (ADRs), but the majority must be purchased on overseas stock exchanges. Adding international stocks to an investment portfolio enhances diversification since U.S. and international markets do not typically move in tandem. In addition, the higher expected growth rates of many emerging market economies (developing countries) offer the potential for higher relative returns with stocks issued by companies in emerging markets. Because of the difficulty of dealing with foreign stock exchanges and foreign currencies, the best way to invest in international stocks is through an international stock mutual fund. Most international funds invest throughout the world. Some invest only in one country or region. *Global stock funds,* however, invest in both international and U.S. securities.

A couple of other stock categories may also play a role in your investment arsenal:

✦ **Sector funds.** Also called specialized funds, these funds concentrate on a single industry, such as energy, precious metals, health care, banking, or biotechnology. Since they are not diversified across multiple industries like the typical mutual fund, sector funds are inherently riskier, yet at times an investor may want to make a pure play on stocks in a single industry.

✦ **Speculative stocks.** These stocks are subject to wide price fluctuations and are typically associated with companies that are not well known, but that have products that are rumored to be on the verge of technological breakthroughs—typically, these days, in the areas of high technology, medicine, biotechnology, mining, and alternative energy. The operative word is "rumored," because these highfliers live or die by the rumors. Even well-known companies that have suffered substantial adversity could be considered speculative. If you have a yen for speculative stock, you'll benefit from the down-to-earth ideas and recommendations in Appendix III.

Top tip for investing in stocks. It's hard to go wrong in the stock market over the long run by spreading your stock money around among the four categories discussed above. At any one time some categories are doing better than others, but it's impossible for anyone to predict, although a lot of people try, and they usually end up poorer for their efforts. So the best thing to do is have some money in each category. Once you come to the epiphanic moment when you realize that no one can accurately predict the future, you'll understand why that's the best strategy for winning the stock market game.

Diversification Part III: Investing in different securities within each category. When you diversify by investing in many different stocks or bonds instead of just one, you reduce the impact of any one stock's or bond's eroding your money. You're spreading around your risk. The most efficient way to do this is with mutual funds, which automatically invest in many, if not hundreds, of different individual securities. It's also fine to invest in individual stocks and bonds, but to be diversified you'll need to hold on to several individual stocks in different industries (financial services, energy, technology, for example) and several different bonds with different issuers (corporations, U.S. government, municipalities, for example). Many investors don't have enough capital to properly diversify with individual securities, particularly individual bonds, but they can with mutual funds.

By carefully disseminating your money among the various investment types and categories, you will avoid the substantial risk of investing too much money in a single category that plummets in value. That's the essence of diversification.

IT'S A MATTER OF STYLE

Within each of the stock fund categories—large-cap, mid-cap, small-cap, and international—mutual fund managers adopt one of three "management styles":

- **Growth.** Managers who favor growth investing choose companies whose revenues and earnings are accelerating. These companies are often the best performers in strong bull markets.

- **Value.** Managers of value funds favor companies whose stocks are undervalued. Perhaps the companies are temporarily out of favor with Wall Street or they possess unusually valuable, but as yet unrecognized, assets. Value stocks don't usually perform as well as growth stocks in rapidly rising markets, but they also don't fall as much in declining markets.

- **Blend.** Finally, some managers prefer to find investment opportunities wherever they lurk, so they will use a blend of both growth investing and value investing.

When evaluating funds for possible addition to your portfolio, find out the fund manager's investment style. The easiest way is to check one of the mutual fund monitoring services at the library. Aggressive investors tend to favor funds that utilize the growth style; more conservative investors prefer value funds; and others prefer managers who mix it up. Finally, investors who want to hedge their bets may select one growth-style fund and one value-style fund in each stock fund category or pick a blend fund. If you invest in individual stocks, bear in mind that stocks themselves usually either fall into the growth or value category as well.

Investment Strategies for Active Investors

This appendix contains a potpourri of suggestions designed specifically for active investors.

✦ **A low-risk way to indulge your speculative proclivities.** If you want to speculate, do it in a controlled fashion through a "YG2BK" account.

✦ **Income investors prefer preferred stocks.** Preferred stocks are too often overlooked as a way to earn some high-dividend income.

✦ **Avoiding gargantuan stock losses with limit orders.** Another straightforward, albeit overlooked, way to protect against wallet-emptying stock calamities.

✦ **The role of mutual funds in actively managed portfolios.** This is for those who believe the malarkey that mutual funds are not a good place for your money. Professional investors and the megarich alike use mutual funds in their portfolios.

✦ **Thinking about hedge funds?** Since hedge funds are now being offered to the hoi polloi as well as the aforementioned tycoons, I'll put in my two cents to help you make an informed decision.

✦ **Profiting from the baby boom generation.** Baby boomers control so much wealth that they will greatly benefit several industrial sectors over the next few decades. Some likely beneficiaries are mentioned so that you can profit from your own largesse, thereby giving you even more money to spend on the products and services provided by these boomer-benefiting industries.

✦ **Income-producing real estate: an ideal baby boomer investment?** It's not too late for you to consider investing in real estate, so I'll lay out a plan, warts and all, because it can be a time-consuming and risky undertaking.

Are you an active investor or an obsessive investor? If you're not sure (it's a fine line), take heed of the following advice from John Train: "The people who sustain the worst losses are usually the ones who overreach. And it's not necessary: steady, moderate gains will get you where you want to go."

A Low-Risk Way to Indulge Your Speculative Proclivities

A recent news article noted that a stock market rally had greatly increased the amount of individual investor money flowing into stock sectors that had been the strongest, and out of sectors—in both stocks and bonds—that had been lagging the leaders. As any good contrarian will tell you, this behavior sends a strong signal that the leaders are going to start to lag and the laggards are going to start to lead. It also reminds me of a talk show caller who rebuked my customary caution by saying (at the peak of the 1990s bull market, no less) that it made no sense investing in the international stock funds that I was recommending because they were making only 15 percent when he could make over twice that in technology funds.

YG2BK to the rescue. Whether they use an investment adviser or do it on their own, many investors like to speculate on risky investments— investing on the basis of a stock tip or investing in a really hot mutual fund (yes, that's speculating as well). There's nothing wrong with speculation so long as you don't bet your financial future on it.

Definition of a speculative stock: a stock that a whole lot of people own, but they have no idea why they own it. So my suggestion, if you are inclined to speculate, is to carve out a small portion of your total investment holdings, put it in a separate account, and do your speculative thing. You might want to call it your YG2BK portfolio, which stands for "You've got to be kidding!" because that's what your spouse or colleague at work or bridge partner or investment adviser is likely to say when you proudly announce the latest addition to your special account.

How much? The proportion of your total investment holdings that might go into your YG2BK account depends on how much you can afford to lose. Ten percent doesn't seem excessive, and if you have prodigious holdings, you might be able to raise that to 20 percent. But don't go overboard, even if you think you have a Midas touch.

SUCCESS STORY: SMALL-CAP STOCK BONANZA

Here's the success story of an investor who took his modest Keogh plan account to great heights: "I had always been fascinated with small-company stocks, so when I was in my mid-forties, I started investing in them in a retirement account. Over the years, it has grown to over three hundred times my original investment. But it was scary along the way, because I had large positions in just a handful of stocks. My portfolio got so large that when I reached my early sixties, I transferred half of it to my broker, because I wanted to avoid a potential debacle just before I retired. Incidentally, the debacle never happened, but now that I'm retired, I still don't regret taking the money off my table and giving it to my broker." This is the exception, but I hope you can also become a happy exception with your YG2BK holdings.

Income Investors Prefer Preferred Stocks

Some savvy investors are boosting their income through preferred stocks. But first, a definition. A preferred stock typically pays a fixed dividend. Like common stocks, preferred stocks represent partial ownership in a company. Preferred shareholders receive their dividends before common stockholders. While there are some preferred stock mutual funds, you may want to buy individual preferred stocks. This is a tricky business, though, so you'll most likely need the help of an investment professional who can identify high-quality preferred stocks that meet your needs and explain the complex tax rules surrounding them. Suffice it to say, though, that many pay attractive dividends of 5 to 7 percent or even more, and some, but not all, preferred stock dividends qualify for the lower 15 percent tax rate on dividends. Remember, however, that these are stocks, so, while there's typically no major move up or down in preferred stock prices, there is always a possibility of losing principal, particularly if the company runs into financial tribulations.

Selecting preferred stocks. Preferred stocks require some investigation, similar to the criteria by which you would evaluate bonds. Here are three important considerations:

1. **Quality.** Preferred stocks receive credit ratings like bonds. As with bonds, it's best to stick with higher-rated preferred stocks—those considered, in rating parlance, "investment grade."

2. **Taxation of dividends.** If you buy preferred stocks in a taxable brokerage account (as opposed to a retirement account), opt for those preferreds whose dividends qualify for the 15 percent tax rate. Most preferreds dividends are subject to the same federal tax rates as corporate or government bond interest, but about 20 percent receive the more favorable rate.

3. **Call protection.** Also similar to bonds, preferred stocks are callable, meaning the issuer can buy them back at the issue price anytime after a stated "call date." You should avoid preferred stocks whose prices are above the call price if the call date is either in the near future or has passed. For example, avoid a preferred stock that is trading at $27 per share but is callable at $25 next year, since, if the stock is called, you'll lose $2 per share. On the other hand, if you can buy the same stock at $24, you'll profit from a call, so this might be a decent preferred stock to own.

A. **Call date.** The date after which the company can call in its shares. Many preferred issues are never called, but if the call date has passed, the issuer could still call the shares in at any time.

B. **Call price.** The price you'd get if the company calls in its shares.

C. **Current price.** The price at which you can buy the shares today.

So investing in preferred stocks is not child's play. The following checklist will help.

PREFERRED STOCK CHECKLIST

Yes   *No*

❑   ❑   1. Is the stock issue rated at least investment grade by the ratings agencies?

❑   ❑   2. Is the dividend rate attractive compared with bond yields and other alternative investments?

❑   ❑   3. If the issue will be held in a taxable brokerage account, are the dividends subject to the 15 percent federal tax rate on dividends?

❑   ❑   4. Is there adequate call protection to protect against a loss of part of the original investment shortly after making the investment?

w w w

Avoiding Gargantuan Stock Losses with Limit Orders

Stocks are curious things. The stock indexes could be rising like bottle rockets, but that doesn't necessarily mean all of your stocks are doing the same. Stocks can fall and fall precipitously with no advance warning. I spoke with two retired gents a few years ago who had invested most of their money in a handful of high-flying technology stocks in the late 1990s. They held on too long. One had lost over 60 percent and the other over 80 percent of his money. The financial pages of the newspapers are rife with examples of even blue-chip stocks whose prices have imploded. Anyone who has held such issues, including yours truly, wishes to have bailed out sooner—far sooner.

Putting your sell decisions on automatic. Fortunately, imposing a sell discipline on stock you own or intend to buy usually doesn't require you to check the stock prices every day or week. You can instruct your stockbroker to automatically sell most mainstream stocks at a specified price with a *stop order*. First, a brief primer on the kinds of stock orders:

+ A **market order** is an order to buy or sell a stock at whatever the going price may be.

+ A **stop order** becomes a market order once the stock's price reaches or passes the specific price stated on the stop order. However, the price stated on your stop order is not guaranteed. The order to sell is triggered once the price you specify is reached, so you will receive the next price. If the stock is diving, the next price could be substantially lower, but that might not be so bad since it at least gets you out of a potentially disastrous further drop in the stock's price.

+ A **limit order** is a trading order that authorizes a purchase or sale of stock only at a specified price level.

+ A **stop limit order** will be filled only if the stock gets to the price that you stipulate, and only if it can be filled at that price. The problem with a stop limit order is that if the stock you hold is really plummeting, your order might not be filled, thereby defeating the purpose of setting a limit order in the first place.

Determining when to bail out. Before you enter a stop order, you need to decide in advance a level below which you don't want to own the stock anymore. You do this by setting a price at which you will sell the investment. Some set a price that's 10 percent below current market, while others set lower stop-order prices. Don't set the price too close to the current price of the stock and thus avoid getting "whipsawed"—selling a stock that has suffered a temporary small decline only to see the price rebound soon thereafter. Also, you may choose to set a limit order on only a portion of a stock holding in case you don't want to get rid of all the shares at once.

Example. Ingrid Investor just bought a stock for $40 a share and wants to avoid a big loss on it. She sets a "stop loss" price on the stock of $30, or 25 percent below the purchase price. This disciplined approach to selling forces her to incur a manageable loss to prevent suffering a monstrous loss.

If the price rises . . . Now, if Ingrid's stock rises—and I sure hope it does—she will move the limit order price up as well. For example, assume the share price rose to $60. As it was rising, she also moved the stop-loss price upward to where it is now $45—still a 25 percent decline. But in this event, if she's forced to sell, Ingrid will still make a profit on her $40-per-share investment.

Taxes be damned. The possibility of having to pay capital gains taxes often gets in the way of selling a stock that is plummeting. But don't let the tax tail wag your stock dog. A lot of investors who are holding on to stocks that have dropped 75 percent or more would—or should have—been delighted to pay the capital gains from selling their positions shortly after the stock began to deteriorate.

Some people fall in love with a stock (the Enron employees simply loved their stock), and if the stock declines significantly, they patiently wait for it to regain its past glory. But an objective observer would probably conclude, "The odds of a stock quickly recouping its lost value after it has suffered a major price drop are far lower than the odds that the stock will continue to decline." No one wants to sell at a loss, but a moderate loss is a lot better than a gargantuan loss.

The Role of Mutual Funds in Actively Managed Portfolios

Many active investors prefer to invest in individual securities—stocks, bonds, CDs, etc. Nevertheless, mutual funds do and should play a valuable role in actively managed accounts. Even investors of considerable means, including many professional stock and bond traders, are finding mutual funds to be an important component of effective diversification and portfolio management. Mutual funds can be used in a variety of ways in larger portfolios.

✦ **To diversify concentrated portfolios.** Mutual funds can be used to diversify a portfolio that is heavily weighted in one or a few stock issues. For example, some baby boomers have been given large blocks of stock by parents or grandparents through gifts or inheritance. Others have substantial portions of their wealth tied up in the stock of the company they work for. Reduce the risk of having too many investment eggs in a single basket by shifting some of the concentrated stock investment into well-diversified mutual funds, index funds, or exchange-traded funds.

✦ **To quickly invest in sectors of interest.** Even experienced investors will probably have some difficulty deploying sufficient resources quickly into a particular industrial sector. For example, an investor whose stock investments consist primarily of value-oriented manufacturing stocks may want to diversify into technology and health care stocks. The quickest way to acquire a diversified portfolio of tech stocks would be to invest in a technology fund, and, for health care exposure, a health care of fund.

✦ **To invest in stock groups that are difficult to manage on an individual-stock basis.** Active stock investors typically concentrate on domestic large-cap stocks. But in other important stock sectors it is costly to assemble a diversified group of individual issues. *Small-company stocks* and *international stocks,* for example, are widely considered important components of a well-diversified stock portfolio, yet experts opine that a seven-figure investment is required to put together an adequately diversified portfolio in either of these categories. Mutual funds will provide the investor with instant diversification and professional management.

✦ **To enhance portfolio liquidity.** The immediate marketability of mutual fund investments is a further advantage to investors, who may have some impediments to raising cash quickly with their directly owned investments.

✦ **To reduce current taxes on investment income.** Active stock investors may be saddled with large tax bills on their investments, particularly if they are trading frequently, resulting in high-taxed short-term capital gains. Moving a portion of this money into tax-friendly index or exchange-traded funds could reduce the annual tax bill.

✦ **To alleviate the chore of management.** Often, active investors find that they lack the time to manage their investments adequately, but still prefer to invest on their own. A major attraction of mutual funds, for investors of all stripes, is the active, experienced management of the fund assets. As you enter your peak earning years and begin to amass a larger portfolio, you may conclude that it's time to use mutual funds in your portfolio.

Thinking about Hedge Funds?

Your vigilant scribe is always skeptical of newfangled investment opportunities, or oldfangled investment opportunities offered to a new cohort of investors. Hedge funds have been around for decades, but they were strictly for the superrich, certainly not for the likes of you and me. But after a couple of lousy years in the stock market, voilà, hedge funds started to be offered to the financially downtrodden— a bionic alternative to anemic stock market returns. But are hedge funds a worthy addition to your investment portfolio? Do you know what a hedge fund is? Not understanding an investment has never been a barrier to investors' plunking down their money.

It's not easy defining a hedge fund because there are so many categories of hedge funds, each of which necessitates further explication. One common element across the hedge-fund population is that the outsize expectations of hedge-fund profits have not been matched by consistent performance.

Pick your own poison. Hedge funds are like mutual funds in that they both consist of a pool of money contributed by a coterie of investors. But there the similarity ends. Hedge funds are usually not subject to the reporting requirements and the scrutiny of the SEC and other regulatory authorities, nor must their managers be registered investment advisers, although the regulators may end that immunity. Absent government regulations, hedge-fund managers usually invest aggressively in a variety of securities and use a myriad of strategies, including options, futures, currency trading, foreign securities, short selling of stocks (i.e., profiting from declining stock prices), and buying on margin (i.e., using borrowed money to increase the investment pool).

Some advantages and even more risks. The major advantage of hedge-fund investing is diversification beyond the garden-variety stocks and bonds that dominate the portfolios of most investors. Generally, the more diversification in a portfolio, the better. The hedge fund, as an asset class, can provide further diversification because these investments often do not move in tandem with run-of-the-mill stock and bond markets. Another advantage is the variety of hedge-fund offerings.

The major drawbacks of hedge funds are their extreme volatility, high fees, and the lack of disclosure standards for investors. The kinds of investments made by hedge-fund managers are inherently volatile, and add the customary use of borrowed money to increase the pool of money being invested, and you have a fund that could suffer enormous losses if the manager places a bad bet. Since hedge funds are not heavily regulated, the dearth of disclosure is particularly problematic. Finally, any hedge-fund investment should be considered illiquid because the premature sale of the investment would, at best, be difficult.

Some other red flags surround hedge-funds as well, which are becoming worrisome to the SEC and other regulatory bodies. Financial institutions that tout a particular hedge fund may have a lot of financial incentive to do so because they may act as the broker for the hedge fund's many transactions and may receive fees that are not fully disclosed. How some hedge funds value their portfolios has also been a concern, resulting in some substantial write-downs of fund asset values. Big investors—billionaires, universities, etc.—can afford to hire firms to check out a hedge fund before an investment is made and to ride herd on it thereafter. But average investors have to rely on the salesperson to perform due diligence, and that's a potential problem.

Hedge funds for mere mortals. As noted above, until recently, hedge funds were available only to "substantial" investors willing and able to fork over $1 million into a single fund. But a disappointing stock market combined with financial institutions' lusting for new revenue sources in a bear market have given birth to hedge funds for souls who have as little as $25,000 to invest. For those who want to join the hedge-fund mania but who lack the stomach for investing so much with a single manager, Wall Street has something just for you: a fund of hedge funds. A fund of funds offers even more diversification by providing access to a wide variety of hedge-fund strategies. That's a pretty good idea.

The upshot. I've always said that every investor is entitled to take a flier now and then—a YG2BK investment—as described on page 349. If you can comfortably afford to lose $25,000 or whatever investment you make in a hedge fund, then it might be a worthwhile arrow to add to your investment quiver. At a minimum it will give you something to brag about at the watercooler or on the golf course. But don't look at hedge funds as a way to recoup past investment losses. True, hedge funds have on average beaten the average stock mutual fund pretty consistently over each of the past fifteen years. But there have been well-publicized bankruptcies of some hedge funds, and others have returned pennies on the dollar to their investors. Those managers who are more successful at controlling volatility all too often produce mediocre performance while reaping prodigious fees. Caveat emptor.

HOW TO JUICE UP YOUR INTERNATIONAL STOCK HOLDINGS

Investing in international stocks is an essential component of a well-diversified portfolio. The easiest way to do so is by owning a traditional international stock fund that invests in large-company stocks that trade throughout the world on the major foreign stock exchanges. But if you really want to make the most of your overseas investments, three other categories of international stocks are worth considering.

- **International small-company stock funds.** Both U.S. and foreign small-company stocks have been excellent performers, and this happy situation should continue.
- **Emerging markets funds** tread in waters that are usually not on the traditional international-stock-fund radar screen. Emerging markets are economies on the way to becoming major forces in the world, such as China's and India's. There's plenty of opportunity

for fishing in these waters, and that's just what the
manager of an emerging markets fund will do.

- **International real estate funds** invest in overseas
  properties (global real estate funds invest in both foreign and U.S. properties), taking advantage of the
  flourishing real estate markets in many foreign countries.

Profiting from the Baby Boom Generation

A demographic behemoth. You're part of a juggernaut. The baby
boom generation has dominated the U.S. marketplace at each stage
of its life cycle. Baby boomers will reinvent what it means to be retired. This economic leviathan has the resources and, when retired,
will have the time to launch an unprecedented discretionary-spending
spree. The statistics are eye-popping:

- ✦ By 2010, boomer annual spending will be $1 trillion more than
  that of the eighteen-to-thirty-four age group.

- ✦ While boomers account for 42 percent of U.S. households, they
  account for 50 percent of all spending.

- ✦ While you've been told for years that you and your boomer co-
  horts are spending yourselves into financial oblivion, you control
  two-thirds of the nation's wealth—a total of $28 trillion. Sub-
  tract out your debt, and that works out to an average net worth
  of over $300,000 per baby boomer, or $600,000 per baby boomer
  couple. This is hardly impoverished.

Wow! Sounds like an investment opportunity to me.

Playing the baby boomer demographic. As the baby boom generation reaches its peak wealth years and enters retirement, several

sectors of the economy will most likely prosper since the combination of high discretionary income, increasing leisure time, and aging (alas, there's nothing we can do about that) will be like manna from heaven for some industries. Savvy boomers will want to focus some of their own wealth on these industries.

✦ **Health care.** The more mature baby boomers are now beginning to enter the age where pharmaceutical, hospital, and other health care expenditures will dramatically rise. While boomers will be big consumers of drug products, price pressure on drug costs may offset the additional revenue from baby boomer pharmaceutical usage. Other areas of the health care industry will probably be big beneficiaries, however. That's why investing in a health care fund may be preferable in this feast-or-famine industry. Let a professional seek out sectors within the industry that are particularly promising. Biotechnology is one such sector that seems to offer a lot of promise for "boomer nation."

✦ **Travel and leisure.** Say what you will about baby boomers, but hedonism is not an area that they eschew, and the travel and leisure industry is likely to benefit mightily. Hotel and travel companies that cater to this monstrous and affluent leisure class are likely to thrive, as are restaurants.

✦ **Financial services.** The financial services industry is salivating over the jillions of dollars that boomers will be rolling over from workplace retirement plans into IRAs and annuities. It's a perfect storm. Retiring baby boomers will also be seeking out financial advice as never before. Lenders will also benefit from continued borrowing, primarily by younger boomers, many of whom will, unwisely, continue to finance the good life.

✦ **Technology.** Technology stocks have been beaten down badly and have recovered only a fraction of their past halcyon levels. So even without the influence of the baby boom generation, technology is an attractive industry if you can forget what happened to your tech stocks at the beginning of the decade. But experts expect the technology industry to receive an additional push from retiring boomers. This is shaping up to be a major crisis for employers, who will be hard-pressed to replace such experienced workers. Technology, particularly software, could be the panacea as companies invest in it heavily to help counter the void left by retiring boomers.

✦ **Real estate.** Real estate stocks have boomed, but they should play a role as a long-term investment at any time. Boomers are much more mobile than their forebears. Second homes are in vogue with this cadre, and housing changes through relocation and downsizing will benefit certain segments of the real estate industry, particularly in the Sun Belt. The inclination of baby boomers to buy apartments in urban areas is also worth noting.

How to play these (and other) sectors. If you're a stock picker, you are well advised to consider some stocks in the above industries as worthy additions to your holdings. If you'd prefer to cast a wider net, a lot of sector mutual funds and exchange-traded funds are available. Please visit the special reader Web site for some tips. **w w w**

Income-Producing Real Estate: An Ideal Baby Boomer Investment?

The following section provides a lot of guidance for would-be real estate investors, as well as some tips for those who are already property owners. Although this area may not appeal to you, real estate has long been one of the best ways for people of average financial means to create retirement security, if not become filthy rich. True, being a landlord is no picnic, particularly for overscheduled baby boomers, but a lot of people don't seem to mind it.

Growth + rising income = a wonderful retirement cash-flow generator. Retirees who own income-producing real estate may enjoy the best of both worlds: rising asset values unencumbered by capital gains taxes until sold later in life, and a rising source of income through rent increases to help meet rising living expenses. Consider the following example of a boomer couple that has a small property with big retirement-income potential.

Example. Leslie and Lester Lessor hope to retire in a couple of years at sixty. They own a small apartment building whose mortgage will be paid off at the time they retire. The Lessors expect this building to be a major contributor to their retirement income. They plan to sell the property when they're eighty and use the proceeds to provide income for the rest of their lives. Leslie prepared the following table to summarize their plans:

AGE	PROPERTY VALUE ASSUMING 6% ANNUAL APPRECIATION	NET OPERATING INCOME ASSUMING 4% ANNUAL INCREASES
60	$400,000	$35,000
70	700,000	52,000
80	1,200,000	77,000

Here's Lester's take on their plan: "This is an ideal retirement investment. Our income will rise through rent increases at the same time the property is appreciating. If we can sell the building twenty years into retirement for $1,200,000, we'll net about $900,000 after taxes and commissions. We could stick that money in 5 percent bonds, earn $45,000 per year for the rest of our lives, and pass on the $900,000 to our nieces and nephews."

Own it yourself. Any way you cut it, buying individual properties is the best way to own real estate. It provides the greatest potential return and is how a lot of wealthy families in this country got wealthy. That said, owning it yourself is the riskiest way to get into real estate. It's your neck that's on the line and no one else's. And it's also not for those who don't want to deal with pesky tenant problems.

It's best to begin small. Make sure you are genuinely cut out to be a landlord and to deal with the sometimes vexing details involving tenants and property. Also, don't become overextended with debt—which could result in disaster the next time a downturn occurs as vacancies rise and the property price drops.

Q&A: IS A VACATION HOME A SOUND REAL ESTATE INVESTMENT?

You may think that a vacation home constitutes a real estate investment. Vacation homes may be a great source of relaxation, but they're usually mediocre investments, unless you're planning to retire to your vacation home or you're well enough off to be able to divide your retirement years between two places. People who buy a vacation home as an investment usually believe the breathless assertions of the real estate salespeople that it will have great rental potential. Sure, you may be lucky enough to rent it for $1,000 a week, but did the broker tell you that the peak rental season lasts only two weeks? And that those are the two weeks when you want to use the place? Or people who buy vacation time-shares—with few exceptions the quintessential bad real estate investment—probably believe they can actually swap their half-bedroom time-share in northern Canada for an ocean-front palace in Monte Carlo. Don't get me wrong, there may be a good reason to buy a vacation home or time-share, mainly for enjoyment, but don't count on its being an outstanding investment. You'll be a lot better off renting a place instead. The owners will be grateful for getting some cash out of their vacation home albatross.

What Type of Property?

Many different types of income-producing properties are available to you. But some are clearly better than others, as I will explain below.

✦ **Residential rental property.** A residential rental property can be anything from a single-family home to a large apartment building. Location, condition, and occupancy rates will all affect the property's value, as can local and neighborhood population trends and zoning changes. As you probably know, the most important consideration in any real estate parcel is location. This truism is particularly crucial for residential real estate. While a few savvy real estate investors have been able to benefit by taking early stakes in "turnaround neighborhoods," this sort of gambling is best left to a professional.

❑ **Single-family homes and condominiums.** These are often the first investments that come to mind for new real estate investors, but they almost always make lousy real estate investments. The reason is that it is difficult to find properties that are priced low enough that the rental income is sufficient to cover mortgage and operating expenses. You'll soon tire of pumping money into a property that is not self-supporting. And if you invest in such a property, you are in essence placing a heavy bet that the property will appreciate smartly and soon. That's a big gamble.

❑ **Multifamily homes and apartments.** The opportunities for success are much greater with multifamily apartments than with single-family homes and condos. Included in this category are small two-, three-, and four-family homes that are often, but not necessarily, owner-occupied. In fact, if you want to purchase your own home and get into the rental real estate game, you can accomplish both at the same time by buying a small apartment building—a duplex or triplex. Multifamily dwellings require a greater initial investment, but the cost per dwelling unit is lower, so the investment makes much greater investment sense. Multifamily units are relatively easy to finance if you have sufficient money to make the down payment, since lenders see the potential rental income as protection on their loans.

✦ **Commercial property.** Office buildings, shopping centers, and industrial real estate all offer investors with substantial resources an opportunity for significant gains, albeit at significant risk. But with the exception of small, well-located, and fully occupied properties, commercial real estate is best left to the experts.

Check out the special *You Can Do It!* Web site for more information on evaluating a property, the keys to success in buying real estate, and avoiding mistakes in real estate investing. **w w w**

ALTERNATIVES TO OWN-IT-YOURSELF REAL ESTATE

Investing in individually owned income-producing real estate requires a tremendous commitment, and you need to be realistic about the challenges. Perhaps it's because of the difficulties associated with real estate investment and management that this sector has provided such tremendous wealth-creation opportunities. But most people simply aren't inclined to make that commitment. Passive methods of participating in the important real estate sector include real estate investment trust (REIT) stocks and real estate mutual funds. Another alternative for the time-challenged but affluent baby boomer is to invest in undeveloped land (see the following section). Finally, making sensible improvements to the family domicile can be a worthwhile incremental real estate investment.

WHAT ABOUT UNDEVELOPED LAND?

You may think that undeveloped land could be an ideal first-time real estate investment, but it is often the worst. Why? Raw-land purchases often end up being raw deals unless you plan to commercially develop the property later on or perhaps build a retirement residence on same (see page 205). Successful investors in undeveloped land need deep pockets—and more. Since undeveloped land doesn't generate any income, your money will probably be tied up for a long time. It's difficult to finance undeveloped land for more than a few years. In addition, finding the right kind of property takes some real expertise. Another cautionary note: large parcels of land that sell for peanuts usually spell trouble, not bargain. The price is cheap for a number of good reasons—lousy location, difficult access, bad drainage. So if the land you want to purchase has more moose per square mile than people, don't expect to make any money on it. Land in particularly desirable areas, on the other hand, is always expensive to purchase.

Property Evaluation Checklist

The following checklist highlights important considerations in making a successful real estate acquisition.

- ❏ **Run and rerun the numbers.** A thorough financial analysis based on actual data and realistic assumptions is essential. Guides and Web sites on real estate investing provide a variety of tools to quickly assess the economic viability of a property and to more carefully evaluate attractive candidates. **w w w**

- ❏ **Location is important.** An objective assessment of the "qualitative" features of the property is just as essential as a rigorous financial analysis. First-time real estate investors often find that the properties they can afford are in unattractive neighborhoods, overlooking the oft-repeated maxim of the three keys to a successful real estate investment: location, location, location.

- ❏ **Inspect the property.** A thorough inspection of the property by a highly qualified inspector is crucial to determine what will be required to repair, maintain, and improve the property. Don't skimp on property inspection fees.

- ❏ **Be realistic about fix-up and maintenance costs.** More than adequate reserves should be readily available to provide for fix-up and maintenance. You should also be realistic about the skills and time necessary to do the work yourself. If it's been a while since you've had a saw or a screwdriver (not the liquid kind) in hand, don't conclude that you can be the property's repair person.

- ❏ **Be realistic about the responsibilities of property ownership and management.** Here's an important question to ask yourself prior to buying an income-producing property: "Do I have the stomach and the time to be a good landlord?" The responsibilities—and the potential liabilities—of property ownership are all too often overlooked by neophyte investors.

❏ **Consider a worst-case scenario.** As with any investment or business decision, before committing to a real estate investment you should consider the financial implications of a worst-case scenario (e.g., major repairs and high vacancies amidst a deteriorating real estate market). Do you possess the financial and psychological wherewithal to sustain the investment under unfavorable conditions?

Index

Special Reader Offers

The special reader Web site that can be accessed through www.
jonathanpond.com (see page xix) will help you keep up to date
on the information and suggestions presented throughout *You
Can Do It!* In addition, you can take advantage of special offers
and discounts that Jonathan D. Pond makes available, including:

- ✓ Discounts on Jonathan's products and services
- ✓ Newsletter and audiotape offers
- ✓ Notices for Jonathan D. Pond TV and radio appearances
- ✓ Special discounts on Jonathan D. Pond lectures and seminars
- ✓ Access to Jonathan's weekly market updates and flash reports

To find out more and to be kept informed of special reader
offers in the future, visit:

www.jonathanpond.com/specialoffers.html

Special Reader Offers

The special reader Web site that can be accessed through www.jonathanpond.com (see page xix) will help you keep up to date on the information and suggestions presented throughout *You Can Do It!* In addition, you can take advantage of special offers and discounts that Jonathan D. Pond makes available, including:

✓ Discounts on Jonathan's products and services
✓ Newsletter and audiotape offers
✓ Notices for Jonathan D. Pond TV and radio appearances
✓ Special discounts on Jonathan D. Pond lectures and seminars
✓ Access to Jonathan's weekly market updates and flash reports

To find out more and to be kept informed of special reader offers in the future, visit:

www.jonathanpond.com/specialoffers.html